The World of
TONI MORRISON

The World of
TONI MORRISON

A Guide to Characters and Places in Her Novels

Gloria Grant Roberson

Greenwood Press
Westport, Connecticut • London

Library of Congress Cataloging-in-Publication Data

Roberson, Gloria G.
    The world of Toni Morrison : a guide to characters and places in her novels /
    Gloria Grant Roberson.
       p. cm.
    Includes bibliographical references (p.) and index.
    ISBN 0–313–32380–1 (alk. paper)
       1. Morrison, Toni—Characters—Dictionaries. 2. African Americans in
    literature—Dictionaries. 3. Morrison, Toni—Settings—Dictionaries. 4. Setting
    (Literature)—Dictionaries. I. Title.
    PS3563.08749 Z844   2003
    813'.54—dc21   2002035333

British Library Cataloguing in Publication Data is available.

Library of Congress Catalog Card Number: 2002035333

ISBN: 0–313–32380–1

First published in 2003

Greenwood Press, 88 Post Road West, Westport, CT 06881
An imprint of Greenwood Publishing Group, Inc.
www.greenwood.com

Printed in the United States of America

The paper used in this book complies with the
Permanent Paper Standard issued by the National
Information Standards Organization (Z39.48–1984).

10 9 8 7 6 5 4 3 2 1

To Toni Morrison for her literary genius,
without which none of this work would have been possible

To my deceased mother, Lillie Alzona Cofield Grant,
who taught me love of family and reverence for God Almighty, who guides
my life

CONTENTS

PREFACE

The impetus for this project was a research assignment I had undertaken as a charter member of the Toni Morrison Society (TMS). I was asked by Dr. Carolyn Denard of Georgia State University in Atlanta, Georgia, the founder and then president of the TMS to be the bibliographer for the annual *Toni Morrison Newsletter—Bibliography Issue*, and I served in this capacity for three years. I normally began my research with an extensive literary search for appropriate citations within the current year, and, in review and compilation of the material, I noticed that there was a great deal of scholarly discourse about Morrison's novels, but 1) there were redundancies in literary themes and 2) the scholarship was often centered around the main fictional characters without providing much exposure to the supporting fictional characters who, in my opinion, also deserved recognition in literary examination. As a librarian, I thought for some time about how I could contribute to the scholarship on Morrison's work in a way that would provide a reference tool to encourage more in-depth review of her novels. This guide to Morrison's characters, people, and places is my contribution to that cause.

This book will help researchers and readers identify characters and thus, perhaps, common themes within and across Morrison's seven novels. I hope that it will introduce to some and highlight for others Morrison's fictional characters and expose similarities among people, places, and cultures once thought unrelated. Through the heart and mind of the

African American experience, Toni Morrison promotes an examination of intercultural ideas that challenges the true meaning of humanity through the pages of her writings. As a writer, Morrison introduces the reader not only to the black experience, but also to the tapestry of cultural and intercultural variations and similarities within the lives of Pecola Breedlove, Macon (Milkman) Dead III, Violet (Violent) Trace, Jadine (Jade) Childs, Lady Jones, and others. Across her novels, one discovers that cultural kinship does not mandate cultural responsibilities. For example, the fictional character of Lady Jones in *Beloved* was a privileged and educated mulatto who, with a Bible and a dream, started a home school for less-fortunate black children. Yet, in *Tar Baby*, Jadine Childs, a fictional character of similar stature and distinction, selfishly uses her racial advantages to bandage the insecurities of her own life.

This reference book will identify the historical, philosophical, musical, biblical, literary, and psychological components that support Morrison's fictional characters as they people her novels. Toni Morrison is not only a writer, storyteller, professor, and educator, but also, I suspect, a librarian at heart. The diversity of historical people and facts that frame her characters reveal extensive scholarship, insight, and intellectual inquiry characteristic of her bookish colleagues, librarians.

Toni Morrison is also a teacher at heart; she challenges the reader to learn and experience her world. Having a broad intellectual base of knowledge, Morrison, as a writer, demands complete attention from the reader. Like all great writers, such as Shakespeare, every word, sentence and paragraph is relevant, and often, one reading is insufficient to grasp the story line. Morrison has an enormous range of knowledge about mythology, folklore, American history, philosophy, and religion and she encourages the reader to read between the lines as she introduces new literary concepts.

Toni Morrison's fictional characters live in a complex world containing a wide range of interesting people. However, there are assumptions to background knowledge and facts that often hinder that process. For example, in *The Bluest Eye*, when Claudia MacTeer and Pecola Breedlove raved about Shirley Temple, Frieda MacTeer rebuts them with her preference for Jane Withers. Who is Jane Withers? How many readers are familiar with the cinema of the 1930s and would know that Jane Withers is another child actress who played opposite Shirley Temple in the 1936 movie, *Bright Eyes*. The adorable little orphan (Shirley Temple) was taunted skillfully by the bratty rich girl (Jane Withers), and Morrison uses her popular history knowledge to show Frieda MacTeer's strong dislike for Shirley Temple.

As a novelist, Toni Morrison has a rich spiritual background and often introduces the reader to Christian stories and images through characterizations in her writings. Religion is a cornerstone to the African American experience, and biblical references are imbedded in the novels to give the full flavor of the author's culture. An explanation to biblical terms and passages will help to bridge the gap between writer and reader. For example, the name "Beloved" comes from the Bible in the book of the Song of Solomon. Bordered by Ecclesiastes and Isaiah, this eight-chapter book is often referenced in Morrison's novels. In *Beloved*, the spirit announces, "I am beloved and she is mine" (Morrison, 210) and the biblical passage is, "My beloved is mine, and I am his: he feedeth among the lilies" (Song of Sol. 2:16). Another religion-related reference is illustrated in a conversation in *Paradise*, where Toni Morrison quotes briefly Saint Augustine, Bishop of Hippo in the spiritual battle between the Reverends Senior Pulliam and Richard Misner. Baptist, Reverend Misner, is furious with his Methodist brother Pulliam and relies on the words of Saint Augustine for solace. Toni Morrison is so comfortable in her knowledge, that she teases the reader by mentioning only the first name of this great theologian, "Augustine." A descriptive review of the African-born (Algeria, 354–430 AD) early Christian leader enables the reader to understand the relevancy to Morrison's book. When I first read *Paradise*, being a librarian, I immediately ceased reading so that I could go and research "Augustine" in several places. Now I hope that readers can turn to just one book, this one, to research unfamiliar references.

Toni Morrison develops central characters that do not live in a vacuum because they breathe and interact with others within the narrative structure of each book. As they move throughout the novel, these characters reveal layers of emotions that consume the reader's imagination. For example, First Corinthians Dead in *Song of Solomon* comes alive with the help of Henry Porter, as she desperately searches for a life outside of her spinster existence within her male-dominated dysfunctional family. Henry Porter, a town drunk, is transformed into a modern-day Prince Charming for his " 'Corrie," a lonely lady in distress. Between these two people from diverse backgrounds, Morrison creates a love scene that rattles the soul. She unearths a passion that transcends social and economic backgrounds.

Morrison strongly believes in forming unusual relationships within her novels: Sula Mae Peace and Nel Wright Greene in *Sula*, Jadine (Jade) Childs and William (Son) Green in *Tar Baby*, Guitar Bains and Macon (Milkman) Dead III in *Song of Solomon*, Consolata (Connie) Sosa and So-ane Blackhorse Morgan in *Paradise*, Pecola Breedlove and Claudia and Frieda MacTeer in *The Bluest Eye*, Sethe Suggs and Amy Gordon in *Beloved*, and Dorcas Manfred and Joe Trace in *Jazz*. By taking the time to examine all of Morrison's fictional characters, the reader discovers commonalities among people that otherwise might be thought of as nonexistent. By examining more closely Morrison's method of fictional character development, one may see her talent as a novelist and story-

teller magnified. Most important, it provides a more comprehensive understanding of her work. It is my hope that in this guide to the world
of Toni Morrison, one will be able to see and examine these relationships
across novels and create dialogues with others in a broader review of
Morrison's works.

SCOPE AND ORGANIZATION

The aim of *The World of Toni Morrison: A Guide to Characters and Places
in Her Novels* is to provide a comprehensive guide to the works of Toni
Morrison by concentrating principally on the characters, people, and
places of her seven novels. The 803 entries should, ideally, be read in
conjunction with the coded parent-novel, in order to deepen the reader's
understanding of both the nature of the parent-novel and of the character's, people, or place's affiliation and position in it. The volume of
literary critical studies surrounding the major characters in Morrison's
works is extensive, and this reference tool will lend credibility to the
minor characters, denoting plot relevancy for both groups. Together with
those studies, these entries will help to serve as a sort of guide through
Morrison's fiction and to open new literary avenues for critical thinking
about her works.

In an effort to get what I believe is a true sense of Morrison's people
and places, I deliberately avoided reading the criticism surrounding
Morrison's works. As the *Toni Morrison Society Newsletter* bibliographer,
I was well aware that the volume of scholarship surrounding her works
was widespread, but, I avoided other critical influences in an effort to
protect a clean slate for myself. I wanted to submerge myself in the
community of Morrison's people and plots to establish a relationship
with Eva Peace in *Sula*, Lady Jones in *Beloved*, Miss Della Jones in *The
Bluest Eye*, and the list goes on and on.

In addition, this book will help the reader to understand how Morrison
uses a wide range of literary, cultural, political, philosophical, historical, theatrical, and scientific elements to lend credibility to her fictional
characters and plots in a way that challenges the reader to understand
the era therein on the pages of her novels. This reference tool will help
the experienced Morrison researchers to expand their perceptions of the
characters, people, and places in her seven novels and, for the novice
Morrison reader, it will provide paths for exploration.

Types of Entries

Each entry appears in alphabetical order by fictional or historical surname or place name. If there is no surname, the entry is listed according
to how the name is used within the text. In cases where more than one

name has been used in the text, cross-references show under which name the full entry appears (see below).

Fictional Characters

All major and minor characters, including pets, people, and places within the seven novels are included.

Real People and Literary Characters

In addition to the fictional characters, many of the entries are for real people or literary characters mentioned in the seven novels. Morrison's fictional characters are rich with an association of notables from many disciplines. There are biblical notables like Saint Augustine, Bishop of Hippo, philosophical giants like Henry David Thoreau, sociologists like W.E.B. DuBois, and the list goes on. A brief biographical sketch is given for each person; for literary characters, there is a brief identification of the character and its relevance to the Morrison novel.

Animals

Animals are listed only if given a name within the novel. For example: Here Boy, a dog, is an entry because he is Baby Sugg's pet in *Beloved*.

Cross-References

Throughout the book, cross-references are indicated by an explicit invitation to "see" another entry. Cross-references show variants of names and the name under which the full entry appears. For example, "Betty" is cross-referenced to "Teapot's Mamma" (from *Sula*), because that name is how she is perceived in the book.

Page Numbers Cited in Entries

In the entries, page numbers refer to the page in the Morrison novel that supports the description in the entry. If there is an author given in parentheses along with the page number—for example (Du Bois, 76)—it indicates that the author's name and source will be found in the bibliography at the back of the book.

Appendix

An appendix lists all of the Morrison novels and the characters, people, and place names that belong to each of her seven novels.

NOVEL ABBREVIATION CODES

For each entry, the symbol in brackets that immediately follows each name is the coded identifier for the parent-novel. For example, ERNIE PAUL [TB] indicates that this character is found in *Tar Baby*.

BE   Morrison, Toni. (1970). *The Bluest Eye*. New York: Holt, Rinehart, Winston.

BLV   Morrison, Toni. (1987). *Beloved*. New York: Knopf.

JZ   Morrison, Toni. (1992). *Jazz*. New York: Knopf.

PA   Morrison, Toni. (1998). *Paradise*. New York: Knopf.

SS   Morrison, Toni. (1977). *Song of Solomon*. New York: Knopf.

SU   Morrison, Toni. (1973). *Sula*. New York: Knopf.

TB   Morrison, Toni. (1981). *Tar Baby*. New York: Knopf.

ACKNOWLEDGMENTS

To God go the glory.

I am deeply indebted to my family—husband Clifford; and children Gloriane (Tobi), Clifford Daniel (Danny), and Cynthia (Cindy), and her husband Edward (Eddie) Johnson whose love, encouragement, and belief that I could, sustained me. My appreciation goes to the Faculty Peer Review Committee and Adelphi University, Garden City, New York, for the sabbatical leave and the research grant that supported my work. My thanks go to Dr. Carolyn Denard and the Toni Morrison Society, because, without Carolyn assigning me to the *Newsletter* bibliography, I would have never recognized the need for this project.

My appreciation goes to: Jonathan Lass, my assistant "extraordinaire" for his flexible schedule and calm demeanor in the face of many rewrites; to Belaynesh Solomon, Pam Griffin, and Kristi Kobloth for patience and willingness to help; to my neighbor/friend, Kathleen Baker, for her proficiency and good temperament; to Muriel Herring for her artful advisement; to all of my fellow faculty members in Adelphi University's Swirbul Library who supported my efforts and never let on how tired they were of hearing about Toni Morrison's characters, people, or places; and to Anne Thompson, development editor at Greenwood, for her editorial expertise, support, and encouragement, and Arlene Belzer and Alicia Lutz of Coastal Editorial Services for all their editing assistance.

A

AARON POOLE. *See* POOLE, AARON [PA]

ABLE FLOOD. *See* FLOOD, ABLE [PA]

ABLE WOODRUFF. *See* WOODRUFF, ABLE [BLV]

ABU SNAKE CHARMER [BLV]. The crowd was eager to see Abu Snake Charmer at the carnival outside of Cincinnati, Ohio, visited by Sethe, Denver, and Paul D. (48).

ABYSSINIAN BAPTIST CHURCH [PA]. This historic black church in Harlem, New York, was founded in 1808 by a group of African American and Ethiopian shopkeepers who refused to accept segregation in the house of the Lord. The Abyssinian Baptist Church has long been rich in the culture of black history and wholly dependent upon the "Lord of our weary years" (159).

ACE FLOOD. *See* FLOOD, ACE [PA]

ACTON [JZ]. Dorcas Manfred became romantically interested in Acton during her illicit relationship with Joe Trace, a married older man in the neighborhood. Acton was young, arrogant, and desirable. As soon as

Acton began to pay attention to Dorcas, she plotted ways to break off the affair with Joe Trace. The excitement of openly dating someone closer to her age and sought after by her friends outweighed any gifts received in secret from an aging salesman of Cleopatra Products.

However, dating Acton came with judgmental comments about her hair, dress, and behavior, which Dorcas misinterpreted as caring. In reality, Acton was self-centered and took pleasure in controlling his female companions. Acton's selfishness was evidenced clearly when, while the couple passionately intertwined on the dance floor, Dorcas was shot by her then former lover, Joe Trace. Acton's ego took center stage as he bitterly complained about the blood on his shirt as Dorcas lay dying on the floor (188–89, 192).

ADA WILLIAMS. *See* **WILLIAMS, ADA & FOWLER [BE]**

ADOLF, UNCLE. *See* **UNCLE ADOLF [TB]**

AFRICAN WOMAN [TB]. This unique character served as a symbol of ethnic pride on foreign soil. The African woman was a chic, lanky, and poised black woman that entered a Parisian market to purchase less than a dozen eggs. She moved about the market with a flair, catching everyone's attention with her manner, stature, and sunshine-colored tunic. She wore symbols of African pride etched on her skin. Upon departing, she glanced back with disdain in the direction of Jadine Childs, another black shopper, and spat.

The African woman's brazen gesture was meant to insult the American woman whose heart and traits contradicted her hue. Jadine was disturbed by the offensive display of vulgarity because, unconsciously, she had wished to bond with her African sister. After the incident, feelings of isolation and loneliness forced Jadine to plan a visit to L'Arbe de la Croix. There she could find the validation and emotional stability needed with her only relatives, Ondine and Sydney Childs (45–47).

AISHA [TB]. Jadine Childs wanted to show off Son (William Green), her new boyfriend, to Aisha, one of her New York City modeling friends (223).

AJAX [SU]. Ajax was the oldest of seven cherished sons parented by a single mother who intrigued her children with the knowledge of metaphysical customs. Maturing into a confident young man, Ajax was quite popular with the opposite sex, but only his mother and airplanes captivated his heart. All other relationships were mainly sexual or superficial, at best (126).

Sula Mae Peace's reputation for adventure and independence reminded Ajax of his mother's free spirit. Being raised in a home with extreme social latitude made it easy for Ajax to steal a bottle of milk from a neighbor to gain entry into Sula's lair (127–28). As quickly as the affair began, it ended under the weight of Sula's need to control her lover (131).

Shortly after Ajax left town, Sula found his driver's license and discovered that his name was not "Ajax" at all, but "Albert Jacks." Sula was disappointed that their intimacy lacked substance because she did not even know his proper name. Honest in his desire to lease, but not own, Ajax never meant to deceive her. Sula was looking for love and Ajax was just looking (135–37).

ALBERT JACKS. *See* AJAX [SS]

ALBERT SCHWEITZER, DR. *See* DR. ALBERT SCHWEITZER [SS]

ALBRIGHT, FRANK [PA]. Frank Albright was the husband of Mavis and father of Sally, Frankie, Billy James, and Merle and Pearl, deceased twins. He was a controlling (27) and abusive (22) husband who drank too much. Frank had a big fancy car that doubled for his bedroom when he arrived home intoxicated. The neighbors knew the residence needed a lawn mower, but Frank's ego needed a Cadillac (28). Frank banned Mavis from driving his prized possession, but she stole it to run away from home (25).

Many years after Mavis left home, she met her daughter, Sally, who revealed that she was always afraid of her father because of his attempted sexual advances toward her (314).

ALBRIGHT, MAVIS [PA]. Mavis Albright was the wife of Frank, and mother of Sally, Frankie, Billy James, and Merle and Pearl, deceased twins. During a newspaper interview, Mavis reported that a five-minute errand to the market resulted in the death of her twins in an overheated car (23). She stole her husband's Cadillac and left home because she feared that her three other children planned to harm her (25). Traveling to her mother's house in Paterson, New Jersey (30), Mavis found food, money, fuel, and aspirins (32), but no sympathy for a mother that had left her children (31). Moving on further west, with the aid of hitchhikers (33–35), Mavis finally ran out of gas near the Convent.

After meeting Consolata Sosa (Connie), Mavis resolved to remain within the confines of the Convent. She traveled back to watch the children at school but, undetected by them, she did not stay (258). Under Connie's supervision, Mavis had responsibilities, attention, and a place for herself and the spirits of her deceased twins to dwell (258). Mavis was prideful of her close relationship with Connie. After the Mother

Superior's death, Connie became despondent and began to drink heavily. Mavis was very protective, and a flippant remark from Gigi about Connie's mental state erupted into a physical fight between the two women (167–68).

Mavis was socially comfortable in the Convent and was there the night the men from Ruby came with guns (283).

ALBRIGHT, MERLE & PEARL [PA]. Merle and Pearl were the deceased twin infants of Mavis and Frank Albright and sisters of Sally, Billy James, and Frankie. The story told was that they were smothered to death in an overheated car while their mother, Mavis, was inside the store for a short time shopping for dinner. Later, Mavis learned that criminal charges had been filed against her in connection with the death of her twin infants (23).

ALBRIGHT, SALLY, FRANKIE, & BILLY JAMES [PA]. The three remaining children of Mavis and Frank Albright after the death of the twins were Sally, Frankie, and Billy James. Their mother left home in the middle of the night after convincing herself that the children wanted to physically harm her. Frank Albright was an abusive and distrustful man, so the children basically were left to fend for themselves. Years later, Mavis returned to take a look at them on the school playground, but they were unaware of her presence (25).

ALCORN, MISSISSIPPI [PA]. Alcorn, Mississippi, was where Gigi, frustrated with her life, placed a telephone call to her grandfather, who advised her to come home (65).

ALFRED, GEORGIA [BLV]. Paul D. was filled with agony at losing the emotional support of his Sweet Home friends. Heartbroken and alone, he lashed out in anger. Defiance brought imprisonment with forty-six other captives on a chain gang in Alfred, Georgia. Restricted by chains, Paul D. and the men endured the cruelty of welding a hammer by day and sleeping boxed in a shallow pit by night. The lead prisoner was called Hi Man because he signaled the beginning and the end of a sadistic morning ritual that fulfilled the erotic appetites of guards who viewed slaves as defenseless cretin. In Alfred, Georgia, Paul D. learned the hard way that those in authority can restrict the body, but never the mind (41).

One day, nature freed the prisoners with her mighty thunder by creating mud as an exit from hell. The Cherokees cut their chains and aided their flight out of Georgia, but the experience was branded in Paul D.'s conscious forever. The security of a "tobacco tin" safeguarded the only memories that touched Paul D.'s heart (106–12).

ALGERIA [TB]. Dr. Robert Michelin was banished from Algeria, a country in northern Africa, bordering the Mediterranean Sea, between Morocco and Tunisia. The population of Europeans there was less than 2 percent, as most of the natives were of Arab descent (15).

ALICE MANFRED. *See* MANFRED, ALICE [JZ]

ALICE MANFRED'S BROTHER-IN-LAW [JZ]. Dorcas' father, and Alice Manfred's brother-in-law, were killed brutally in the East St. Louis riots. He was a responsible businessman who, as a bystander, just happened to get in the way of a rioter's anger (57).

ALICE MANFRED'S SISTER [JZ]. Alice Manfred's sister was the mother of Dorcas. After hearing of her husband's death, she took comfort in her home, only to die in a house fire deliberately set by the same rioters who killed her husband. In the East St. Louis riots, the fire was fueled by hatred and ignorance and the arsonists probably knew that fire engines would not reach a black neighborhood in time to save the life of a woman already traumatized by the loss of her husband (57).

ALICE, MISS. *See* MISS ALICE [BE]

ALICE PULLIAM. *See* AUNT ALICE [PA]

ALICE TULLY HALL [TB]. Son arrived in New York City with past memories of the Alice Tully Hall, one of the nation's leading concert halls at the Lincoln Center for the Performing Arts. The hall was named for Miss Tully (1902–1993), Corning Glass Works heiress and a professional singer, who supported music and the arts through her generous contributions (216).

ALICIA. *See* CELESTINA & ALICIA [TB]

ALIGHIERI, DANTE (1256–1321) [BE]. Young Elihue Micah Whitcomb (later "Soaphead Church") admired the works of Dante Alighieri to the point that he wanted to find his own Beatrice (169). Dante, an Italian poet, was born in Florence and died in Ravenna, Italy. He was the son of Alighieri di Bellincione Alighieri, a notary belonging to the Guelph family. Dante's first book, written in 1292, was *Vita Nuova*, or *New Life*, a book of verse and prose that recounted his love for Beatrice Portinari (1265–1290), a girl he first saw at age nine.

Dante and Beatrice first met as adolescents and the two did not speak until they were teenagers. Nevertheless, Dante cherished Beatrice with the kind of passion so intense it defied time and reason. In his 1961 study of Dante, Charles Williams wrote, "Beatrice was, in her degree, an image of nobility, of virtue, of the Redeemed Life, and in some sense of Almighty God himself" (Williams, 8).

After Beatrice's death at a young age, Dante intensified his efforts to capture her spirit in many ways throughout his poetry. In a sense, Dante wrote about the mysteries of love and romance like many other poets of his time. Evidence of how Beatrice inspired Dante is embedded deeply throughout his works. Dante's main philosophy centered on the idea that all virtues and all vices proceed from love.

ALMA ESTEE. *See* **ESTEE, ALMA [TB]**

AMANUENSIS [SS]. According to the *American Heritage Dictionary of the English Language*, 4th edition, an "amanuensis" is, "One who is employed to take dictation or to copy manuscript" (*American Heritage Dictionary of the English Language*, 55). In the beginning, First Corinthians Dead told her family that she was Ms. Michael-Mary Graham's "amanuensis" to hide the fact that she was hired as her maid/domestic. Ms. Graham was impressed greatly with her new hire and later expanded First Corinthians' duties to include typing lessons. Thus, fiction was supplanted by fact, but by then First Corinthians had met Porter, the love of her life, and any and all career goals were altered (187).

A.M.E. ZION & GOOD SHEPHERD BAPTIST CHURCHES [TB]. In Son's hometown of Eloe, Florida, there were only two churches in the all black community. The A.M.E. Zion and Good Shepherd Baptist churches served a population of over two hundred parishioners, dependent on the level of spiritual awareness from week to week (136).

AMY DENVER. *See* **DENVER, AMY [BLV]**

ANARCHIC [TB]. After the death of his wife, Cheyenne, Son was anarchic in nature, as he wandered around the world to avoid prosecution in Eloe, Florida (166). According to the *The Living Webster Encyclopedia Dictionary of the English Language*, an "anarchist" is "a variation of 'anarchist' is one who advocates violent revolution against the established order as a prerequisite of freedom" (38).

ANDREW [TB]. William "Son" Green was teased by his friends because they mistakenly thought that the time he spent in the home of Miss Tyler—who was Andrew's aunt—was for sex. Andrew was Son's buddy. In reality, Son wanted access to her piano, not her person. When the outgrowth of his musical talent became apparent, his friends recognized their blunder (136).

ANGELINO, LUKE [BE]. Luke Angelino was the student in Pecola Breed-love's class who was seated next to Marie Appolonaire. Pecola refers to Luke and Marie as examples of the unfairness in a seating arrangement that left her without a partner (45).

ANGEL MAN [BLV]. "Angel man" was a term of endearment that Denver used for her father, Halle Suggs. Born during her mother's flight from the brutality of Schoolteacher and Sweet Home, Denver knew her father only through the stories told by Baby Suggs, her grandmother. Denver viewed her father as an "angel man" because she was brought up on tales of his bravery, compassion, love, and commitment to his mother and friends at Sweet Home, and this made a young girl proud (208–9).

ANNA DJVORAK. *See* DJVORAK, ANNA [SS]

ANNA FLOOD. *See* FLOOD, ANNA [PA]

APOLLO POOLE. *See* POOLE, APOLLO [PA]

APPOLONAIRE, MARIE [BE]. Marie Appolonaire was the classmate of Pe-cola Breedlove who occupied a desk with Luke Angelino. As the only student in the class who sat without a partner at a desk, Pecola felt slighted and ostracized (45).

ARABIAN NIGHTS DANCER [BLV]. The Arabian nights dancer was one of the eight performers at the carnival outside of Cincinnati, Ohio, visited by Sethe, Denver, and Paul D. (48).

ARAPAHO GIRLS [PA]. The Christ the King School for Native Girls (Convent) provided shelter and schooling for girls from the Arapaho tribe. Nomadic in tradition, the Arapaho Indians depended heavily on the buffalo for food. The southern Arapaho tribe lived with the Cheyenne on assigned land in Oklahoma. They fought and hunted on horseback, lived in skin tepees, practiced little agriculture, and had similar tribal ceremonies as the Kiowa. Their dress code was moccasin, breech-cloth, and buckskin dress (10).

ARMISTICE DAY [JZ]. More than six years after the armistice was enacted, Violet Trace went to a church armed with a knife to war with the dead (9, 91).

As outlined in the *New Encyclopedia Britannica* (*NER*) an "armistice" is "an agreement for the cessation of active hostilities between two or more belligerents" (*NEB*, 569). The years 1914–1918 are very significant in American military history because they denote the beginning and the end of World War I, also known as the Great War. It is important to note that the armistice was requested by Germany and granted by the Allied forces. The first European war began in 1914 involving Germany, England, and their Allies. Many of those in the armed forces never returned, so when news that the war was over, there was pandemonium in the streets. It was not until 1919 that President Woodrow Wilson made November 11 the official Armistice Day, in honor of the many who had lost their lives fighting in World War I.

ARNETTE FLEETWOOD SMITH. *See* SMITH, ARNETTE FLEETWOOD [PA]

ARNOLD FLEETWOOD. *See* FLEETWOOD, ARNOLD (i.e., FLEET) [PA]

ATENAS [PA]. Sister Mary Magna, accompanied by five nuns and three children, including young Consolata (Connie) Sosa, traveled to the United States on the *Atenas*, an American flagship owned by the United Fruit Company. The *Atenas* dealt in foreign trade with U.S. possessions and territories (224).

AUDREY [BE]. Maureen Peal told a story to the MacTeer sisters and Pecola Breedlove about a little black girl by the name of Audrey who requested a Hedy Lamarr hairdo. The beautician was very candid in letting the enamored young Audrey know that her texture of hair made the request for a white movie star's coiffure impossible (69).

AUGUST CATO. *See* CATO, AUGUST [PA]

AUGUSTINE, SAINT, BISHOP OF HIPPO (354–430 AD) [PA]. Outraged by Rev. Pulliam's distortion of God's meaning of love at the wedding of Arnett Fleetwood and Coffee (K.D.) Smith, Rev. Misner called upon the teachings of St. Augustine, one of the great leaders of the Christian faith (145). St. Augustine's greatest inspiration was his devout mother, Saint Monica, who prayed constantly as her son struggled with his lack of faith. At the age of thirty-two, the prayers of his mother were answered as St. Augustine of Hippo began a life of Christian commitment, study, and thanksgiving. St. Augustine delivered over four hundred sermons throughout his life. His extensive writings are the foundation of Christian education.

The passages referred to by Rev. Misner come from the *Tractates on the Gospel of John*, which is the English-language translation of St. Augustine's *Joannis Evanagelium Tractatus*, the complete commentary on the gospel. It is there that he chastises the minister against self-importance and compares vanity with the works of Satan.

St. Augustine wrote:

But he who is a proud minister is reckoned with the devil; but the gift of Christ is not contaminated, which flows through him pure, which passes through him liquid, and come to the fertile earth. . . . For the spiritual virtue of the sacrament is like the light: both by those who are to be enlightened is it received pure, and if it passes through the impure it is not stained. Let the minister be by all means righteous, and seek not their own glory, but His glory whose ministers they are. (Augustine, 5.15)

Rev. Misner saw the relevance of St. Augustine's wisdom in Rev. Pulliam's behavior as guest minister at the wedding.

AUNT ALICE [PA]. Alice Pulliam was the wife of Rev. Senior Pulliam and aunt of Kate Harper Golightly. As most of the wives in Rudy, Oklahoma, Alice followed her husband's direction in matters of religious and community issues. She was called "Aunt Alice" affectionately by Kate (158).

AUNT FLORENCE [SS]. Aunt Florence was Mrs. Bains' sister who invited her grandnieces and grandnephews to visit in the South during the summer after their move up north. Young Guitar loved hunting in the South. He was a good marksman and enjoyed having the opportunity to partake in the sport. However, he recounted to Milkman a story about a shooting incident that occurred during a visit with Aunt Florence which he deeply regretted. Guitar knew that it was wrong to take the life of a doe. He felt that a boy/man could kill almost anything, but not a doe, which symbolizes the gentleness of motherhood (85).

AUNT JEMIMA ACT [SS]. Milkman was ashamed because he needed both his father and his aunt to get him out of jail. When Pilate came in with her "Aunt Jemima" act, he knew that she had demeaned herself deliberately because of him (209).

An Aunt Jemima act involves behaving in a subservient manner toward the white man. In some cultures, Aunt Jemima is only the black woman who provides the recipe to make delicious pancakes; The pancake flour is Aunt Jemima and Aunt Jemima is the pancake flour. However, among people of color, Aunt Jemima was a humiliating role of a black woman who allowed the white man to get rich from her southern recipe for pancakes. The smiling image of a black woman on the pancake box only added insult to injury (53).

Few know that in 1889, the Aunt Jemima pancake mix was introduced by Chris L. Rutt and Charles G. Underwood in St. Joseph, Missouri. The two men had bought the Pearl Milling Company and needed a product to sell. The idea of a self-mixing, self-rising pancake flour seemed feasible. Later, in 1893, Rutt and Underwood saw the vaudeville performance of a black-faced actress singing the song "Aunt Jemima" and wearing a head-rag and a bandana. The positive reaction to the ethnic image launched Nancy Green, the black woman playing Aunt Jemima for the world. Ms. Green traveled around the country making pancakes at exhibitions as the smiling black woman and Rutt and Underwood made millions.

AUNT JIMMY. *See* **GREAT AUNT JIMMY [BE]**

AUNT PHYLLIS [BLV]. Aunt Phyllis was the midwife from Minnowville who was summoned by Mr. Garner when Sethe Suggs' delivery time was near. Aunt Phyllis came to assist in the delivery and then returned to Minnowville.

Sethe was lonely for woman talk, as Mrs. Garner and Aunt Phyllis were the only two women in her life, but the opportunity never came for her to visit Aunt Phyllis in Minnowville (159).

AUNT ROSA [TB]. Aunt Rosa was Son's aunt from his mother's side. Aunt Rosa lived in Eloe, Florida, and she opened her home to Son and his lady friend when they visited Eloe. Unaccustomed to a young lady sleeping in the nude, Aunt Rosa insisted on providing Jadine Childs with a cover-up. Aunt Rosa was firm and polite, but Jadine felt insulted having her lifelong habit of sleeping naked judged and amended by an old woman in Florida (252–53).

AUNTI JULIA [BE]. Aunti Julia was the senile relative of Della Jones, Mr. Henry Washington's former landlady, who walked the streets day and night. Everyone knew of her mental instability, but the county hospital classified Aunti Julia as harmless and took no action. Mrs. MacTeer and her friends jokingly renounced that notion, commenting on how frightening Aunti Julia could be roaming around in the middle of the night (14).

B

BABY FISHER. *See* FISHER GIRL [BE]

BABY SUGGS. *See* SUGGS, BABY [BLV]

BACH, JOHANN SEBASTIAN (1685–1750) [TB]. In the greenhouse of Valerian Street at L'Arbe de la Croix, his Caribbean home, violin music by Johann Sebastian Bach was played to encourage the growth of plants (12). Valerian believed that exposing the plants to soothing music speeded up their progression.

BAINS, CENCY [SS]. Cency was the mother of Guitar Bains who picked up and left her children after her husband was killed in a work-related accident. Mrs. Bains, her mother-in-law, assumed responsibility for the family Cency abandoned (21).

BAINS, GUITAR [SS]. Guitar Bains was a friend of Milkman and a member of a secret society known as the Seven Days. A contest, a store window and a little boy's desire became a name and an identity (45). There were several events in Guitar Bains' life that set the stage for turmoil and anger. His father's death was unexpected and left Guitar with a lifelong aversion for sweets and white authority (61). Raised by his grandmother after his mother left her family, Guitar also witnessed the tyranny of a black businessman's intimidation to render them homeless because of rent money they didn't have (22).

Guitar became the object of Milkman's hero-worship for three reasons: he rescued him from a beating from four boys (264), he was older, and he got him into his aunt Pilate's home (36–45). The two friends were inseparable . . . until their values clashed. At first Guitar was inquisitive about Milkman's aunt Pilate, but as time evolved, he began to resent her. The patronizing "Aunt Jemima" act that Pilate employed to get Milkman and himself out of jail disgusted him, as did his mother's reaction to the white boss who brought news of his father's death (224). In addition to Guitar's aversion for white people, he also disliked symbols of black elitism. Milkman's efforts to invite Guitar to Honore, an affluent beach community frequented by the Dead family, were always rejected. Guitar did not wish to socialize with uppity blacks that visited elite resorts. In earnest, Guitar felt places like Honore were worthy of destruction by dynamite (103).

Guitar's disclosure of his membership in the Seven Days, a secret society of seven black men who avenged the murders within their race by random executions of white people, shocked his young friend. Guitar rationalized his actions as a byproduct of love, but Milkman disagreed and credited hate (154–61). Each member of the Seven Days was assigned a specific day. Guitar was the Sunday man and he vowed to avenge the death of blacks by killing whites on Sundays.

Four little black girls had been bombed in a church during Sunday services, and Guitar needed money for explosives to avenge their deaths (173). Milkman offered to include Guitar in the plan to steal Pilate's gold. However, what Milkman thought was gold was only a dead man's bones. Suspicion and disappointment distorted Guitar's perception of revenge and killing, which evolved in time and purpose. Killing on Sunday became any day, and his prey changed from innocent whites to Milkman, his best friend (279). Since Guitar Bains was an expert hunter, it is unlikely that he aimed at Milkman and killed Pilate (85, 336).

Perhaps by killing Pilate, Guitar was also killing the mother who had disappointed him.

BAINS, MRS. *See* **MRS. BAINS [SS]**

BARGEMAN THE [SU]. Steeped in racial prejudice, the white bargeman who found the body of Chicken Little, a black child, naturally assumed that the boy's uncivilized parents had caused his death. In superiority laced with ignorance, the bargeman deduced that all colored people were merely barbarians without regard for human life, especially that of children.

After carting the child's body to nearby Porter's Landing, he became annoyed when he was told that there were no blacks living there. The bargeman flatly refused to transport the body on to Medallion, Ohio, so someone else complied (63–64).

BAY BOY [BE]. One of four boys who teased Pecola Breedlove as she left school one day. Hurling insults at their defenseless classmate, they did not stop until the MacTeer sisters interceded. Claudia MacTeer lashed back by calling Bay Boy a "bullethead." All of a sudden, the threat of taking on three girls instead of one quieted his loud teasing (67).

Junior, son of Geraldine and Louis, admired Bay Boy for his intimidating traits. However, Geraldine did not share her son's hero-worship and prohibited any social contacts leading to friendship (87).

BEATRICE [BE]. Soaphead Church thought that he had found his "Beatrice" when he married Velma (169). To find one's Beatrice is to find the love of one's life, as Dante Alighieri did. The names of Dante Alighieri (1265–1321) and Beatrice Portinari (1265–1290) were romantically linked like Romeo and Juliet, but not for the same reasons. Unlike the Shakespearean lovers, Dante and Beatrice were not lovers, as the couple met as children and barely knew each other.

In Florence, during the thirteenth century, the custom was for parents to arrange the marriages of their children. So, both Dante and Beatrice were married to other people. Neither marriage was threatened by Dante's fervor, as there was no evidence that Beatrice ever returned Dante's affections.

Dante first saw Beatrice at age nine, and nine years later he saw her again. Those two brief meetings constituted love for Dante Alighieri. Beatrice's early death at age twenty-four heightened Dante's obsession, and thereafter she became a symbol of God's love, divine revelation, and Christ's salvation. According to Charles Williams, "Love then, however he [Dante] speaks of it, is a quality—a quality of himself towards Beatrice" Williams, (18). In his writing, Dante used Beatrice to tell the world about goodness and love. All that was holy and precious was embodied in Dante's devotion to Beatrice.

Dante had six sons and one daughter, Antonia. Influenced, by her father, after he died with malaria in 1321, she took her vows as a nun and chose the name of Sister Beatrice.

BEATRICE [TB]. Soldier's (Son's friend) young daughter was one of the children Jadine Childs photographed in Eloe, Florida (272).

BEAUCHAMP, LUTHER [PA]. Luther Beauchamp was the husband of Helen and parents of Royal and Destry (84–85). As one of the New Fathers of Ruby, Oklahoma, Luther was one of the trustful men that Pious

DuPres called on after learning of the raid on the Convent women. He knew that Luther could be counted on to help avert a disaster (284).

BEAUCHAMP, OSSIE [PA]. As one of the New Fathers of Ruby, Oklahoma, Ossie Beauchamp took an active role in the road to street honoring celebration. It was Ossie who owned horses, organized a horse race to earmark the occasion, and donated his military decoration (Purple Heart) as the prize to the winner of the race. Ossie loved the people of Ruby, Oklahoma, and did everything he could to endorse their progress. Contributing the Purple heart demonstrated that Ossie had greater pride in his community than in his country.

After World War I, there was news of many black soldiers returning to the South and being disrespected and treated badly by civil authorities after defending their country in military service.

Ossie was elated when young Coffee (aka, K.D., short for Kentucky Derby) Smith won the race and became the new owner of the Purple Heart (10).

BEAUCHAMP, REN [PA]. Pious DuPres asked Ren and his brother Luther Beauchamp to join the efforts to stop the men of Ruby from inflicting pain on the Convent women (284).

BEAUCHAMP, ROYAL (CALLED ROY) & DESTRY [PA]. Roy and Destry were the sons of Luther and Helen Beauchamp. The Oven, a communal cooking site, was first erected by Zechariah Morgan and the Old Fathers and served as an historical icon of survival and unity for the New Fathers of Ruby (114). As the years passed, the young people wanted to update the Oven's motto and meaning, but the older population resisted change, so it became a subject for generational debate (114). The first meeting about the Oven was to discuss clarification of the wording for its motto, and the boys were eager to defend their position. Roy was the spokesperson, and even though his delivery was seen as disrespectful by some of the adults. He argued that the motto, "Beware the Furrow of His Brow," lacked the courage and conviction of former slaves who fought hard to build a community out of nothing.

In harmony with his brother, Destry suggested that the motto on the Oven should be changed to, "Be The Furrow of His Brow." When Nathan DuPres accused Destry of wanting to be God, he denied the allegation, respectfully recanting that adherence to God's laws made them His instruments, not His rivals. The young people wanted, "Be the Furrow of His Brow," on the Oven to forge a closer relationship with God through love and obedience. The adults wanted "Beware the Furrow of His Brow" to maintain their history and because the word "beware" gave God total dominance in their lives through fear. Representing the young people of Ruby, Roy and Destry Beauchamp spoke about the need for adjustments in a changing society (85–86). But Steward Morgan ended the discussion by threatening to shoot anyone who touched the wording on the Oven (87).

The second meeting was after the fist representing militancy was painted on the Oven. Defiantly, Roy Beauchamp addressed the need to launch protest activities against white supremacy by updating the Oven's motto and adding African to the American in their cultural identity (104).

BEAVER RIVER [BLV]. The sight of Lu/Sethe's swollen feet put Amy Denver in mind of a corpse she once saw while fishing in the Beaver River (34).

BEAVERS, LOUISE (1908–1962) [SS]. Initially, Milkman thought that his aunt Pilate had performed admirably when she got them out of jail. Pilate had come into the police station with a lowly demeanor to collect the items stolen from her home by Guitar and Milkman. Milkman initially likened her behavior to that of Louise Beavers and Butterfly McQueen, actresses of the 1920s and 1930s (205). Pilate was family, and her demeaning behavior in the police station embarrassed him. Milkman's comment was disparaging because both Beavers and McQueen played menial film roles as mammies, cooks, and maids.

Louise Beavers began her career in 1927 in the silent film *Uncle Tom's Cabin*. In the role as Delilah, the maid in *Imitation of Life*, she sells a pancake recipe to her employer that results in wealth and security for the white woman (205).

BECK MORGAN. *See* **MORGAN, BECK [PA]**

BECKY (DOG) [SS]. The hound that Small Boy brought to lead the duo pack of dogs in the hunt for coon was called Becky. It was understood among the men that under Becky's lead, a successful hunt was guaranteed. The prey imagined, however, turned out to be a bobcat. Becky and the hounds trapped the animal in a tree until the men skillfully shot it down (272, 280).

BEDE CLAYTON [JZ]. Newly married, Joe and Violet Trace worked together on the barren land that belonged to Harlon Ricks. Ricks sold the land and the Trace's debt to Clayton Bede. According to Bede, interest and supplies pushed the Trace's original debt from $180 to $750. It took hard work and nearly five years for Joe and Violet to cancel the padded bill (126).

BEECHNUT [SU]. Beechnut was the site of the long-term care facility into which Sula Mae Peace signed her grandmother, Eva Peace. Sula remarked to her friend Nel that the home was "Out by Beechnut" (100).

BEECHNUT CEMETERY [SU]. The people of Medallion would not go to the white undertaker to see the body of Sula Mae Peace. Instead, they went to the burial site to visit Sula's grave in the colored section of the Beechnut Cemetery (150).

BELLE, TRUE [JZ]. True Belle was the mother of Rose Dear and May and grandmother of Violet Trace and five other grandchildren. As the faithful servant of a very pregnant Miss Vera Louise Gray, True Belle was the first to know about the forthcoming mulatto infant, who would banish an unmarried daughter from home and hearts of outraged parents. The only parental empathy for the unwed mother-to-be came in the form of money and an opened door (140–41).

For True Belle, traveling to Baltimore with Miss Vera Louise meant leaving her husband and children behind in the care of an older relative. The big city and the delight of pampering young Master Gray eased True Belle's guilt of leaving two girls to grow up without her. She adored Golden Gray, and, when he reached manhood, she encouraged him to go search for his father (140–43). Later, when a neighbor gave her the urgent news of her daughter Rose Dear's poverty and distress, True Belle altered her plans. True Belle feigned sickness to gain her freedom and rejoined the family who needed her (98, 138).

BELOVED [BLV]. Beloved was the spirit of the deceased infant killed by her mother, Sethe Suggs. As an infant under the age of two (4) she lost her life only to return eighteen years later as the spiteful spirit of a young woman. The house of 124 Blueston Road and the spirit of the infant were already at odds, but, Sethe, the mother who took her life, and Denver, the sister she never knew, cried out for her physical presence to appear (4). Baby Suggs was dead, Buglar and Howard were gone (3), and Here Boy, the pet dog, cowarded outside in the yard (12) as Sethe and Denver summoned forth the ghost who created so much havoc in their lives (4).

Denver's loneliness was revealed in her attentiveness to the mysterious young woman who came into their lives with a mighty thirst after a day of carnival fun with Sethe and Paul D. (57). As time progressed, Beloved's jealousy of Paul D. and her unnatural reverence for Sethe became apparent to Denver. Denver witnessed Beloved's aggression toward Sethe when tried to choke her in the Clearing (101). Beloved resented anyone who took Sethe's attention away from her. Murdered as an infant, she had been denied life, and Sethe had to pay for her loss. In an effort to eliminate Paul D., she used seduction as a tool (117, 207). [Later,

Beloved's humming of a song that Sethe sang to an infant confirmed suspicions about kinship for a guilt-ridden mother (176).] Once Beloved revealed her true identity to Sethe, the atmosphere in 124 became one of obsession, revenge, and blame (241).

Denver saw the imbalance in authority and knew that she had to get help in order to save her mother's life from the vindictive spirit who demanded retribution. Pregnant with the residue of pain and suffering, Beloved finally left 124 when the women from the community arrived to help (261).

BEN (DOG) [PA]. Steward Morgan had Ben and Good, two collies, on his ranch. The coat of these Scottish dogs are considered their crowning glory. Twice a year, Steward's nephew, K.D., enjoyed bringing the dogs into the town of Ruby, Oklahoma, for special grooming (54).

BENNIE [PA]. As a hitchhiker in need of a ride to California, Bennie caught a ride with Mavis Albright in her newly repainted Cadillac. Bennie was pleasant as she sang songs and encouraged detours to "soul restaurants" for what she considered "real food." As a ruse, Bennie suggested that Mavis use the bathroom and departed without even a good-bye. In leaving, she took Mavis' raincoat and boots as souvenirs of the trip (35).

BERNADINE. *See* DOLLS [JZ]

BERTHA REESE. *See* REESE, BERTHA [BE]

BEST, DELIA [PA]. Delia Best was the wife of Roger, mother of Patricia, and grandmother of Billie Delia Best. She came to Ruby, Oklahoma, with her child to build a life with the man whom she loved, but color consciousness and ignorance made her an outcast. Delia Best died in childbirth amongst men who hesitated to help a woman whose husband was out of town (197–98).

BEST, FAUSTINE [PA]. Faustine Best was the infant daughter who died in childbirth with Delia Best, wife of Roger Best (198).

BEST, FULTON & OLIVE [PA]. Olive and Fulton Best lost all but one of their children to influenza and other sickness. The future for Roger, the surviving son, looked very bleak. News from the Morgan twins of a plan to resettle encouraged Roger to send for his family. However, when Roger's mulatto sweetheart and child arrived in Haven, his parents reacted negatively and with disdain (30, 201).

BEST, PATRICIA (CATO) [PA]. Patricia Best was the daughter of Roger and Delia Best, wife of Billy Cato, and mother of Billie Delia Cato. As a child, Pat felt like a foreigner living in her hometown of Ruby, Oklahoma. Her father finally married Delia, her mother, one of the women living in Ruby, Oklahoma, known only by her first name. She had pale skin, noticeably someone outside of the "eight-rock" family grouping (197, 207). This union after Pat was born caused tongues to wag and eyes to stare within the community. There were no blatant signs of condemnation, but anyone with mulatto characteristics and without the eight-rock characteristics of coal complexions with hair to match was very conspicuous.

The circumstances surrounding Delia's death during childbirth greatly contributed to Pat's feelings of exile. Roger was out of town and Delia desperately needed transportation to the hospital in Demby. Pat realized that the women of Ruby had tried very hard to find help for her mother, but their male counterparts had not. Filled with excuses in the wake of a medical emergency, the men only came to help her after her death (197).

Marrying Billy Cato, one of the eight-rock children, offered only a short-lived solution to Pat's identity problem. As Pat Best Cato, she gained espousal status within the community. However, after her husband's early death and her daughter's birth, feelings of inferiority resurfaced because their child was a constant reminder of racial commingling (196).

The anguish and sorrow that follows narrow-mindedness restricted a mother's love and prevented the protection of a child. The sadness and irony lies in Pat's desire to embrace the town's biases in judging her daughter. Pat Best simply redirected the pain and suffering of her own childhood into maternal disapproval and displeasure for Billie Delia. In a sense, Pat was only reconstructing her own childhood. Her father never sheltered her from the pain of bigotry, so she neither thought nor knew how to protect her daughter. Billie Delia was reared under the suspicious and critical eye of her mother, who eventually drove her away. The mother-and-daughter bonding was splintered before it had time to fully develop.

Pat Best convinced herself that the genealogy project was a noble gesture to the town. However, she did burn the materials once she documented the imperfections in the eight-rock clan (217).

BEST, ROGER [PA]. Roger Best was the son of Fulton and Olive, husband of Delia, father of Patricia, and grandfather of Billie Delia. The move from Haven to Ruby, Oklahoma, curbed Roger's medical plans, but reunited him with his sweetheart and their illegitimate child. Delia and his daughter both had light skin with mulatto features, which bothered a few of the New Fathers. Roger chose not to react to the ignorance (201). The good people of Ruby gossiped when Delia was his first corpse after mortuary school (196), but Roger disregarded their concern. As a despondent husband, he was too busy blaming himself for being away at school when his beloved Delia died in childbirth (198).

As one of the New Fathers of Ruby, Roger was respected for his entrepreneurial ventures that provided important services to the town. Roger's van doubled as a hearse, and he was always available when someone passed on. He was not one of the nine men that raided the Convent, but he was not without blame. Roger Best did not help the image of the women at the Convent when he spoke negatively about them to the men of Ruby and even fabricated tales of Gigi's seductive behavior toward him on the ride to the Convent to pick up Mother Superior's body. In essence, Roger encouraged the fears and suspicions among the men that prompted the raid (275).

BETTY. *See* **TEAPOT'S MAMMA [SU]**

BETTY [TB]. Betty was one of Jadine Childs's friends from New York City. Betty was a lesbian openly, but when she met Son, Jadine's boyfriend, she considered changing her lifestyle to include men. In essence, Son's masculine charm and sex appeal forced Betty back into the closet (223).

BEULAH [TB]. In a conversation with her husband, Valerian Street, Margaret compared Ondine Childs, the couple's housekeeper, to the stereotypical black maid in *The Beulah Show*, a half hour situation radio comedy of the early 1940s (31). The show and the main character were both named *Beulah*. As a character, Beulah was stereotypically a southern black female domestic endowed with the happy go lucky demeanor. According to John Dunning who wrote extensively on historical radio programming, "She [Beulah] was a novelty character and sustained by a white man doing a black woman's voice" (Dunning, 1998). The original radio voices of Beulah were two white men: first, Marlin Hurt and then later Bob Corley. Hattie McDaniel (1895–1952), the first African American to receive the Academy Award for her role as supporting actress in the role of Mammy in *Gone With The Wind* in 1940, was the first black actress cast in the role of Beulah on a nationally syndicated radio show. As an accomplished actress and singer, she was extremely funny in the role of Beulah as the domineering black maid in the home of the Hendersons, a white family.

After McDaniel's stint on radio, the *Beulah Show* evolved to television and until the end in 1954, four additional black actresses (Ethel Waters [1896–1977]), Louise Beavers [1908–1962], Amanda Randolph [1896–1967], and later her sister, Lillian Randolph [1914–1980]), were employed during a time when the roles for black women were scarce. According to Dunning, "It was not until Hattie McDaniel took the part in a nightly CBS serial format that Beulah outgrew her novelty status and emerged as a character of some staying power (Dunning, 1998).

BIG DADDY (I.E., RECTOR MORGAN) [PA]. Rector Morgan was the son of Zechariah (Big Papa) and Mindy and husband of Beck and father of twins, Deacon and Steward, Elder and Ruby. As a young lad, Rector was of great assistance to his lamed father when the families were forced to leave Fairly, Oklahoma. Worried about where his people would go, it was Rector that Zechariah chose to accompany him into the wilderness to pray (96–97). Later, as a young man, Rector and Able Flood became partners in a banking enterprise that failed.

BIG MAMA [BE]. Big Mama was Claudia and Frieda MacTeer's grand-mother. Reminiscing, Claudia recalled how much she preferred the good feelings of Big Mama's kitchen to the gift of a doll at Christmas (22). As an impressionable little girl, Claudia wanted a heartrending experience for Christmas, not a present. It was also understood that Mrs. MacTeer's intolerance of the behavior of loose women was handed down from Big Mama (77).

BIG PAPA. *See* MORGAN, ZECHARIAH (I.E., COFFEE SMITH) [PA]

BIG PAPA [BE]. Big Papa was the grandfather of Claudia and Frieda MacTeer. Claudia's fond memories of being serenaded with violin music by Big Papa while sitting on furniture crafted just for her far outweighed the enjoyment of a doll received at Christmas (22).

BILLIE DELIA CATO. *See* CATO, BILLIE DELIA [PA]

BILLY CATO. *See* CATO, BILLY [PA]

BILLY JAMES ALBRIGHT. *See* ALBRIGHT, SALLY, FRANKIE & BILLY JAMES [PA]

BILLY, UNCLE. *See* UNCLE BILLY [SS]

BIRDIE GOODROE. *See* GOODROE, BIRDIE [PA]

BIRDS OF VIOLET TRACE [JZ]. Violet Trace had two birds, a canary and a parrot. The parrot she just called "My Parrot," and when she called to him he would say, "Love you." In a confused state, Violet went searching for the birds that she had deliberately discarded (27).

BISHOP ALLEN [BLV]. The 124 Bluestone address was vacant when Baby Suggs arrived because Bishop Allen had reassigned the previous minister to a congregation farther North. Initially 124 Bluestone had housed a family with eighteen children before Baby Suggs took occupancy (146).

BITTY FRIENDSHIP CATO. *See* CATO, BITTY FRIENDSHIP [PA]

B.J. BRIDGES. *See* BRIDGES, B.J. [TB]

BLACK JAKE. [SS]. *See* DEAD, MACON I. In a conversation with Milkman, Susan Byrd referred to his grandfather, Old Macon Dead I, as "Black Jack." She remarked that he was "black as coal" (321).

BLACKHORSE, BITTY. *See* CATO, BITTY FRIENDSHIP [PA]

BLACKHORSE, CELESTE [PA]. Wife of Drum Blackhorse and mother of Thomas, Peter, and Sally (95).

As one of the leaders of the group of people ejected from Fairly, Oklahoma, Drum Blackhorse withstood the humiliation and rejection of men with whom they'd thought would share cultural bonds and by whom the'd expected to be embraced. Pity from those along the way was unacceptable, so the wayfarers, fortified with pride, continued on their journey. When the group found a hungry child, they ensured a proper burial for a mother whose life was cut short. Drum Blackhorse was valiant in his efforts to pitch in to help (189–90).

Walking single file, Drum and Thomas Blackhorse served as beacons for the rest (96). In the camps they encountered on the way, the people were hostile and unfriendly. Basic human needs were denied, even for the pregnant women in their group. Armed with stamina and stubbornness, their suffering only served to reinforce their commitment to one another.

BLACKHORSE, DRUM [PA]. Drum Blackhorse was the husband of Celeste and father of Thomas, Peter, and Sally. Imbued with a pioneering spirit, Drum Blackhorse pitched in to help whenever the need arose. After his political aspirations were abruptly halted in Mississippi, he reverted to tending the land (193).

BLACKHORSE, ETHAN [PA]. Ethan Blackhorse was Drum Blackhorse's brother. In preparing the genealogy of the citizens of Ruby, Oklahoma, Pat Best was puzzled when she found a line was drawn through Ethan Blackhorse's name in the family Bible (188).

BLACKHORSE, PETER [PA]. Peter Blackhorse was the son of Drum Black-horse, husband of Bitty Cato, and father of Fawn Blackhorse Cato. When August Cato asked Peter Blackhorse for the hand in marriage of his young daughter, Fawn, he consented in spite of the fact that the peti-tioner was a much older man and his wife's biological uncle and, therefore, Fawn's grand uncle (197).

BLACKHORSE, SALLY. *See* POOLE, SALLY BLACKHORSE [PA]

BLACKHORSE, THOMAS [PA]. Thomas Blackhorse was the son of Drum Blackhorse, husband of Missy Rivers, brother of Peter Blackhorse and Sally Blackhorse Poole, and father of Soane and Dovey Blackhorse Mor-gan. Thomas walked single file with his father, as they led the caravan of people forced to leave Fairly, Oklahoma (96).

BLEACHED NIGGER [BLV]. Edward Bodwin was always active in his cam-paign against slavery. Once, he was humiliated by white racists in Ar-kansas who painted his face black and labeled him a "bleached nigger."

BLIND RACE [TB]. Gideon told Son the tale about the blind people, cap-tives who went blind when they saw Dominique, the French pronunci-ation for the Commonwealth of Dominica. Later, the Isle des Chevaliers was named for the blind people. As the story goes, after a wrecked sea vessel, many of the slaves, horses, and Frenchmen aboard drowned. Un-able to see, the blind people and horses that survived managed to get to shore in spite of the tide. Gideon told Son that Mary Therese, but not himself, was a descendent of the blind race. She saw with the mind instead of the eye. The fact that they had the same mother, but different fathers saved him from the affliction (152).

BLIND TWINS [JZ]. Musical guitar duo who played in the beauty parlor that Dorcas, niece of Alice Manfred, frequented (131).

BLOOD BANK DISTRICT [SS]. The "Blood Bank District" was the area of town where violence and blood commingled with stained streets and shattered lives (32).

BLUE JACK. *See* JACK, BLUE [BE]

BOB (DOG) [BE]. Bob was the dog that belonged to Bertha Reese, Soap-head Church's god-fearing landlady. Bob was an old and tired dog that needed the kind of extra care that was impossible to get from a woman who was just as old and tired. Handicapped by deafness, Bertha Reese just managed to feed Bob on a regular basis.

Soaphead Church, the eccentric boarder, was nauseated by the mere sight of the dog and plotted ways to get rid of him. In a cowardly fashion, he used the gullibility of Pecola Breedlove, who wanted blue eyes, to kill Bob. According to Soaphead's deception, Pecola was to feed the dog contaminated meal, and the reaction of his body would indicate whether God would or would not grant her request for blue eyes the following day. Infected, Bob went into convulsions, which verified to Pecola that pretty soon she would have the blue eyes she so desired (117).

BODWIN, BROTHER & SISTER [BLV]. The Bodwins were abolitionist siblings of Scottish descent. Raised by a father who believed in God and his goodness, the Bodwins hated slavery and went out of their way to help those in bondage (260, 137). For Baby Suggs, the Bodwins provided friendship, a house/home, and employment; for Sethe, a job at Sawyers Restaurant upon her release from jail (204); and for Denver, the memory of the Bodwins' past gifts and kindnesses to her grandmother, which encouraged her to seek employment within the household when the family needed food (255).

BOON, WINNIE [TB]. Winnie Boon, Drake's grandmother in Eloe, Florida, was one of the "pie ladies" in the church. Drake was a good buddy of Son (295).

BOSTON, MASSACHUSETTS [BLV]. When Amy Denver found Sethe in the woods, she was in route to Boston, Massachusetts, to find some velvet fabric. However, spurred on by memories of her mother, Amy Denver left Sethe, claiming Boston as her home (85).

BOTTOM, THE [SU]. The upper section of Medallion designated for the housing of black people. The Bottom was not down, but up in the hills, since the slave master reneged on his promise and refused to relinquish fertile ground to the slaves. To appease the slaves, the slave masters used the rationale that the land was valuable as God's scenery when looking down from heaven. At the mercy of the white landowners, the slaves made the most of a trying situation (5).

BOW-TIE [TB]. Bow-tie was Mary Therese Foucalt's name for Sydney. Mary Therese was a woman hired to work in L'Arbe de la Croix, in the home of Valerian and Margaret Street, under the supervision of the servants, Ondine and Sydney Childs. Mary Therese took exception to African Americans and enjoyed insulting them every chance she had. In an effort to minimize their superiority over her, Mary Therese renamed them—Sydney became Bow-tie and Ondine became Machete-Head (108).

BOYBOY [SU]. Boyboy was the husband of Eva and father of Hannah, Eva (Pearl), and Ralph (Plum). Boyboy met Eva, married her, and moved to Ohio. Only five years and three children later, his passion for women, alcohol, and spousal abuse led to abandonment of his family (31–32). Boyboy left them without much food or money, showing lack of remorse then and later.

A few years later, a well-dressed scoundrel of a husband and father returned for a visit in the company of another woman. The conversation was superficial between the estranged couple, as Boyboy failed to comment on Eva's missing leg or the well-being of his children. Upon leaving, he was seen whispering to his female companion and laughing out loud. At that point, the repressed hatred that a wife felt toward a husband who could leave her alone with three children and no food erupted and took root. Eva knew that the double boys in "Boyboy," validated the absence of manhood in a weak husband (36–37).

BRADEE, MR. *See* **MR. BRADEE [SS]**

BRANDTS, THE [TB]. Jadine Childs and Margaret Street were chatting about an invitation from the Brandts, the Streets' neighbors, to come to the Caribbean during the Christmas holidays (65).

BRANDYWINE [BLV]. After Mr. Garner died, Schoolteacher, his wife's brother-in-law, came to Sweet Home to manage the plantation. One of the changes he made was to sell Paul D. to a man by the name of Brandywine. Times were turbulent, and Paul D. was belligerent and distraught over the death of some of his Sweet Home buddies. Trying to even the score, Paul D. attempted to murder Brandywine as he was being transported across Kentucky (106).

BREAKSTONE, CALVIN [SS]. Milkman met Calvin Breakstone in Shalimar, Virginia, on the hunt. As a skillful hunter, Calvin was paired with Milkman, the novice. Calvin was adroit at stalking and knew the importance of listening, the need for extreme quiet, and the need to communicate simultaneously with his fellow hunters and hunting dogs in pursuit of prey.

Calvin was a jovial man and playfully teased Milkman about his inexperience as a hunter. Calvin thought that Milkman, as a novice woodsman, accidentally had discharged his rifle in fear, but that was not the case (271–84).

BREEDLOVE, CHARLES [BE]. Great Aunt Jimmy was furious with the parents of the infant she rescued from demise after only four days, so she refused to recognize their biological kinship to the child in his naming.

Instead, she deliberately named young Cholly after her brother, Charles Breedlove (133).

BREEDLOVE, CHOLLY [BE]. Cholly Breedlove was the husband of Pauline and father of Sammy and Pecola. Four days after he had entered the world, Cholly's young and foolish mother decided that he should leave. In an attempt to end her infant son's life, she chose the neighborhood garbage dump. Great Aunt Jimmy rescued him, cast his mother out of the home, named the infant for her brother, and spent the remainder of her life taking care of young Cholly Breedlove (132).

Working at Tyson's Feed and Grain Store with Blue Jack—an old man with stories of life, adventure, and women—afforded Cholly the only male-bonding experience in his life. The two men spent many hours together, but the memory of Old Blue's generosity in sharing the heart of a watermelon at an Independence Day picnic stayed with Cholly long after July 4 (133–35).

In his journey from boyhood to manhood, Cholly experienced humiliation and anguish which colored his entire life. A sexual encounter with a young girl (Darlene), was interrupted in the woods by armed white men who mocked his masculinity. Cholly longed to tell his old friend about what happened in the woods, but by then the trials in Blue's life had intensified his drinking (147–51).

Running away from the prospects of fatherhood at age fourteen, Cholly Breedlove went in search of Samson Fuller, the father he never knew. Whatever empathy he had hoped for never came, as his biological father only cursed and belittled him (147–48, 155–56).

Meeting Pauline Williams, the young girl with a deformed foot, in Kentucky, awakened Cholly's desire for marriage and a new life (160). However, the responsibilities of fatherhood were foreign to Cholly, so when he sired two children, he was unable to be a parent to them. Low self-esteem, loss of employment, and alcoholism rendered him incapable of functioning as a protective and nurturing husband or father (161). Later, after sexually violating his daughter, he deliberately set a fire to destroy their home (17). Cholly Breedlove ultimately died a broken man (5).

BREEDLOVE, PAULINE WILLIAMS [BE]. Pauline Williams Breedlove was the daughter of Ada and Fowler Williams, wife of Cholly Breedlove, and mother of Sammy and Pecola. At age two, a rusty nail entered her foot and, subsequently, martyrdom entered her life. As a young girl, the appeal for order and precision was borne in Pauline's preoccupation with her own consciousness (111). When Pauline met Cholly, a light-eyed songster who playfully touched her deformed foot, she fell head-over-heels in love. Cholly and Pauline married and moved up north for better work opportunities (113).

The move north brought a change in life that strained the marriage. Cholly went to work while Pauline suffered from loneliness and a lack of sociability, which led to isolation and arguments. The lure of fantasy, glamor, and acceptance was found at the movies in the company of Clark Gable and Jean Harlow (123). Even the birth of her two children could not altar Pauline's need for attention. As an employee in the Fisher family, she was afforded all of the social and personal attributes needed to bolster a shallow ego. As a domestic within the Fisher home, Pauline felt important and socially stimulated. However, these feelings of heightened self-esteem were costly for her husband and children. When Cholly's drinking increased, Pauline became sole financial provider, and the halo she wore became enjoined with her spirit of martyrdom.

Pauline was addressed formally as "Mrs. Breedlove" by her children and informally nicknamed "Polly" by the Fisher family. Religion became the crutch that served to promote Pauline's dominance over the frequently intoxicated Cholly (126). As a single parent in a two-parented household, Pauline's preoccupation with self robbed young Pecola and Sammy Breedlove of the emotional security they needed to become well-adjusted people (111–26).

BREEDLOVE, PECOLA [BE]. Pecola Breedlove was the daughter of Pauline and Cholly Breedlove and Sammy's sister. When she was born, Pecola's mother saw ugliness instead of beauty (126). The material nurturing needed by a little girl was not coming from Mrs. Breedlove, Pecola's mother, whose emotional stability was sustained by detaching herself from family responsibilities. There was no one to give Pecola the hope that she needed to believe in herself as a viable human being. Mrs. Breedlove was the Fisher housekeeper extraordinare who doted on the little Fisher girl. So, little sad Pecola was like a kite on a long string, floating aimlessly through adolescence in search of buoyancy.

Throughout the novel, everything happens *to* Pecola Breedlove. The simple act of buying candy became a generational and cultural battle. Pecola, in her innocence, simply ingested the rudeness of a narrow-minded old man (48–49). Looking at the characters within Pecola's existence from a feminist point of view, one sees that the females (except for conceited little Maureen Peal) were not as mean-spirited as their male counterparts.

Misses China, Marie, and Poland, the three ladies of the night who lived upstairs, accepted Pecola because she came into their home wanting nothing but conversation and attention (51–57). The MacTeer females were loving and protective in their desire to shield Pecola from further pain and embarrassment. Claudia and Frieda MacTeer actually tried to fight Pecola's battles when the odds were against her. Maureen Peal feigned friendship until she saw an opening for victimization and insults (67–73).

In sharp contrast, the males exploited poor Pecola to the point of threatening her sanity. Junior and Soaphead Church both took advantage of Pecola in order to hurt animals. Pecola could not have known that Junior was a deviant waiting to affect harm on his mother's prized cat (89–93). Soaphead Church advertised that he had spiritual powers, and Pecola was desperate to believe (173–75). The most damaging thing that can happen to a little girl is to experience sexual abuse by her father, and Cholly Breedlove betrayed Pecola in a way that defied human decency (161–63).

Pecola Breedlove looked outside for beauty because she was never taught to look inside. She didn't need blue eyes; she needed kindness and attention from those who cared to help her overcome her stigma of loneliness by building her self-esteem.

BREEDLOVE, SAMMY [BE]. Sammy was the son of Pauline and Cholly and brother of Pecola. Sammy was the older child, so he took the full emotional impact of living in an embattled and dysfunctional home with parents who nurtured their needs at the expense of those of their children. He was a young boy who wanted a father, but that was not what he had. When his parents fought, Sammy was a scapegoat for the perceived victim and the abuser. In his disoriented pain, Sammy sought comfort in the ability to hurt others, often suffering more than his victims (39). Twenty-five times within fourteen years, Sammy ran away from home, only to return more defeated than he was when he left (43). Solutions for Sammy were not found in flight, so he was forced to endure the constant bickering and disruption between his parents. It is interesting that there is little interaction between sister and brother, indicating that everyone in the household went for themselves. His father was always drunk and seldom productive, so Sammy often sided with his mother. Sammy embraced the notion of his father's death ending the misery of living in fear and humiliation (46).

BRIDE OF POLAR BEAR [TB]. Margaret Lordi, the young woman who was to become the bride of Valerian Street of the Street Brothers Candy Company of Philadelphia, first was featured as the Bride of Polar Bear in a parade when she rode a float accompanied by a polar bear (51).

BRIDGES, B.J. [TB]. B.J. Bridges was a former teacher of Michael Street. Michael's mother, Margaret Street, invited Bridges to spend the Christmas holidays with the Street family in the Caribbean so that she could entice her son to come home for the holidays. Valerian, Michael's father, thought the idea was absurd and angrily voiced his opinion (66, 89). The arrival of communication announcing Bridges' inability to come for Christmas settled the dispute (194).

BROOD POOLE. *See* POOLE, BROOD [PA]

BROOD POOLE SR. *See* POOLE, BROOD, SR. [PA]

BROTHER (TREE) [BLV]. Sweet Home had many beautiful trees, but one was special to Paul D., and he referred to it as "Brother." When Sethe told Paul D. that Amy Denver, the young white woman who had found her in the woods, had compared the scars on her back to a chokecherry tree, Paul D. immediately reacted with disdain, because he viewed trees as symbols of strength and comfort. Not only was Brother, a source of security and shade, but also it provided fond memories of his good times with his Sweet Home buddies. Paul D. rejected the white girl's fusing trees with pain—it contradicted his linking of trees of joy (21).

BROTHER & SISTER BODWIN. *See* BODWIN, BROTHER & SISTER [BLV]

BROTHER BODWIN. *See* BODWIN, BROTHER & SISTER [BLV]

BROTHER OTIS (1941–1967) [PA]. Mavis enjoyed the music of "Brother Otis" on her ride back with the gas station attendant after getting the gas. Brother Otis was Otis Redding, a gifted young soul singer of the 1960s. He died at an early age when his plane crashed into a Wisconsin lake on December 10, 1967. One of his most popular recordings, "Sitting on The Dock of the Bay," was recorded just three days prior to his death. The soulful music of Otis Redding is still cherished today (45).

BROTHERS, THE [JZ]. Two dancing brothers snubbed Dorcas at a party by turning up their noses and walking away when she was eager for a dance (67). The rejection by the brothers encouraged Dorcas' affair with an older man who showed an interest in her.

BROUGHTON, MR. *See* MR. BROUGHTON [TB]

BROWN GIRLS, THE [BE]. To underscore the elitism of Geraldine, wife of Louis and mother of Louis Jr., Morrison describes the "brown girls" at length. They were a special breed of young black girls who had cultural and social advantages. Accustomed to the finer things in life, the brown girls were envied by those less fortunate and less cultivated. They embraced the jealousy of underlings as badges of honor, and they stressed that their silver-spoon status was denied others within their race. Male attention and relationships were expected, and they occurred within socially accepted timetables. Intimacy came with politeness, appreciation, and conditions of expediency. The brown girls wore the best clothes, went to the best schools, and met the best people. Geraldine brought her brown-girl snobbiness to Lorain, Ohio, along with the cat that she cherished more than her family (81–86).

BROWN, NERO [SS]. Nero Brown was one of the men who Milkman assumed was a member of the Seven Days, the secret society that avenged the death of blacks. He was convinced of Nero's membership in the Seven Days when he saw him riding in a car with the other members: Henry Porter, Empire State, Railroad Tommy, Hospital Tommy, Guitar Bains, and a man whom he did not recognize (211).

BROWN, SALLY [TB]. Sally Brown was the mother of Cheyenne (Son's wife). When Son returned to Eloe, Florida, after eight years of running from the law, Soldier and Drake gave him news of his former mother-in-law's death. Son's visit with his father provided more details about Sally Brown's worshipping in church after the death of her daughter while publically banishing a shotgun at night. As a mother, Sally Brown wanted to avenge Cheyenne's death. She was grieved at losing her daughter at the hands of Son who used a car to kill her. The knowledge of Cheyenne's blatant adultery was insignificant, except that Sally Brown did not discriminate in her need for revenge. In addition to Son, the husband/murderer, she also wanted to inflict pain in the life of the teenager/lover caught in the marital bed of her daughter (248–49).

BUBBA (PIG) [JZ]. When the Hunters Hunter returned home, Honor, the boy watching over his animals, reported that Bubba, the pig, had been very difficult to handle (169).

BUCKLAND REED. *See* **REED, BUCKLAND [SU]**

BUD [JZ]. Joe Trace took a break from delivering his Cleopatra Products in the neighborhood to observe the recreational activities of C.T. debating with Bud (69).

BUDDY, MR. *See* **MR. BUDDY [BLV]**

BUDDY WILSON. *See* **WILSON, BUDDY [BE]**

BUFFALO MEN [BLV]. Buffalo men was the name the Cherokee Indians gave the forty-six black men on the chain gang (111–12). In his book describing the life of the buffalo soldier, historian William H. Leckie writes, "The origin of the term 'buffalo soldier' is uncertain, although the common explanation is that the Indian saw a similarity between the hair of the Negro soldiers and that of the buffalo. The buffalo was a sacred animal to the Indian, and it is unlikely that he would so name an enemy if respect was lacking" (Leckie, 26). Both the black men of the Tenth Regiment, United States Calvary and later the 92nd Infantry Division adopted the name and wore emblem of the buffalo proudly as part of their regimental crest.

BUFORD, MR. *See* MR. BUFORD [BE]

BUGLAR SUGGS. *See* SUGGS, BUGLAR [BLV]

BULLET HEAD [BE]. "Bullet Head" was the derogatory name Claudia MacTeer called Bay Boy, one of their classmates, when he and his friends were taunting Pecola Breedlove (66).

BUTLER FAMILY [SS]. The Butlers were the family of rich white landowners who tricked Old Macon Dead into signing away Lincoln's Heaven, his farm in Montour County. The Butlers murdered Old Macon Dead because he refused to turn over Lincoln's Heaven to them after his many years of his hard work (52).

BRYD CROWELL (CROW) [SS]. Crowell Byrd was the son of Heddy, brother of Sing, and father of Susan Byrd. Born to Heddy, his Indian mother, he later changed his name to Crowell Byrd (232).

BYRD, HEDDY [SS]. Heddy Byrd was the Indian mother of Crow and Sing Byrd. Heddy and her children lived in a house near Solomon's Leap. When Solomon, the flying African, dropped his son, Jake, after taking off for Africa, Heddy found him. This happened before Crow was born, and Heddy wanted a male child. She raised young Jake with her family. Ryna, Jake's mother, lost her mind when her husband flew away, so Heddy raised Jake as her own (323–24). As an Indian woman, Heddy was unhappy when her daughter, Sing, ran away to marry Jake, the black child whom she had raised (284).

BYRD, MARY. Mary was the wife of Crowell (Crow) and mother of Susan Byrd (289).

BYRD, SING. *See* DEAD, SING BYRD [SS]

BYRD, SUSAN [SS]. Susan Byrd was the granddaughter of Heddy, daughter of Crow (Crowell Byrd), and niece of Sing (wife of Macon Dead I). When Milkman visited the first time, Susan divulgeed very little in front of her gossipy friend, Grace Long (287). On his return visit, she was free to talk without the presence of Ms. Long. It is then that she explained the link between Heddy (the Indian woman), Solomon (the flying African), and Ryna (320–25).

C

CAIN, WOODROW [BE]. In concert with Bay Boy, Buddy Wilson, and Junie Bug, Woodrow Cain encircled Pecola Breedlove and chanted rhythmic insults. In anger, Frieda MacTeer interceded by bashing Woodrow over the head and threatening to disclose embarrassing information about his bedtime problem to his friends if he did not leave Pecola alone. Needless to say, Frieda took the sting out of Woodrow Cain, the bully (66).

CAIN, MRS. *See* MRS. CAIN [BE]

CALIBAN (S) [TB]. Caliban is cited as an example of a vagabond like Son. He roamed around the world for eight years without name and country (166). In William Shakespeare's *Tempest*, Caliban, son of Sycorax, the original possessor of Prospero's island, is a retarded slave. The name "Caliban" is derived from the word "cannibal."

CALINE POOLE. *See* POOLE, HURSTON & CALINE [PA]

CALVIN BREAKSTONE. *See* BREAKSTONE, CALVIN [SS]

CANAAN. *See* HAM'S SON [SU]

CANDY DANCE [BE]. Frieda and Claudia MacTeer choreographed dance steps and movements that followed the eating of sweets. The goal was to make Rosemary Vilanucci, the girl next door, jealous. The dance was supposed to let Rosemary know that they had candy and she did not (76).

CANDY KING [TB]. Margaret playfully called her husband, Valerian Street, the Candy King (31).

CARL [TB]. As an inquisitive country man, unaccustomed to and impressed by fur blend sweaters and fancy boots, Carl drove Jadine and Son into Eloe, Florida. Occasional glances from the driver's mirrored view of the backseat prompted inquiries comparing northern and southern attire (245).

CARLOS [PA]. Carlos was the handsome janitor/sculptor working at Pallas Truelove's high school who saw the vulnerability of a lonely teenager and took advantage of it (166). The shy and overweight girl from a well-to-do family was skillfully manipulated by Carlos (178).

Once trust in the relationship was established, the two planned to visit Dee Dee, Pallas' hippie-type mother in New Mexico. Carlos and Dee Dee were closer in age and got along very well. They shared interests in art, lifestyle, and, ultimately, selfishness and immorality. One day, Pallas found the lovers together, and it broke her heart (166). Pallas fled the house, never to see either one of them again (168–69).

CARNIVAL ACTS [BLV]. When Sethe, Denver, and Paul D. visited the carnival outside of Cincinnati, Ohio, they watched Abu Snake Charmer, Arabian Nights Dancer, Giant, Midget, One Ton-Lady, Two-Headed Man, and Wild African Savage (48).

CARY, SIMON. *See* REVEREND SIMON CARY [PA]

CATHERINE JURY. *See* JURY, CATHERINE [PA]

CATHERINE THE GREAT (1762–1796) [TB]. Jadine Childs found it humorous that Son believed that the antique jewelry worn in a modeling layout was actually a present to her from the eighteenth-century German princess who became the empress of Russia. When told that Catherine the Great had been dead for over two hundred years, Son shielded his embarrassment by shifting the discourse to the value of the earrings. The difference in educational attainment between Jadine and Son was evidenced clearly by this scene (117, 123).

CATHOLIC FOUNDLING HOME [JZ]. Pregnant with a black man's child, young Vera Louise Gray made plans to put the child in a Catholic Foundling Home. It was understood that unwanted births of white girls automatically went to the Catholic Foundling Home.

At the child's birth, however, the shamed Vera Louise Gray was so proud of the infant with golden skin and matching hair, she canceled all plans for giving the mulatto child away (148).

CATHERINE BLACKHORSE. *See* JURY, CATHERINE BLACKHORSE [PA]

CATO, AUGUST [PA]. As an older man without a wife, August Cato asked Thomas and Peter Blackhorse for the hand in marriage of Peter and Friendship's young daughter, Fawn. Within the Ruby community, this kind of arrangement was called a "takeover" because, biologically, August Cato was Fawn's great-uncle: he was her mother's grandfather's brother. Billy Cato, husband of Patricia Best and father of Billie Delia, was the only child born of this union (196).

CATO, BILLIE DELIA [PA]. Billie Delia Cato was the daughter of Patricia Best and Billy Cato (deceased), granddaughter of Roger and Delia Best and Fawn and August Cato, and great-granddaughter of Friendship (Bitty) and Peter Blackhorse and Sterl and Honesty Jones Cato. In addition to her maternal grandmother's mulatto features, Billie Delia inherited a combination of Blackhorse, Best, and Cato blood. Born with biracial traits impossible to mask, Billie Delia grew up under a cloud of doubt. To her mother, she was a constant reminder of the racial mixing frowned upon in the town of Ruby, Oklahoma.

At age three, an incident that should have been viewed as innocence became an indictment. A mother's suspicions escalated into an ugly scene with a pressing iron aimed at the head of an innocent child. As a pantyless toddler, eager to ride the horse, Hard Goods, Billie Delia should have not experienced the public criticism or the beating that resulted from her mother's anger as a mulatto outcast of the town (150–51). Billie Delia's desperate exit to the Convent after a fight with Patricia stifled any further communication between mother and daughter (203). She went to the Convent for shelter and protection.

There were those in the town of Ruby, Oklahoma, who thought Billie Delia had a questionable reputation with the opposite sex. The Morgan twins, in particular, labeled her as the "easiest girl" in Ruby, but they were wrong. She was kind and sympathetic to others. Billie Delia supported her friend Arnette even though she knew that her soon-to-be husband, K.D., was trifling and unfaithful (152). Billie Delia had experienced serenity within the Convent, so, when she met a hurt and bewildered Pallas Truelove, she deposited her there, too (162). Bold and defiant under the condemning eyes of the finest citizens of Ruby, Oklahoma, Billie Delia openly intermingled with the Convent women when they arrived at Arnette's wedding reception (158). The older women of the community, like Soane and Dovey Morgan and Anna Flood, saw Billie Delia's generous heart and responded in kind (151).

There were problems when two brothers, Apollo and Brood Poole, both were captivated romantically by Billie Delia. The situation became quite heated and a shooting between the brothers occurred. Needless to say, this certainly did not improve Billie Delia's image in town. Out of control, the brothers finally resolved their problems when Billie Delia left town. The Brood brothers were distant cousins of the Catos and any intimacy with Billie Delia would have violated bloodlines (277).

CATO, BILLY [PA]. Billy Cato was the deceased husband of Patricia Best and father of Billie Delia (198–99).

CATO, BITTY FRIENDSHIP [PA]. Bitty Friendship Cato was the daughter of Sterl and Honesty Jones Cato, the wife of Peter Blackhorse, and the mother of Fawn, who, in a takeover, married August Cato (196).

CATO, FAWN BLACKHORSE [PA]. Fawn Blackhorse Cato was the daughter of Peter and Friendship (Bitty) Blackhorse and the wife of August Cato, who was her grandfather's brother and, therefore, her great-uncle. The mixing of blood within marriages was called a "takeover" in the Ruby, Oklahoma, community. From the marriage of August and Fawn, one son, Billy Cato, was born (196).

CATO, HONESTY JONES. *See* CATO, STERL [PA]

CATO, JUPE [PA]. Obedient to the wishes of Zechariah Morgan and Drum Blackhorse, Jupe did not take the provisions offered by the light-skinned people. The wives and mothers did return to take the food because the children were hungry, but the money remained untouched (195).

CATO, PATRICIA BEST. *See* BEST, PATRICIA (CATO) [PA]

CATO, STERL [PA]. Sterl Cato was the brother of August Cato, husband of Honesty Jones, father of Bitty Cato Blackhorse, grandfather of Fawn Cato (wife of August Cato), and great-grandfather of Billy Cato (father of Billie Delia Cato) (196).

CATO, WILLIAM [PA]. William Cato was one of the "New Fathers" that resided in Ruby, Oklahoma (194).

CCC (CIVILIAN CONSERVATION CORPS) [BE]. Mrs. MacTeer was known to go on verbal tirades about social injustices when she was upset with signs of poverty that affected her home and family. The missing milk that Pecola Breedlove drank set her off, and her daughter, Claudia, knew to leave the room before she got around to the callousness of Roosevelt and the CCC (Civilian Conservation Corps) (25).

The CCC began in March 31, 1933, with an executive order under the presidency of Franklin Delano Roosevelt. The main purpose of the organization was to solve some of the problems in the country after the Great Depression. The plan was to get men to safeguard the natural resources of the United States. Georgia was one state that wanted to exclude blacks, but Roosevelt quickly put a stop to that.

CECILE SABAT. *See* SABAT, CECILE [SU]

CELESTE BLACKHORSE. *See* BLACKHORSE, CELESTE [PA]

CELESTINA & ALICIA [TB]. Celestina and Alicia were twin great-aunts of Joseph Lordi who were summoned by the Lordis to validate the bright yellow hue of young Margaret's hair (56).

CENCY [SS]. *See* BAINS, CENCY [SS]

CESTAIRE, AIME (1913–) [TB]. During romantic interludes, Jadine Childs read to Son from the works of Aime Cestaire, a French writer and politician. Independent in thought, Cestaire wrote most of his poetry in his native language without rhyme and metaphoric style. Cestaire's works are extensive and include plays like *Une Tempest*, his take on the Shakespearean play *The Tempest* (229).

CHARITY FLOOD. *See* FLOOD, CHARITY [PA]

CHARLES BREEDLOVE. *See* BREEDLOVE, CHARLES [BE]

CHARMAINE [PA]. After growing up without her, Sally Albright saw her mother, Mavis Albright, in a restaurant. In a daughter's eagerness to close the time gap between her and her mother, Sally informed her mother that she no longer lived at home, but was now sharing an apartment with her friend Charmaine (314).

CHE [PA]. "Che" was the name given by Grace (GiGi) to the infant son Arnette Fleetwood aborted at the Convent (250). On her wedding night a few years later, Arnette, in a confused state, returned to the Convent to reclaim the dead child (241).

CHEROKEE INDIANS [BLV]. The Cherokee Indians were a valiant band of native Indians who resisted conformity and set out on their own to carve out a life in the wilderness. Many of them were ill, but that did not hinder them from helping to free the forty-six enchained Buffalo Men who wandered into their camp covered in mud (111).

CHEYENNE [TB]. Cheyenne was the deceased wife of Son (William Green). Jadine Childs was curious as to why Son left Eloe, Florida, in such a hurry. Son told her the story of how he was responsible for Cheyenne's death (174).

Against the advice of his friends, Son married the good-looking and sexually alluring Cheyenne (254). One evening he returned from work and found his wife in bed with a teenager. Outraged, Son rammed his car into the house, and Cheyenne died in the fire that engulfed the bed (224). Son tried to save her, but to no avail. The widower, was later charged with first-degree murder and left town to escape incarceration (176).

CHICKEN LITTLE [SU]. Chicken Little was an innocent and playful little boy who happened along one day during a period of boredom and mischief for Nel Wright and Sula Peace (59). That fateful day, reckless child's play ended Chicken Little's short life as Sula challenged her strength as Nel stood by and watched (59–61).

Sula tried to swing him in the air above the water, but the weight of Chicken Little was too much; and he slipped from her grip and vanished into the river (59–61). Days later his body was found downstream in Porter's Landing and brought home to Medallion. The corpse of Chicken Little was so disfigured that only his absence identified it (64).

CHICKEN WILLIAMS. *See* **WILLIAMS, CHICKEN [BE]**

CHILDREN IN CHRISTMAS PLAY [PA]. The children on the stage for the Person's Yuletide play in Ruby, Oklahoma, were Royal and Destry Beauchamp; Hope, Chaste, Lovely, and Pure Cary; Linda DuPres; Peace and Solarine Jury's two grandsons; Ansel and Fruit; Joe-Thomas and Dina Poole; Drew and Harriet Persons' son, James; Payne Sands' son, Lorcas; and two of Timothy Seawright's grandsons, Steven and Michael Seawright (208).

CHILDREN OF BABY SUGGS [BLV]. Baby Suggs' children were Patty, Rosa Lee, Ardelia, Tyree, John, Nancy, Famous, and Halle (143).

CHILDREN OF ZECHARIAH & MINDY FLOOD MORGAN [PA]. Zechariah and Mindy Flood Morgan's children were Pryor, Rector, Shepherd, Ella, Loving, Selanie, Governor, Queen, and Scout Morgan (191).

CHILDS, JADINE (I.E., JADE) [TB]. Jadine Childs was the niece of Ondine and Sydney Childs, employees of Valerian and Margaret Street. Culturally advanced by a European education and lifestyle, coupled with exposure to the world of modeling and glamour, Jadine wore an air of superiority. The scene in the Parisian market when the African woman spat at her served to shatter her air of dominance (46, 288). Rooted in one world, seeking the security of another, her life was filled with inner conflict (146).

Self-centered in thought and actions, Jadine cared for her aunt and uncle, but not with the same intensity they showed for her. The Childs thought of Jadine as a daughter with a full range of maternal emotions, yet, Jadine was indifferent to pertinent details about their lives (68).

More than once, Jadine heard her aunt complain about her feet (160), yet she selected fancy footwear as her Christmas gift (90). The true benefactors of the Sorbonne education she wore so proudly also escaped her. When Jadine was twelve, Sydney and Ondine became her surrogate parents. Out of responsibility and love, they spent their life savings on her education, yet Jadine lauded Valerian Street as her benefactor (226). She did not realize that Valerian's contributions resulted from the toil and request of her aunt and uncle.

Son, the stowaway turned lover, was below social standards for Jadine, but his masculinity more than compensated for this deficiency (126). Jadine was being wooed by Ryk, the European suitor, and the passion paled in comparison (90). Meeting Son in all of his crude blackness ignited emotions in her long suppressed. Jadine wanted the passion of a black lover, but only on her terms. There were class, intellectual, and cultural differences between the couple, but Jadine thought she had the upper hand and could mold Son to her liking. She soon found out that Son's personality was too strong for makeovers. On one hand, she mocked his maverick lifestyle and mannerisms; on the other hand, Jadine was captivated by his magnetism.

In a short time, Son recognized characteristics and mannerisms about Ondine and Sydney that Jadine simply overlooked (265). After the fatal Christmas dinner scene, Son left for New York with Jadine to follow. As lovers, Son and Jadine had an intense intimacy, but it was short-lived because their personalities clashed. Jadine was unhappy with the visit to Eloe, Son's hometown. Together in New York again, they found the intimacy that was once freely given had become forced. Jadine returned to her world of modeling in Paris as she fled the disappointment of love gone wrong (280). Stopping at L'Arbe de la Croix on the first leg of her trip aboard, Jadine received some sound advice from Ondine about what it takes to be a real woman. Listening was as foreign to Jadine as sincerity, so she boarded the plane to Paris without the understanding she needed to enhance her selfish life. (281).

CHILDS, ONDINE (I.E., NANADINE) [TB]. Wife of Sydney and aunt of Jadine, Ondine Childs worked beside her husband in the Street home in Philadelphia for years. Once they relocated to the Isle des Chevaliers, she relied heavily on the assistance of the Island people to maintain the Street house. Tired feet and advanced years heightened Ondine's dependence on Yardman and the Marys, who were peculiar, but lessened the burden of managing the Street household (41). When Valerian dismissed those, without consultation, on whom Ondine relied, she took it personally. Technically, he was the boss, but Ondine became so enraged, she blurted out the horrible secret of Mrs. Street's abuse of their son, Michael. Rage gave way to reason as the Childs were financially dependant on their employment with the Streets (207).

Ondine loved Jadine, but in her heart she knew that her niece was selfish. When Jadine returned from New York, en route to Paris, Ondine tried to explain to her about the relationship real women have with their mother figures (281), but the message escaped Jadine, falling on deaf ears (290). The one and only constant force in Ondine's life was the love and devotion of her life partner and husband, Sydney.

CHILDS, SYDNEY [TB]. Sydney Childs was the husband of Ondine and uncle of Jadine. In partnership with his wife, Sydney worked for the Street family for over fifty years. He was a proud Philadelphian and wore his work ethics with pride. Both older men with younger wives, Sydney and Valerian trusted each other and communicated with respect. That is, until Valerian fired Ondine without consideration or consultation. When questioned about his actions, Valerian verbally disrespected Ondine. Without fear of reprisals, Sydney chastised Valerian during a heated discussion about the matter (207).

Family and pride were of great importance to Sydney (163). When his brother's child was orphaned, he and his wife adopted Jadine as their own. It was nothing for them to invest their life savings in pursuit of her education (193). Sydney's disappointment matched his wife's when he was forced to confront Jadine's selfishness.

CHINA. *See* MISS CHINA [BE]

CHINA [SU]. China was a woman in Medallion who was well known for promiscuity and whose earlier death was compared to Sula Peace's. The comparison was made to confirm and verify that notoriety did not alter community sympathy and support during bereavement (172).

CHIPPER & SAMPSON (DOGS) [BLV]. Chipper & Sampson were pet hounds owned by the two nephews of Schoolteacher (149).

CHOCOLATE EATER [TB]. Mary Therese Foucalt called Son (William Green), the "chocolate eater" because at night he roamed around the grounds of L'Arbe de la Croix eating chocolate candy kisses. Mary Therese Foucalt, the old island woman, also credited Son with the on-slaught of ants that arrived shortly after he did. Mary Therese had advance knowledge of his presence on the island because the chocolate eater's arrival came to her in a vision. Therese let all of her island friends know of her dislike for American blacks, but she could not hide her adoration of the "chocolate eater" (104).

CHOKECHERRY TREE [BLV]. At first, Amy Denver summoned strength from her God when she saw Sethe's lacerated back, then she mustered up the words to describe what she saw to Sethe (whom she called "Lu") as a wound that looked like a chokecherry tree. A chokecherry is a reddish-brown shrub-like tree. The bark ranges from gray to brown and from smooth to somewhat scaly (79).

CHOLLY BREEDLOVE. *See* BREEDLOVE, CHOLLY [BE]

CHRIST THE KING SCHOOL FOR NATIVE GIRLS [PA]. After the embezzler left in a hurry, the nuns started the Christ the King School for Native Girls, but everyone in Ruby, Oklahoma, called the school the "Convent" (224).

CHURCHES IN RUBY, OKLAHOMA [PA]. There were three churches in Ruby, Oklahoma: Mount Calvary Baptist, Rev. Richard Misner; Holy-Redeemer, Pentacostal Rev. Simon Cary; and New Zion Methodist, Rev. Senior Pulliam.

CINCINNATI, OHIO [BLV]. Mr. Garner brought Baby Suggs from Sweet Home in Kentucky to the Bodwins in Cincinnati, Ohio. The house at 124 Bluestone Road was the beginning of Baby Suggs' new life as a free woman. In time, two of her grandchildren arrived and, later, her daughter-in-law, with yet another grandchild. The future looked bright as Baby Suggs reached out with love to her neighbors. However, visitors from Kentucky brought horror and fear that threatened the peace (141–45, 135).

CIRCE [SS]. Circe was the well-known midwife who worked for the Butlers, a wealthy white family who raised dogs and bushwhacked Macon Dead I for his land (52, 232).

Circe's reputation for birthing both white and black infants was well known throughout the country. The only mother she ever lost during childbirth was Sing Byrd Dead when Pilate was born. She assisted both Macon II and Pilate as infants, and again as orphans after their father's tragic death. Squirreled away in the Butler home, Circe gave them food and shelter. After a few days, the children set out on their own.

When Milkman visited Circe years later, he found an old woman living in a broken-down mansion amongst canines. She revealed to Milkman how the Butlers destroyed people in order to maintain their opulence. In the end, they gained nothing, as their precious home literally went to the dogs. Circe was appalled when Mrs. Butler chose to commit suicide, rather than experience the life of a servant. In a vengeful manner, Circe retaliated by letting the dogs in to destroy her cherished mansion.

Circe filled in many of the blank spots in the Dead family history, and Milkman understood more about his history after his visit (242–47).

CISSY & FRANK [TB]. Cissy was Valerian Street's sister, and Frank was her husband. When Cissy met Margaret, her brother's young wife, she criticized her, stating that only a loose woman wore crosses as jewelry. Cissy even went so far as to demand that she take it off. After that, the sisters-in-law did not get along. Margaret was angry, and retaliated by denying Cissy visitations with her one and only nephew, Michael (69).

CLARISSA & PENNEY [PA]. Clarissa and Penney were two teenage Indian girls who attended the Convent school, but resisted the confinement of religious life. They found the religious sisters controlling, but liked Connie because she had once led a carefree life like theirs. When they realized that Connie was sneaking off to meet a man on Friday afternoons, in amusement and intrigue, they covered for her (231). News of the Convent/school's financial problems and impending dismantlement please the girls. When the school actually closed, Clarissa and Penney were sent East for schooling. Along the way, freedom from restrictions and religious rulings came with a detour in Arkansas. Clarissa and Penney later mailed Connie the money she had loaned them to aid their new life (240–41).

CLARK, WINSOME [JZ]. Winsome Clark wrote one of the letters stolen by William "Sweetness" Younger, the delinquent nephew of Malvonne Edwards. Writing to her husband, she advised him that, because of insufficient funds, she was forced to return home with their children. Reading the letter and sensing its importance, Malvonne added a stamp to speed it on its way to the unknowing husband (42–43).

CLAUDIA MACTEER. *See* MACTEER, CLAUDIA [BE]

CLAYTON, BEDE. *See* BEDE, CLAYTON [JZ]

CLEARING, THE [BLV]. The Clearing is the place in the woods where Baby Suggs gathered the townspeople for worship. Baby Suggs summoned children, mothers, and fathers, each in their own grouping, to use the trees as their pews and listen to behavioral instructions. The gatherings proved to be an emotional release for people. In the Clearing, Baby Suggs taught the crowd how to love themselves in spite of racial woes. She believed that God's love was greater than any white man's loathing (86–87).

When Baby Suggs died, Sethe insisted on the Clearing as her burial site, but town ordinances prevented it (171). It was also where Sethe went to pay tribute to her husband, Halle (89).

CLEOPATRA PRODUCTS [JZ]. Cleopatra Products were the female cosmetics that Joe Trace sold (26, 128).

COFFEE SMITH. *See* K.D. [PA]

COFFEE SMITH. *See* SMITH, COFFEE (I.E., PRIVATE SMITH) [PA]

COFFEE SMITH. *See* MORGAN, ZECHARIAH (I.E., BIG PAPA) [PA]

COLBERT, CLAUDETTE (1905–1996) [BE]. Born Lillian Claudette Chauchoin, Claudette Colbert was the movie star of the 1930s who played the lead role of the white widow who befriended and hired the black maid who had the mulatto daughter named Peola Johnson in the 1934 film *Imitation of Life*. Maureen Peal recognized the similarity in Pecola Breedlove's name and Peola Johnson's name (67). *Imitation of Life* was adapted from Fannie Hurst's novel of the same name.

COLES, REVEREND. *See* REVEREND COLES [SS]

COLONEL WORDSWORTH GRAY. *See* GRAY, COLONEL WORDSWORTH [JZ]

COMMITTEE ON CIVIL RIGHTS. *See* TRUMAN, HARRY S. [SS]

COMPTON, PRAISE [PA]. Along with Missy Rivers, Fairy DuPres, and Ella and Selanie Morgan, Praise Compton helped when Lone DuPres was found, a hungry infant, standing in front of the house with her deceased mother inside. A covering for the child was needed, and Praise accommodated by ripping away part of her skirt (190).

CONNIE. *See* SOSA, CONSOLATA [PA]

CONSOLATA. *See* SOSA, CONSOLATA [PA]

CONVENT, THE [PA]. The official name of the Convent was the Christ the King School for Native Girls. When the Sisters of the Sacred Cross secured the property, they tried to conceal all of the erotic fixtures that earmarked an embezzler's den. The vulgar display of sexual ornaments had insulted their religion. The Convent was seventeen miles outside of Ruby, Oklahoma, an all-black town populated by 360 people. Once a school for Indian girls, the Convent later became a refuge for troubled souls (4, 232).

COOP [SS]. "Coop" was the nickname for Revered Cooper of Danville, Pennsylvania (256).

COOPER, ESTHER. *See* MRS. ESTHER COOPER [SS]

COOPER, REVEREND. *See* REVEREND COOPER (I.E., COOP) [SS]

COPPER VENUS [TB]. Jadine Child's modeling name was "Copper Venus." Son overheard Mary Therese Foucalt, one of the women who worked for the Streets, talking to herself about Copper Venus and approached Jadine for answers (115).

CORA [SU]. Cora was the friend of Dessie who resisted the chatter about catalogues and new rugs, preferring to hear gossip about Shadrack and Sula Peace. She listened attentively about how, out of respect for evil, Shadrack curtsied to Sula Peace in public one day (116).

CORRIE. *See* DEAD, FIRST CORINTHIANS [SS]. "Corrie" was the pet name given to First Corinthians by her lover, Henry Porter (195).

COTTOWN, TENNESSEE [JZ]. Miss and Mrs. Dumfrey carefully hid the fact that their family was originally from Cottown, a little "one-horse" town near Memphis. In an effort to disassociate themselves from Cottown, they hurtfully shunned a hometown neighbor (18–19).

C.P.T. [JZ]. Sheila (Malvonne Edwards' cousin) chastised Joe Trace for his tardiness in bringing her order of Cleopatra Products by using the slang term C.P.T., which means "Colored People Time" (69).

CREEK NATION [PA]. Deacon and Stewart Morgan saw the decline in living conditions and were determined to relocate their families and the Oven from Creek Nation after their stint in the army. There is a tribal government located in east-central Oklahoma known as the Muskogee Creek Nation. The Creek Nation boundaries include eleven counties: Creek, Hughes (Tukvpvtce), Mayes, McIntosh, Muskogee, Okfuskee, Okmulgee, Rogers, Seminole, Tulsa, and Wagoner (6).

CROWELL BYRD. *See* BYRD, CROWELL (I.E., CROW) [SS]

C.T. [JZ]. Joe Trace found the conversations and antics between C.T. and Bud an amusing distraction in a busy day of peddling Cleopatra Products around the neighborhood (69).

CUNY [TB]. Son (William Green) made reference to the City University of New York (CUNY) when he arrived in New York from the Isle des Chevaliers (216).

D

DADDY MAN [PA]. Gigi called her father "Daddy Man" when she saw him again after many years (309–10).

DADDY SAGE [JZ]. One of the letters in a batch of mail stolen by Malvonne Edwards' delinquent nephew was addressed to Daddy Sage. The contents of the letter addressed to Daddy Sage were quite steamy and cause Malvonne some concern. The sexually explicit communication between two people whom she knew lived in the same building, prompted Malvonne to send the letter on its way with a note of caution (44).

DANTE. *See* **ALIGHIERI, DANTE [BE]**

DARLENE [BE]. Darlene was the young girl at Aunt Jimmy's funeral whom Cholly Breedlove invited to go down to the gully. As the two attempted intimacy, two white men interrupted with laughter and incitement. Darlene covered her face as the men pointed guns at the couple in an attempt to force Cholly into a demonstration of his sexual powers. After the incident, Cholly took his frustrations out on Darlene. In seven words, Cholly totally disregarded and dismissed anything that Darlene might have been feeling about the embarrassing incident. He simply said, "We got to get, girl. Come on" (144–49).

DAUDET ALFONSE (1840–1897) [SS]. First Corinthians Dead did not want anyone to know that her employment with Miss Michael-Mary Graham, the noted poetess, was that of a maid. She went to work in high heels carrying a book and a bundle of changing clothes to support the deception.

First Corinthian's choice of *Contes de Daudet* (*Stories of Daudet*) was an excellent decoy, as french literature written in 1893 was not something a black woman traveling to a job as a domestic would carry to read on a bus (190).

The author, Alfonse Daudet, was a French writer of short stories, plays, and poetry. He wrote about life in Southern France and the mysteries of human relationships. Daudet also wrote *Les Amoureuses* (The Lovers) (1858); *Le Petit Chose* (*The Little Thing*) (1868); (*Chapin Le Tueur De Lions Lions*) (1863); *Chapatin the Killer of Lions*) (1863); and others.

DAUDET, CONTES de (STORIES OF DAUDET). *See* DAUDET, ALFONSE [SS]

DAVID [PA]. David was the limousine driver employed by Leon and Norma Keene Fox. When Mr. Fox was out of town, David solicited young girls to do "special jobs" for Mrs. Fox. He spotted Seneca at the bus stop and approached her with the proposition of work. Mrs. Fox had instructed David to look for a smart girl in the street. As soon as Mrs. Fox received news of Mr. Fox's return, David was to deposit Seneca back at the bus depot (136).

DAWN [TB]. Dawn was a New York City friend of Jadine Childs. As an aspiring actress, Dawn sublet her apartment to Jadine while she was on the West Coast for a filming. As were all of Jadine's girlfriends, Dawn was impressed with Son and his masculine charm (261).

DEACON MORGAN. *See* MORGAN, DEACON [PA]

DEAD, FIRST CORINTHIANS [SS]. First Corinthians was the daughter of Ruth and Macon Dead II, and sister of Magdalene called Lena. At age forty-two, First Corinthians found that her college education at Bryn Mawr could not reduce the loneliness and boredom in her life. Leaving the confinement of her home, she sought the maid's position with Michael-Mary Graham, the state poet laureate. She made a good first impression and was hired immediately. In order to hide her position as a servant from her highbrow family and the community, she pretended to be a secretary. The deception was complete with a change of clothes and a scholarly book of short stories by Alfonse Daudet, the french writer, which she carried under her arm as she boarded the bus (187–89).

On the public bus, First Corinthians was exposed to Henry Porter who attempted to communicate with her. At first, she resisted the advances of her father's tenant who drank too much wine on occasion, but she later succumbed to his persistent and earthy charm. Porter was considered undesirable for most of the town's women, but especially the granddaughter of the town's only black doctor and the second daughter of Macon and Ruth Dead. Corinthians was careful to conceal her interest in him because she knew that a relationship with a man like Porter would make life unbearable at home. However, Milkman, her brother, saw her exiting Porter's car and alerted their father, who raised a ruckus. Only the happiness found with Porter caused Corinthians to leave the Dead home and move in with the man who affectionately called her "Corrie" and who revitalized her life (187–202, 334).

DEAD, HAGAR. *See* **Hagar [SS]**

DEAD, MACON I (I.E., OLD JAKE) [SS]. Macon Dead I was the husband of Sing, father of Macon II and Pilate, and grandfather of Magdalene called Lena, First Corinthians, and Macon Dead III (Milkman). The youngest son of the flying African, Macon was born with the name "Jake."

When Jake lifted off with his father, Solomon (Shalimar), for the trip back to Africa (322), the flight for two was unsuccessful, and the young boy was dropped and found by Heddy, the Indian woman who raised him with Sing, her only daughter (320–22). Later, Sing and Jake married and moved up north. The Freedmen's Bureau accidentally renamed Jake when he registered as an ex-slave. Thus, Jake became Macon Dead, and it is under that name that Macon II and Pilate were born (53). His wife's death during childbirth left him devastated and unable to hear her spoken name (43). In dreams, Jake tried to give Pilate what she had been denied: knowledge of her mother. Pilate thought her father wanted her to sing, and she did. In reality, spiritually he was introducing his daughter to the mother she never knew (333). Later, Jake was killed defending Lincoln's Heaven, the land that he loved (42).

DEAD, MACON II [SS]. Macon Dead II was the husband of Ruth Foster; father of First Corinthians, Magdalene called Lena, and Milkman; and brother of Pilate. As a husband, father, and brother, everything that Macon Dead II did centered around making money and displaying opulence. He communicated to his son that money was the key to success and happiness (163).

In a close look at Macon's childhood, one sees events that dramatically altered his character. A young boy's admiration for his father was assaulted by tragedy and loss (42). Working side by side, father and son cultivated the farm rich in natural resources and game, only to see it threatened and ultimately robbed (51). Witnessing the tragic death of his beloved father at the hands of greedy landowners changed an innocent lad into a desperately materialistic man. However, the same greed that compelled the Butlers to kill caused Macon to value money and real estate more than family. A dead man in a cave, a satchel of gold, and dreams of replacing his father's farm clashed with his young sister's principles. Pilate could not deal with stealing a man's gold after taking his life. The riff between sister and brother lasted a lifetime, and they went separate ways (169–71).

Later, Macon's marriage to the doctor's daughter was merely business, not romance. The twenty-five-year-old prospective suitor saw opportunities abound to increase his fortune. The psychological problems that came with his teenage bride weighed heavily on the marriage. Macon wanted to love his family, but loving was disappointing and hurtful. Macon missed being with Pilate and the security of interacting with his father, whom he adored.

Macon married the doctor's daughter hoping to advance socially and financially. He felt cheated, however, when his wife came with the psychological problems that repulsed him. His disappointment was evident in his displays of disrespect toward her in front of their children. One incident caused his son, Milkman, to assault him physically. In order to salvage the relationship with his son, Macon revealed personal aspects of his marital discord and then encouraged him join his business (70–74).

In his youth, Macon II took good care of his baby sister, Pilate (40–41, 51). Both children suffered after the death of their father, but each in a separate way. Being the older son, Macon II worked closely with his father and in his grief, also materialistically resented the lifestyle lost, whereas Pilate suffered more from the emotional loss of a parent. When Macon discovered the gold after killing the man in the cave, he envisioned ways to buy another home. However, the two siblings fought as Pilate wanted no part of the corpse's gold. It was many years before Macon Dead II and Pilate would meet again.

Macon II's problems with Pilate and a loveless marriage to Ruth, the doctor's daughter, hardened his heart toward women. Consequently, his relationship with two daughters, Magdalene called Lena and First Corinthians was cold and superficial (169–71).

DEAD, MACON III (I.E., MILKMAN) [SS]. Macon Dead III, aka "Milkman," was the son of Macon and Ruth Foster, brother of Magdalene called Lena and First Corinthians, nephew of Pilate, first cousin of Reba, and second cousin of Hagar. When Pilate visited her brother and met Ruth, her sister-in-law, for the first time, she saw that there were serious problems within the marriage. Experienced in witchcraft, Pilate advised Ruth about seduction and ways to make Macon desire her. As result, Ruth became pregnant. Early on, even in the womb, the child's life was threatened as Macon tried to force his wife into an abortion (125–27). Milkman was determined not to give up his childhood in the wake of a dysfunctional home life. He looked for alternatives to replace the love and security he missed because of the problems in his parent's marriage. Subsequently, every pleasure or pain that touched his life centered around his need to break the intergenerational cycle of distrust and unhappiness.

His name, "Milkman," was the result of his mother's obsession with breast-feeding him until his feet touched the floor (14–15, 78). In conformity with his gender, Milkman adopted his father's posture toward and about women (75). As the breadwinner, his father was domineering and his mother and sisters were delicate, boring, and passive. At the age of twelve, Milkman found another hero in Guitar Bains, who rescued him from an altercation with four boys. Guitar was older, fearless, and wise as he ventured into the home of Pilate Dead, the aunt who simultaneously intrigued and frightened Milkman (35–39, 264).

His friendship with Guitar was seeded in immaturity, but later harvested a mature and insightful young man. As Milkman evolved, his need for a hero dissipated. He began to listen to Guitar with a more critical ear. The idea of the Seven Days, their mission, and Guitar's membership upset Milkman and created a serious breach in their relationship (159–61).

His relationship with Pilate, Reba, and Hagar gave Milkman a new sense of pleasure. At home, his mother, Magadalene called Lena, and First Corinthians were three somber, uptight women, but the three women in Pilate's house were free spirited and interesting (79). Pilate and Reba were so relaxed in their social and moral thinking that Milkman's incestuous relationship with Hagar was accepted without condemnation. There was freedom at Pilate's house, whereas, within his family, he was only a pawn to be manipulated. Both parents took advantage of kinship to influence Milkman's thinking with intimate details of their marital relationship that only confused and annoyed him.

When Milkman discovered that Pilate's gold was really a bag of bones, he went to the cave in Virginia. He had heard stories from his father, but was unaware that his family ties were so strong in that region. As he traveled, he found hospitality and warmth in Danville, Pennsylvania, but in Shalimar, Virginia, he was assaulted by a stranger and received a threatening message from Guitar Bains (229, 261–62). As Milkman embraced the richness of his ancestry, he was forced to release boyhood notions of friendship and loyalty. Ironically, it was away from home that

Milkman took the time to understand his relationships with the women in his life. Emotionally armed with generational pride, he returned home and escorted Pilate back to bury her father's bones. However, Guitar's lunacy erupted as he fired the bullet that ended Pilate's life (333–37).

DEAD, MAGDALENE CALLED LENA [SS]. Elitism came to Magdalene called Lena from being the eldest child of a successful Negro businessman and the granddaughter of the town's most respected Negro doctor. Long before she witnessed Mr. Smith's failed aviation stunt from the roof of Mercy Hospital, Magdalene called Lena had learned how to disregard commoners (5, 12). The Sunday-only rides in the Packard through the better white neighborhood reinforced the Dead family's good fortune and status within the black community (32). The roses that Magdalene called Lena and her sister had worked so diligently to make were scattered in the air during all of the confusion. Neither the eminent birth of their brother nor the antics of a North Carolina Mutual insurance agent promising to fly was as important as collecting the roses they toiled over that were now airborne (5).

Magdalene called Lena was unhappy because she resented her father's dominance in contrast to her mother's passivity and feminine naivete. She was aware of the unhealthy dynamics in her family and tried to control the situation. The sixteen years between she and her mother made the two women more like sisters than mother and daughter. Magdalene called Lena was determined that her father was a brute and became her mother's savior. The decision to forego college for a sedentary life at home was hers, but she placed all of the blame on her father. Magdalene called Lena knew that she could not concentrate on her studies at college with her mind at home. Staying close to her mother was mandatory in order to fend off her father's emotional abuse (215).

Not only did Magdalene called Lena safeguard her mother, but she also shepherded her sister. When First Corinthians could no longer tolerate the unhappiness of a sedentary life and ventured out in the real world to get a job, Magdalene called Lena supported her decision (189). It is interesting that in their home, Magdalene called Lena had found some degree of contentment as a self-proclaimed savior. In the role as martyr, she understood her mother's weakness and her sister's frustrations, so fighting for them became her mission and her mandate.

DEAD, PILATE [SS]. Pilate Dead was the daughter of Sing and Macon I, mother of Reba, grandmother of Hagar, sister of Macon Dead II, and aunt of Magdalene called Lena, First Corinthians, and Macon Dead III Milkman). Early in life, death robbed Pilate of her family. Childbirth was at the expense of her mother's death. Her father's grief was so great that when he buried his wife, he forbade anyone to ever mention her name again (43). When Pilate was twelve, her father was murdered for defending the land he loved (40). Soon after, greed for a dead man's gold caused Pilate's separation from her brother and friend (171).

Alone and defiant, Pilate headed toward Virginia the memories of which charted her path (141). She encountered abuse where there should have been trust, and shame supplanted intimacy (143). Pilate took the time to sort out the priorities in her life and began anew with a spirited and focused agenda (148–49). Throughout her life, Pilate maintained a profound love for family and, eventually, the kinships lossed through death were reborn in her daughter, Rebecca (Reba), and later, her granddaughter, Hagar (147, 150).

The affection of a strong father and the protection of a doting brother imbued Pilate with a genuine love for humanity. She offered food or drink to anyone who entered her living space (149). Pilate was coarse, but kind. She defended Milkman, still in his mother's womb (126); protected Reba from an abusive lover (94–95); celebrated family in light of thievery; belittled herself to secure the release of two robbers from jail (206–7, 209), and created a world for Hagar filled with maternal love (125, 336).

When Pilate lay dying from a bullet fired in hate, her one regret was not knowing and loving more people. The irony in the message from her father's ghost was that Sing was not a song, but a spouse and a mother (208). In compliance and respect for the memory of her father, Pilate sang songs that brought joy to others.

DEAD, REBA. *See* **REBA [SS]**

DEAD, RUTH FOSTER [SS]. Ruth Foster Dead was the daughter of Dr. Foster, wife of Macon Dead II, and mother of Magdalene called Lena, First Corinthians, and Milkman (Macon Dead III). As the only daughter of the only Negro doctor in town, Ruth was economically sound, but socially and emotionally bankrupt. Elitism in a small town came with strings that heightened solitude and confusion. Ruth wanted her father to fulfill all of her emotional needs, but he could not (23). As a motherless child raised by a father who belittled those of lesser social and emotional status, Ruth led a life of isolation and social starvation. In time, she internalized he father's values and unconsciously departed into a world comfortable within the dynamics of a dysfunctional parent/child relationship.

In the beginning of their marriage, Macon Dead II was ambitious and feigned affection for his wife. When her father granted the young Macon Dead permission to court his daughter, it was only because he had tired of her smothering and saw the marriage as his release. Macon plotted for a courtship, which led to marriage, but he soon realized that the social ladder he wished to climb as the son-in-law of Dr. Foster was anchored to the floor (23). Unable to secure funding for a business venture with the railroad, Macon angered and gave up all hopes of civility within the marriage. In addition, witnessing his wife's obsession with her father gave Macon license to embark on a campaign of ridicule toward Ruth that spanned the life of the marriage.

Ruth tried to be a good wife and mother, but emotional problems hindered her efforts. As a wife, she was criticized and belittled openly by her husband; as a mother of two daughters, she was too fragile for self-reliance, and, thus, parental roles were reversed in an effort to protect her; and as a mother to her only son, she robbed Macon III of his name and his dignity by insisting on breastfeeding until his feet were on the floor (12, 13–14).

Ruth easily related to Pilate, her sister-in-law, because she was strong and challenged Macon's authority. It was in Pilate's behalf that Ruth stood up to Macon to get money for Hagar's funeral.

DEAD, SING BYRD (I.E., SINGING BIRD) [SS]. Sing Byrd Dead was the Indian daughter of Heddy; sister of Crowell Byrd, aka Crow; wife of Macon Dead I aka Jake; and mother of Macon II and Pilate. Her mother's efforts to restrict Singing Bird's contact with blacks failed miserably. She fell in love with Jake, the young black man raised in her home, and ran away to marry him. On the pretense of leaving for school, she traveled north with Jake. The accidental renaming of Jake to Macon Dead by the Freedmen's Bureau was seen by Sing as a new beginning in a new land. She gave birth to one son, Macon, and died giving birth to Pilate, her daughter (51). Her husband's grief restricted the speaking of her name ever again (53–54).

DEAL, REVEREND. *See* REVEREND DEAL [SU]

DEAR, ROSE [JZ]. Rose Dear was the wife of an absent husband, daughter of True Belle, sister of May, and mother of five children, of which Violet Trace was the third born. When Rose was eight years old, her mother left to work in Baltimore (141). When she was married and had five children, her husband also departed.

The husband on whom Rose Dear depended just up and left one day, complaining about the frustrations and disappointments of life (138). Because Rose Dear was left alone with the children and unable to ward off the creditors, a part of her mind left with the confiscated furnishings (98). The family was dependent on the generosity of good neighbors for food and shelter. Soon, however, True Belle was summoned home from Baltimore to help the destitute family. Four years later, Rose Dear found relief from the mental torment that consumed her at the bottom of the well by committing suicide (99).

DEE DEE. *See* TRUELOVE, DIVINE [PA]

DEED SANDS. *See* SANDS, DEED [PA]

DEEPER POOLE. *See* POOLE, DEEPER [PA]

DELIA. *See* BEST, DELIA [PA]

DELLA JONES. *See* MISS DELLA JONES [BE]

DENVER. *See* SUGGS, DENVER [BLV]

DENVER, AMY [BLV]. A white girl on her way to Boston in search of material and a dream, Amy Denver stumbled upon Sethe in the woods (32). With Jesus as her anchor and her guide, Amy aided the wounded and about-to-deliver black girl. The appearance of the scars on Sethe's back evoked sympathy and outrage in Amy. Fervently questioning God's intentions, Amy took a detour from her search for velvet to care for Sethe, whom she called "Lu."

When Amy departed for Boston after the birth of Lu's baby, she demanded recognition for her midwifery skills. Sethe was overwhelmed with Amy's attentiveness and already had decided to name her infant daughter after the white girl so filled with compassion (79–85).

DESDEMONA [BE]. As an avid reader, young Elihue Micah Whitcomb, later Soaphead Church, read the works of William Shakespeare (169). In *Othello*, a Shakespearean tragedy about Othello, a Moor (black man) and an officer in the Venetian army, fell in love and married Desdemona, a well-bred young Venetian woman. Desdemona was later murdered by her jealous husband who fell victim to the deceptions and trickery of Iago, his jealous and sadistic ensign. As a Shakespearean scholar, Charles Boyce saw Desdemona in a spiritual context and wrote, "She resembles the angel that opposes the devil in such a play, struggling for control of the central character, who is a symbol of humanity (Boyce, 155).

DESSIE [SU]. Respected as a member of the Order of Elks, Dessie entertained the women in her group with the story of seeing Shadrack, the town's fallen citizen, tip his imaginary hat in respect to Sula Mae Peace, the town's nefarious citizen. All ears were turned to hear the story, as it was no secret that Shadrack was not civil toward anyone. Even for a simple hello, Shadrack chose profanity as his language of choice. For

Dessie, the interaction between Shadrack and Sula Mae verified her knowledge of demonic intercourse, and she swore that her punishment came in the form of the sty that appeared upon her eye the very day she saw Shadrack and Sula Mae Peace exchange greetings (116–17). Ironically, Dessie was one of the first to join Shadrack in his National Suicide Day parade after the death of Sula Mae Peace (158).

DESTRY BEAUCHAMP. *See* **BEAUCHAMP, ROYAL & DESTRY [PA]**

DETROIT, MICHIGAN. *See* **SOUTHSIDE, DETROIT, MICHIGAN [SS]**

DEVIL'S CONFUSION [BLV]. "Devil's confusion" was a phrase Sethe used in conversation with Paul D. meaning that Satan allowed her to look good as long as she felt bad (7).

DEVORE STREET [BLV]. Many of the freed slaves traveling north were given the address of a minister on DeVore Street who used his house as a way station. On DeVore Street they found food, family, and friendship (52).

DEWEY KING. *See* **KING, DEWEY [SU]**

DEWEY PRINCE. *See* **PRINCE, DEWEY [BE]**

DEWEYS, THE [SU]. The Deweys were three very different little boys who lived in the streets until they were taken in by Eva Peace. The oldest was of dark complexion with fine hair, the next was fair with freckles and hair the color of fire, and the youngest was half Mexican with brown skin and dark bangs. The variations in traits did not matter to Eva, as she immediately renamed all three boys "Dewey." When, at age seven, the oldest Dewey was ready for school he and the four- and five-year-olds changed their names to "Dewey King." In time, the physical differences faded, and the three Deweys became inseparable by adopting one personality. It was as if the three boys were blank pieces of paper waiting for someone's *anyone's*, inscription (38–39).

DICE [PA]. Traveling south on the train alone, Dice met Gigi, a woman in search of conversation and a cause. Dice was frail in stature, often evoking sympathy from onlookers. In the dining car of the train, the charge of five cents for frozen water became Gigi's battle of choice. In fairness to Gigi, as Dice's defender, she was able to mask her insecurities well. She was aggressive at challenging the five cents charge demanded for the ice, but in the end Dice actually paid double by sarcastically giving the attendant an extra nickel in protest.

As Dice prepared to leave the train, Gigi was aggressive at helping Dice get his suitcase stored overhead. When he exited the train, his protective traveling buddy said cordially, "Good luck. Watch out, now, Don't get wet." Little did he know that, in anger, Gigi would later refer to him as a "lying freak" (68).

DICK & JANE SERIES [BE]. Morrison begins the novel with excerpts from the Scott, Foresman & Company's Dick and Jane Series introduced in 1930. Each chapter is proceeded by a phrase from the series. The look-say books are peopled with Dick, the eldest child; Jane, the middle child; Sally, originally called "Baby," Mother and Father; along with their pet dog, Spot; cat, Puff (originally Mew); and Tim, the teddy bear.

This story book about a middle-class suburban American white family is used to demonstrate the contrast to the black, poverty-impacted families in the novel. The unrealistic world of Dick and Jane was exposed in 1965 by educator Arthur S. Trace, who wrote *Reading Without Dick and Jane*, about the influence of the series as programmed retardation. According to Trace, "Students will find almost any kind of story more pleasurable and more rewarding than the stories in the Dick-And-Jane type reader" (Trace, 164). Concurring, Carla Williams, in her study of the "Dick and Jane" characters, found that, "For all its popularity and influence, however, the world of Dick and Jane—though it was presented as the norm—did not reflect the lives of the majority of American children (Williams, 1995).

DICK GREGORY. *See* **GREGORY, DICK [TB]**

DICK'S [SU]. Dick's was the store frequented by the children in the Bottom of Medallion, Ohio (129).

DILLINGER, JOHN HERBERT (1903–1934) [BE]. China berated Miss Marie for bragging about her gangster boyfriend as though he were John Herbert Dillinger, the notorious bank robber of the 1930s (54).

Dillinger was "fingered" by Anna Sage, a woman who owned a brothel. She wore a red dress (lady in red) to help the FBI identify Dillinger. He was killed that day, July 22, 1934, at the age of thirty-one.

DINA POOLE. *See* **POOLE, DINA [PA]**

DINAH BABY [PA]. The music of "Dinah Baby" (Dinah Washington) played as Mavis Albright road in the car with the gas station attendant after getting gas for the stranded Cadillac. Dinah Washington (1924–1963), born Ruth Lee Jones, was one of the most influential singers in the history of American popular music. As a blues/jazz singer, she was often hailed as the "Queen of the Blues" (45).

DIVINE TRUELOVE. *See* TRUELOVE, DIVINE (I.E., DEE DEE) [PA]

DJVORAK, ANNA [SS]. Anna Djvorak was the grateful Hungarian patient of Dr. Foster whom she credited with saving the life of her son, Ricky. Out of respect and appreciation, Mrs. Djvorak invited Ruth Foster Dead, Dr. Foster's daughter, to Ricky's daughter (her granddaughter's) wedding. An excited Ruth attended the wedding, and later shared the details of the event with her family. Macon Dead II, her husband, however, depreciated her participation in the event because Ms. Djvorak did not know Ruth's name, always addressing her as "Dr. Foster's daughter." He also ridiculed Ruth's awkwardness as a Methodist guest in the rites of communion at the Catholic wedding ceremony, which led to a family argument, a husband's abusing his wife, and a son's retaliative defense of his mother (65–67).

DJVORAK, RICKY [SS]. Dr. Foster was credited for saving Ricky Djvorak's life by not recommending hospitalization for tuberculosis. The truth was that, as a black man without medical privileges in the hospital, Dr. Foster did not have the authority to admit him. Ricky's mother was confident that Dr. Foster had saved Ricky's life, and she honored his daughter, Ruth Foster Dead, with an invitation to Ricky's daughter's wedding (67).

DOG BREEDLOVE [BE]. "Dog Breedlove" was the disparaging name given to Cholly Breedlove by Mrs. MacTeer because he was viewed as an abusive husband and irresponsible father for starting a fire that put his family "outdoors" (17–18).

DOLLS (I.E., ROCHELLE, BERNADINE, & FAYE) [JZ]. As a nine-year-old child, Dorcas was spending the night with a friend when her mother died in a house fire (57). In the shock that followed, Dorcas was unable to comprehend the loss of both parents. Physically, she attended the funerals for her parents, but emotionally, she mourned for her little homemade wooden dolls, Rochelle, Bernadine, and Faye, that burned in the fire. Dorcas emotionally supplanted grieving for her parents with grieving for her dolls. It saddened Dorcas to think that there was no funeral for Rochelle, Bernadine, and Faye, her incinerated play friends. As a young girl, Dorcas could handle the mourning for her three dolls because they were unreal playthings, whereas the loss of a mother just days after losing a father was too devastating for her to grasp emotionally or mentally (61).

DORCAS MANFRED. *See* MANFRED, DORCAS [JZ]

DORCUS [TB]. Margaret Street was not exposed to many blacks, and Dorcus was the one African American female from her past who did not intimidate her (186).

DOREEN [BE]. Doreen was the little girl whom Soaphead Church lured to his home with her friend, Sugar Babe. Candy, ice cream, and money were used as the bait. In his letter to God, Soaphead Church makes reference to the "newspaper," indicating possible criminal charges for sexual abuse of children (181).

DOSTOEVSKY, FYODOR M. (1821–1881) [BE]. Elihue Micah Whitcomb (Soaphead Church) preferred the works of the Italian author, Dante Alighieri over those of the Russian author Fyodor Mikhailovich Dostoevsky. To begin the comparison, it should be noted that Dostoevsky did not have a "Beatrice" like Dante did. Another marked difference between the two authors is that Dostoevsky had an obsession with religion and man's struggle with good and evil. God's authority is very present in all of his works. It is evident in Soaphead Church's open letter to God that reverence for God and His power were foreign to this man who abused young girls and later chastised God for allowing it to happen (140–45).

Dostoevsky's first novel, *Poor Folk* (1846), dealt with unhappiness and poverty. *The Double* (1846), Dostoevsky's second novel, followed with a depiction of someone plagued by a look-alike who took over his life. In *Crime and Punishment* (1866), guilt and inner turmoil of the main character were fundamental to the story line. Dostoevsky later wrote *The Idiot* (1868–1869), *The Possessed* (1871–1872), and *The Brothers Karamazov* (1880). In each of these works, Dostoevsky continued his preoccupation with moral and political dilemmas that require religious and philosophical insight.

DOVEY BLACKHORSE MORGAN. *See* MORGAN, DOVEY BLACK-HORSE [PA]

DOWING, MAY [TB]. May Dowing is the mother of Son's army friend, Soldier. Many of May Dowing's church sisters affectionately called her "Mama May" (295).

DR. ALBERT SCHWEITZER (1875–1965) [SS]. As a German philosopher, medical missionary, theologian, and humanitarian who devoted his life to the betterment of the masses, Dr. Albert Schweitzer and his work in Africa was the first person Milkman could think of when he attempted to think of notable white people who helped the cause of the black race.

Guitar Bains repudiated, claiming that Schweitzer did not care about the people of Africa with whom he experimented (156). Dr. Schweitzer's missionary work with the natives in Africa was controversial, as the notable black sociologist and leader, Dr. W.E.B. DuBois, voiced his criticism in "The Black Man and Albert Schweitzer": "With a religion that preached love and sacrifice, came a missionary who advocated work and loyalty with one hand, and with the other hand opened the door to compulsory labor, over-taxation, the disruption of the family and the tribe, and the rape of the land and its people" (DuBois, 121).

Dr. Schweitzer answered Dr. DuBois in a letter from Africa on December 5, 1945, commenting, "The problem of the blacks working for the whites is exceedingly complex when seen at a close range" (Schweitzer, 51–52). Dr. DuBois responded from Atlanta, Georgia, in a letter dated July 31, 1946: "It was the American slave-trade carried on by Europeans that degraded and spoiled her [African] civilization (DuBois, 53).

Dr. W.E.B. DuBois had legitimate concerns about Dr. Schweitzer's work, but others celebrated his accomplishments with the natives of Africa. In 1952, Dr. Schweitzer was awarded the Nobel Peace Prize for his work as a missionary surgeon and founder of Lambarene Hospital (Republique du Gabon). (*It should be noted that the mail to and from Africa was hampered by time and distance.*)

DR. FOSTER [SS]. Dr. Foster was the father of Ruth Foster, father-in-law of Macon Dead II, and grandfather of Magdalene called Lena, First Corinthians, and Macon "Milkman" Dead III. Dr. Foster had a professional monopoly as the only Negro doctor, which afforded him and his family a good life, social status, financial comfort, and special distinction to the street where he lived (71–74). As a single parent, he suffered under the weight of his only daughter's emotional and social dependency. When young Macon Dead II came requesting permission to date his daughter, Dr. Foster feigned indifference, but secretly he was eager to be relieved of Ruth's desperate need for attention (23).

Throughout the many problems in the marriage, Macon and Ruth Foster Dead shared a candidness about their respective father and father-in-law. Macon found him condescending and uncaring toward those that idolized him (71), and Ruth honestly saw her father as egotistical and thoughtless (124). Dr. Foster's need for mood-altering drugs and kinship delivery of his grandchildren seems abnormal and strongly suggests serious psychological problems.

DR. MARTIN LUTHER KING JR. (1929–1968) [PA]. Seneca was a teenager when Martin Luther King Jr. was killed. Born to Reverend and Mrs. Martin Luther King, this young man grew to be himself a Baptist minister and the most prominent leader of the civil rights movement of the twentieth century. King's birthday, January 15, 1929, is now a national holiday, Martin Luther King Day (261). Martin Luther King is the first and only African American to hold such an honor.

DR. ROBERT MICHELIN [TB]. A raging toothache in the early hours of the night brought Valerian Street into the home of Dr. Robert Michelin, a French neighbor in town. As two men recently detached from wives and countries, Dr. Michelin and Valerian Street found commonality in alcohol and disappointment. Dr. Michelin was exiled from Algeria, a country ruled by France (15–16).

Dr. Michelin had to decline the Streets' an invitation for Christmas dinner because of the weather, so he missed all of the excitement at their yuletide table (194).

DR. SINGLETARY [SS]. First Corinthians Dead felt that Dr. Singletary and Rev. Coles were the only two Negroes in Southside who could afford a second home in a beach community (33).

DRAKE [TB]. Drake was a close childhood friend of Son and Soldier. The three buddies spent quality time together when Son returned home after eight years on the lam for causing the death of his wife, Cheyenne (246).

DREAMLAND THEATRE [BE]. The Dreamland Theatre was a movie house in Lorain, Ohio (69).

DRUM BLACKHORSE. *See* BLACKHORSE, DRUM [PA]

DUBOIS/WASHINGTON DEBATE [PA]. Reverend Richard Misner believed that the people of Ruby, Oklahoma, were not sensitive to the civil rights movement and actually preferred the philosophy of Booker T. Washington over that of W.E.B. Dubois (212). Two of the greatest leaders in the black community during the nineteenth and twentieth centuries were W.E.B. (William Edward Burghardt) DuBois (1868–1963) and Booker T. Washington (1856–1915). The two men shared prominence, but had diverse positions on the advancement of the black race.

Washington believed that hard work would help to dispel the idea of blacks as buffoons and thieves. On September 18, 1895, he delivered his Atlanta Exposition Address (also called the Atlanta Compromise Address) in Atlanta, Georgia, where he noted that, "No race can prosper til it learns that there is as much dignity in tiling a field as in writing a poem. It is at the bottom of life that we must begin, and not at the top. (Booker T. Washington Papers, 579).

Washington was polite in his desire for social change, but DuBois organized a group of peers to devise methods to demand equality. Taking a different position, DuBois advocated political action with an aggressive civil rights agenda by founding the National Association for the Advancement of Colored People (NAACP). DuBois felt that exceptional men would help to save and protect the Negro race (212).

In "On Being Ashamed of Oneself: An Essay on Race Pride," he wrote:

"The organization is going to involve deliberate propaganda for race pride. That is, it is going to start out by convincing American Negroes that there is no reason for them being ashamed of themselves; that their record is one that should make them proud; and their history in Africa and the world is a history of effort, success, and trial comparable with that of any other people" (Lewis, 80).

DUGGIE'S [JZ]. Joe Trace saw Dorcas for the first time as the teenager buying candy at Duggies, a neighborhood drugstore/restaurant. Initially, he just watched the young girl wondering about the affects of sweets on her skin (68).

DUMFREY WOMEN [JZ]. Violet Trace went looking for the Dumfrey women, the mother and daughter whom she hairdressed at their home on Tuesdays, but they were not home. In a conversation with a neighbor, Violet learned that the uppity twosome were really from Cottown, a small town near Memphis, Tennessee. Their husband and father owned a store and both women had good jobs, so no one was supposed to know from where they really came (18–19).

DUNBAR, PAUL LAURENCE (1872–1906) [PA]. As Deacon Morgan traveled through the streets of Ruby, Oklahoma, the sound of children rehearsing the lines of a Paul Laurence Dunbar poem momentarily took him back to the days of his childhood (110).

The study of Dunbar's works in the South was a common occurrence in segregated, as well as integrated, schools. Dunbar was never a slave, but he heard the stories from the recollections of his parents. Always considered bright, he excelled in school as the only black student serving in scholastic positions of authority. Dunbar's work is best known for the authentic poetic diction of the Negro.

Dunbar published eleven volumes of poetry including *Oak and Ivy* (1893), *Majors and Minors* (1895), *Lyrics of the Hearthside* (1899), *Poems of Cabin and Field* (1899), *Candle-Lightin Time* (1901), *Lyrics of Love and Laughter* (1903), *When Malindy Sings* (1903), *Lil Gal* (1904), *Howdy, Honey, Howdy* (1905), and *Lyrics of Sunshine and Shadow* (1905).

Dunbar's *Complete Poems* were published posthumously in 1913. Dunbar also published fiction: *The Uncalled* (1898), *Folks from Dixie*, (1898), *The Strength of Gideon and Other Stories* (1900), *The Fanatics* (1901), and

The Sport of the Gods (1902). Paul Laurence Dunbar is immortalized for his style of poetry.

DUNFRIE [SS]. As a young man, Old Macon Dead's interview with the Freedmen's Bureau was a series of errors. When asked for his birthplace, Macon replied, "Macon." When asked for his father's name, he responded, "He's dead." For some reason, the Freedmen's representative recorded Dunfrie as his place of birth and Macon Dead as his name (53).

DUNION, MISS. *See* MISS DUNION [BE]

DUPRES, FAIRY [PA]. As a young fifteen-year old, Fairy DuPres found an infant alone near the body of her deceased mother. Young Fairy assumed responsibility for the caring of the child. She named her "Lone" to record how she was found. Never marrying, Fairy less devoted her life to raising Lone. Skillful as a midwife, Fairy taught Lone everything she knew about the subject. When she died, Lone took over the practice (190).

DUPRES FAMILY [PA]. When Lone DuPres overheard the men plotting a raid on the Convent women, she turned first to the DuPres family for help. Not only were these people the ones who saved, raised, and nurtured her; but they also had the gift of patience. As a family, they had suffered the horrors of racial injustice like everyone else. However, the DuPres family processed the pain toward the positive, not the negative. They had always prided craftsmanship over statesmanship, so it was loss of employment that pained them, not political gains. People with skills that contributed directly back to the growth of the community were important to their survival. Often the fear of black labor dominating the market effected their livelihood, but, all in all, the DuPres held fast to God's love and his promises.

The news that Lone DuPres brought was disturbing and any intolerance toward the Convent women took a backseat to the town's outrage of grown men pouncing on unsuspecting women (284).

DUPRES, JUVENAL [PA]. Juvenal DuPres was the father of Nathan DuPres. Like Zechariah Morgan, he was forced to leave a public office in Louisiana (193).

DUPRES, LINDA [PA]. Linda DuPres was the daughter of Pious, and one of the children participating in the Christmas pageant (208).

DUPRES, LONE [PA]. Alone she was found, so "Lone" she became. In the vicinity of her deceased mother, there was no food and no one to care for the orphan (190). Faith DuPres raised Lone and transferred all of her midwifery skills to her in the process. The DuPres family reputation for birthing children was flawed with the delivery of the Fleetwood babies. Each child arrived with a medical problem that defied midwifery competence (271). The good people of Ruby were convinced that the illnesses of Noah, Esther, Ming, and Save-Marie were due to Lone's advanced years.

With reverence and respect, Lone adhered closely to God's calling and man's dilemma. Knowing that nothing just happens, Lone believed that she was endowed with special talents directly from God to help guide his children on earth. Seeing that Connie had the gift, Lone encouraged her to use it to save the life of Scout Morgan when he lay unconscious after a truck accident (245). Devoutly religious, Connie resisted, but saw the need to comply to save Scout's life.

Lone DuPres was aware that many of Ruby's good citizens had traveled the road to the Convent (270). So, when she overheard the men planning a revolt, she quickly gathered help. She began with the DuPres family because they had a history of fairness and trust in caring about others. Lone knew well that God's plan intended for her to act responsibly and get help. He allowed Lone to hear the scheming and plotting of the men at the Oven, for that reason and that reason only (271–86).

DUPRES, MIRTH MORGAN. Mirth Morgan was the daughter of Elder Morgan and deceased wife of Nathan DuPres. The couple never had children, but they opened their home to all of the children in Ruby, Oklahoma (204).

DUPRES, MOSS [PA]. Moss DuPres was the cousin of Nathan DuPres. Moss always became the scapegoat when they honored Nathan as the oldest resident of Ruby. Nathan deferred to his cousin Moss because, according to his recollection, he was older by a couple of years (204). Moss and his family lived some distance outside of Ruby, and he was not as active in town as Nathan (198).

DUPRES, NATHAN [PA]. Nathan DuPres was the husband of Mirth Morgan (deceased) and son-in-law of Elder Morgan (deceased). Recognized as the oldest man in the town, Nathan was well respected in Ruby, Oklahoma. Losing all of his children to the horrors of a destructive storm and then his beloved Mirth, he saw his personal suffering as a way to help others. Nathan's affection for the families in Ruby was evidenced in the many functions he organized to support children's activities. The Children's Day picnic held at his home was a great source of enjoyment for everyone, and no throat went parched during pageant rehearsals when Nathan was around to hand out candy (148). He was long winded when addressing the audience at pageants, but he was loved for his generosity and kindness (204–5).

DUPRES, PIOUS [PA]. Pious DuPres was the son of Booker, nephew of Juvenal, and father of Linda. In the mob going to the Convent, there were no DuPres men, but there was a brother of a daughter-in-law, and that signaled involvement. Pious quickly analyzed the problem and went off to get help. The shame of grown men plotting to hurt women repulsed him and he was determined to stop it (284).

DUSTY (I.E., SANDRA) [PA]. Looking for a ride out West, Dusty approached Mavis Albright's Cadillac in the parking lot of an eatery. Dusty was Mavis' first hitchhiker, and the most talkative. Six symbols of military service graced her neck, and the lives and loves represented were Dusty's main conversation. From Zanesville to Columbus, she ate chocolate-covered marshmallow cookies and chattered about her medals (33–34).

E

EASTER MORGAN. *See* MORGAN, EASTER [PA]

EAST ST. LOUIS RIOTS [JZ]. The riots of East St. Louis took the lives of Dorcas' mother and father (60).

EDDIE TURTLE. *See* TURTLE, EDDIE [PA]

EDISON STREET [JZ]. Vera Louise Gray moved to Edison Street in Baltimore with a servant, True Belle, and an orphan/son, Golden Gray. She made up a plausible story for the neighbors that openly questioned a colored child raised by a white woman (139–40).

EDNA FINCH'S MELLOW HOUSE [SU]. Ice cream parlor up in the Bottom of Meridian, Ohio (51).

EDWARD, BODWIN. *See* BODWIN, BROTHER & SISTER [BLV]

EDWARD, KING [SS]. King Edward was the owner of what was once a gas station, but later became a meeting place for friends. He was also a celebrated town hero as a former baseball player for the black league in Shalimar, Virginia (271).

EDWARD, SANDS. *See* NEW FATHERS OF RUBY, OKLAHOMA [PA]

EDWARDS, MALVONNE [JZ]. Malvonne Edwards was the upstairs neighbor of Joe and Violet Trace and aunt of Sweetness (68). Malvonne's attention to neighborhood gossip was matched by her energy for hard work and her compassion for others. When Malvonne found the stolen mail her delinquent nephew left behind, her interest in the lives of those that used the 130th Street mailbox was apparent. She took it upon herself to reroute the interrupted correspondence (41–43).

Initially Malvonne resisted when Joe Trace asked to use her apartment for clandestine meetings with Dorcas, his teenage neighborhood lover. Joe's persistence and persuasion weakened Malvonne, and she finally agreed to the arrangement (45–49). Malvonne was not a good friend of Violet, his wife, but she was never comfortable with the deal. Succumbing to her conscience, it was Malvonne who finally told Violet about the adulterous arrangement (5).

EIGHT-ROCK FAMILIES [PA]. Eight-rock families were blue-black people who lived in Ruby, Oklahoma, and who were tall and graceful in stature. Within the grouping, the eight-rock people assumed elitist status, often distancing themselves from people outside their sect. Initially, members of the eight-rock sect acquired positions within public office positions, but they were often short-lived. (193).

ELDER MORGAN. *See* MORGAN, ELDER [PA]

ELIHUE MICAH WHITCOMB. *See* WHITCOMB, ELIHUE MICAH *and* SOAPHEAD CHURCH [BE]

ELLA & JOHN [BLV]. Ella and John were the Underground Railroad couple who delivered first three unescorted grandchildren, and later Sethe, a daughter-in-law, with the fourth newly born grandchild to Baby Suggs in Ohio (92, 135). Ella was a strong and determined woman who experienced great suffering at the hands of sadistic slave owners, but her spirits were undaunted (113). At 124 Bluestone, it was Ella's courage and quick thinking that saved Brother Bodwin when a disoriented Sethe lunged at him with an icepick (265).

ELLEN [TB]. Ellen was the wife of Soldier and childhood friend of Son in Eloe, Florida.

ELOE, FLORIDA [TB]. Son (William Green), left his hometown of Eloe eight years before arriving at L'Arbe de la Croix. An exclusive all-black community of ninety houses, Eloe had no record of births or political structure. All municipal services were provided by whites from neighboring towns. Agricultural, fishing, and petroleum resources provided income for the working class of the nearly four hundred people.

Son ended his eight-year absence from Eloe to introduce Jadine Childs to his family, and hometown. Jadine's propensity for world travel did not fit into the small town docket, so she left Son there and returned to New York (173–74, 260).

EMANCIPATION PROCLAMATION [BE]. Old Blue Jack entertained young Cholly Breedlove with stories about the life of black folks after the Emancipation Proclamation was signed by President Lincoln, granting freedom to all slaves (133).

EMBEZZLER, THE [PA]. The embezzler was an elusive man who courted fear and built a stronghold with eight sleeping quarters, two huge baths, and storerooms throughout the house. The fixtures displayed his passion for eroticism and pleasure. It only took one celebration and one undercover guest, for the embezzler to be forced to find a new home in a prison cell. The dream mansion became the Convent for the schooling of Indian girls (71).

EMBEZZLER'S FOLLY [PA]. Looking forward to starting a school for Indians girls, Sister Mary Magna and the nuns were dismayed to see the horrible condition of the mansion when they arrived. In the beginning, it did not resemble what their neighbors in Ruby, Oklahoma, would later call the Convent. The Sisters immediately began to change the lurid architecture constructed by a man of unsavory character who designed the place as an "embezzler's folly" for sexual adventures (3, 71).

EMPIRE STATE. *See* STATE, EMPIRE [SS]

ERIE LACKAWANNA RAILROAD [SS]. Macon Dead II just knew that if he got money from Dr. Foster, his father-in-law, he would get rich in a business venture with the Erie Lackawanna Railroad expansion project. Macon had insider information on track placement and all he needed was the money. Dr. Foster, however, refused to fund the project, and this led to years of resentment toward him and his daughter by the entrepreneurial and disappointed son-in-law (72).

ERKMEISTER, MISS. *See* MISS ERKMEISTER [BE]

ERNIE PAUL. *See* PAUL, ERNIE [TB]

ESSIE FOSTER. *See* FOSTER, ESSIE [BE]

ESTEE, ALMA [TB]. Alma Estee was the young girl who sometimes lived with Therese Foucalt in the hills of Place de Ven. Alma Estee was one of the Marys who worked for the Street family on the Isle des Chevaliers with Therese and Gideon. When Jadine Childs was taking a plane back to Paris, she met Alma in the airport restroom, where she worked. At first Jadine did not recognize her, but Alma idly chatted about Son, the chocolate-eating man, who promised to bring her a much desired wig from the States. Jadine wanted to exit the conversation gracefully, so she addressed Alma as "Mary," deposited money in her hand and hurried away. Confident that a few dollars had relieved her of the burden of conversing with the cleaning woman, Jadine did not hear or recognize the young girl's pain in her response. "Alma—Alma Estee" (288–90).

Alma was angry when Son returned to the island without her wig and looking for Jadine. In a vindictive manner, Alma deliberately lied about seeing Jadine on the arms of a man as she boarded the plane for Paris (299–300).

ESTHER COOPER. *See* MRS. ESTHER COOPER [SS]

ESTHER FLEETWOOD. *See* FLEETWOOD, ESTHER [PA]

ETHAN BLACKHORSE. *See* BLACKHORSE, ETHAN [PA]

EVA (CALLED PEARL) PEACE. *See* PEACE, EVA (CALLED PEARL) [SU]

EVA PEACE. *See* PEACE, EVA [SU]

F

FAIRFIELD CEMETERY [SS]. Fairfield Cemetery was the racially integrated cemetery where Dr. Foster was buried. His daughter, Ruth Foster Dead, made regular early-morning visits to her father's grave. The loneliness of being ignored by a husband who despised her drove Ruth to the comfort of the dead. She truly believed that her father was the only person who cared about her. On one such occasion, Ruth was followed to the cemetery in Fairfield Heights by her son, Milkman. (123).

FAIRLY, OKLAHOMA [PA]. Big PaPa and Big Daddy led over seventy-five family members and friends out of Fairly, Oklahoma (95–96).

FAIRY DUPRES. *See* DUPRES, FAIRY [PA]

"FAST ASS" [TB]. Mary Therese Foucault, the island woman that did chores for the Street household did not like most American blacks and demonstrated her contempt by disparagingly renaming them. Mary Therese felt that Jadine Childs was too promiscuous, so she referred to her as the "fast ass" or the "chippy" (108).

FATHER PADREW [SS]. Father Padrew was the priest who officiated at the wedding of Anna Djvorak's granddaughter, of which Ruth Foster Dead was one of the invited guests. When communion was served,

Ruth's confusion was twofold because she was a Methodist; the language of *Corpus Domini Nostri Jesu Christi* escaped her, as did the timing for the placement of the wafer in her mouth. Ruth responded accordingly when Father Padrew repeated the Latin phrase. Later, when Father Padrew approached Ruth after the ceremony, he stopped short of advising her that only Catholics could receive communion when Ms. Anna Djvorak rescued her with a formal introduction of her guest to Father Padrew, as one of her dearest friends (65–66).

FAUBUS, ORVAL (1910–1994) [SS]. The anger surrounding the integration of the Little Rock High School and Arkansas Governor Orville Faubus was a topic of conversation between members of the Seven Days, a group of black men who avenged the death of black people (101).

Linda Brown, a black student living in Topeka, Kansas, had to travel twenty-one blocks to attend an all-black school, when a white school was within two blocks of her home. In *Brown v. Board of Education*, under the direction of Thurgood Marshall, the NAACP challenged the "separate but equal" doctrine and reaffirmed that the doctrine was unconstitutional. The order of integration of public schools was defied by many governors, Orville Faubus being one of them. He ordered the guards to stop black students from entering the school. President Eisenhower over-ruled Governor Faubus and the 101st airborne platoon was sent in to ensure safe passage for the black students. During this period of time there were riots and angry protests.

FAUSTINE BEST. *See* BEST, FAUSTINE [PA]

FAWN BLACKHORSE CATO. *See* CATO, FAWN BLACKHORSE [PA]

FAYE. *See* DOLLS [JZ]

FAYE [JZ]. Wife of Stuck, one of Joe Trace's good friends (224).

FDR. *See* ROOSEVELT, FRANKLIN DELANO [SS]

FEATHER [SS]. As the owner of Feather's Pool Hall, Feather refused to sell Guitar Bains a beer because he was accompanied by his friend, Milk-man. Guitar pleaded, but Feather would not bend because not only was Milkman under the drinking age, but he was also the son of Macon Dead II, a man that Feather did not respect or like (57).

FELICE [JZ]. Felice was a friend of Dorcas Manfred. After sharing many girlish adventures with Dorcas, Felice knew that Dorcas was sneaking off with Joe Trace, an older married man, but said nothing (64–65). The incident with the brothers was humiliating for Dorcas, and Felice understood her need for male attention (66–67). The friendship between the two girls was strained by Dorcas' relationship with Joe Trace, but that was remedied when Acton, a younger man, came on the scene. Acton was known and accepted within their peer group, and the three of them were at the party that fateful night.

When Dorcas was shot by Joe Trace, her rejected lover, it was Felice who finally telephoned for an ambulance (192–93). Some time later, while visiting the home of Violet and Joe Trace, Felice revealed that Dorcas might have lived if she had not refused transportation to the hospital as she lay wounded. Felice also revealed to the Traces that Dorcas was not a nice person because she took advantage of people (212).

FELICE'S GRANDMOTHER [JZ]. Caretaker for her granddaughter while her parents worked a live-in job in Tuxedo, Felice's grandmother was stern in her discipline and opinions of right and wrong (198, 204).

FELICE'S PARENTS [JZ]. Felice's parents worked for a family in Tuxedo and only came home infrequently because of the demands of the job (198).

FIELDS, WILLY [SU]. Eva Peace had to be hospitalized when she threw herself out of the window in an effort to save her daughter, Hannah, from the yard fire. Both women were injured and taken to the hospital, but Hannah was burned badly and closer to death. Eva's wounds were overlooked by the hospital attendants in an effort to save Hannah's life. Old Willy Fields, the hospital orderly, noticed the trail of blood coming from the unattended Eva Peace and immediately called for medical attention. After that incident, Old Willy Fields proudly boasted about how he saved the life of Eva Peace (77).

FINLEY, MR. *See* **MR. FINLEY [SU]**

FINN, HUCK [TB]. Son was compared to the free-spirited character of Huckleberry Finn in Mark Twain's (Samuel *L. Clemens* [1835–1910]) novel *The Adventures of Tom Sawyer*, a story was first published in 1876 (166).

FIRST CORINTHIANS DEAD. *See* **DEAD, FIRST CORINTHIANS [SS]**

FIRST WIFE OF VALERIAN STREET [TB]. The marriage between Valerian Street and his first wife lasted only nine years and two abortions before it was terminated cordially. The memories of the union were not pleasant, yet, in spirit, she chaperoned the retired Valerian in his greenhouse on L'Arbe de la Croix. News of his first wife's death and subsequent burial did not reach Valerian until after the burial. In state of numbness, Valerian tried to recall the color of her eyes (143).

FISHER FAMILY [BE]. As the house servant, Pauline Breedlove had a place of importance within the Fisher Family. The Fishers depended on Pauline for the smooth running of their home. She was given authority and responsibility. The comfort extended to renaming Pauline to Polly. The little Fisher child was nurtured and loved by Pauline at the expense of her own children (127–128).

FISHER GIRL [BE]. The little Fisher girl was the young daughter of the Fisher's, the rich white family for whom Pauline Breedlove worked. The little girl was "Baby" to Pauline, and Pauline was "Polly" to the little girl. It is important to note that the Fisher home was more than employment for Pauline, it was a world that she protected and clung to for emotional and social stability. So, in the Fisher employ, Baby was mothered in a way that undermined the maternal emotions and privileges deserving of biological children.

In Edward F. Frazier's 1939 study of the Negro family, he documented that emotional bonding with the master's child was not uncommon for the female servant. According to Edward F. Frazier, "The attachment and devotion which the 'mammy' showed for the white children began before the children were born" (Frazier, 50). It seems that during the pregnancy, the mistress was cared for by the valued female servant, and that that nurturing extends well into the life of the child. Pauline's caring of the Fisher child mentally helped to cement her place in that world of liberty and position. The little Fisher girl was permitted to address Pauline as "Polly," but the Breedlove children were discouraged from calling her "mother," or any other variation of the word. In or out of the home they were to address their mother only as "Mrs. Breedlove."

The scene in the kitchen when Pauline slapped her biological daughter, Pecola, but consoled Baby, revealed how a mother's mental state can retard the emotional development of an offspring. In anger, Pauline verbally and physically assaulted Pecola, and, in the next moment, she tenderly consoled the little Fisher girl with the promise of another pie. The disparity between the caring and protection of Baby and the neglect and disregard for Pecola is an indication of Pauline Breedlove's dementia (107–9).

FLEET. *See* FLEETWOOD, ARNOLD [PA]

FLEETWOOD, ARNETTE. *See* SMITH, ARNETTE FLEETWOOD [PA]

FLEETWOOD, ARNOLD (I.E., FLEET) [PA]. Arnold "Fleet" Fleetwood was the husband of Mable, father of Jefferson and Arnette, and grandfather of Ming, Noah, Esther, and Save-Marie. The memories of the trip from Fairly, Oklahoma, made Fleet determined to provide a comfortable home for his family in Ruby, Oklahoma. Still, he was unrehearsed for the conversion of his home into a makeshift hospital. The care of his four ailing grandchildren took precedence over everything and everyone else in the Fleetwood home (58).

As a quiet and retiring man, Fleet was a go-along-to-get-along kind of guy. The emergency meeting between the Morgans and the Fleetwoods about Arnette's honor was hosted in his home. Arnold Fleetwood was older, but his son, Jefferson, was angrier. Rev. Misner mediated and Arnold took the backseat, allowing Jefferson to lead the discussion (57–61).

Under the leadership of Steward Morgan, Arnold was one of the nine men who went to the Convent to assault the women. He felt that the frustrations of four sick grandbabies, a wife consumed with their care, and the story of his only daughter's humiliation within the Convent walls justified his actions of revenge.

FLEETWOOD, ESTHER [PA]. Esther Fleetwood was the second child of Sweetie and Jefferson Fleetwood and was named for the great-grandmother, who had attended to their first child so faithfully (295).

FLEETWOOD, JEFFERSON [PA]. Jefferson Fleetwood was the son of Arnold and Mable Fleetwood, husband of Sweetie, and father of Esther, Ming, Save-Marie, and Noah. Watching his wife and mother caring for his four ailing children unnerved Jefferson. A tour in Vietnam had not prepared him for the frustration and despair experienced upon his return to Ruby, Oklahoma (57).

His fifteen-year-old baby sister, Arnette, had been assaulted publicly by her boyfriend, Coffee "K.D." Smith, the only Morgan heir, and Jefferson was out for blood (58). Finally, the distraught and disappointed father had found a vent to channel the anger built up from fathering four sickly children. At one point in the meeting between the Morgans and Fleetwoods, Jefferson threatened to call the meeting off. A settlement finally was reached, and the subsequent marriage of his sister to her offender quieted his rage (59–62).

The stories of his sister's trip to the convent, filled with inaccurate information, made Jefferson a prime candidate to join the Morgan twins in their feud with the women. Accompanied by his father, he crossed the line from defender to destroyer (277). In the sorrow that followed the death of his daughter, Save-Marie, Jefferson stood valiantly beside his grief-stricken wife and family.

FLEETWOOD, MABLE [PA]. Mable Fleetwood was the wife of Arnold, mother of Jefferson and Arnette, mother-in-law of Sweetie, and grandmother to four children. In a strong and caring manner, Mable Fleetwood aided in tending to her sick grandchildren. She understood and empathized with Sweetie. Mable shared the emotional and physical drain of the constant care of the children. As a mother-in-law, she made every effort to lessen Sweetie's stress (60–62).

FLEETWOOD, MING [PA]. Ming Fleetwood was the third child of Sweetie and Jefferson and was named by her father (295).

FLEETWOOD, NOAH [PA]. Noah Fleetwood was the first child born to Sweetie and Jefferson and was named both for his great-grandfather and for the biblical Noah (295).

FLEETWOOD, SAVE-MARIE [PA]. Shortly after the raid on the Convent, Save-Marie, the youngest child of Sweetie and Jefferson Fleetwood passed away. Sweetie would not allow Save-Marie to be buried on the Morgan ranch. Instead, the child was laid to rest in the backyard of the Fleetwood home (295).

FLEETWOOD, SWEETIE [PA]. Sweetie Fleetwood was the wife of Jefferson, mother of four sick children, daughter-in-law of Arnold and Mable, and sister of Luther Beauchamp. The stress of tending to four sickly children drove Sweetie to leave the security of the Fleetwood home and walk aimlessly toward the Convent (124). Seneca felt sorry for the distraught woman and walked beside her all the way (126, 128). The women at the Convent recognized how disoriented Sweetie was and tried to comfort her, but, exhausted, she fell asleep resisting. In a disoriented state, Sweetie awakened to find her husband at the Convent to bring her back home. She verbally assaulted the sisters of the Convent, claiming that they wanted to keep her captive against her will (130).

FLOOD, ABLE [PA]. Able Flood was the grandfather of Anna Flood and partner of Rector "Big Daddy" Morgan in the bank in Haven.

FLOOD, ACE [PA]. Ace Flood was the husband of Charity, son of Able, and father of Anna. He was also the builder and founder of Ace's Grocery Store. His daughter returned home from Detroit to take charge of the business after her father's death (120).

FLOOD, ANNA [PA]. Anna Flood was the daughter of Ace and Charity Flood and the love interest of Rev. Richard Misner. Independent in thought and attire, Anna returned to Ruby from Detroit to see about her father's store. The sight of Rev. Misner, the new young minister, changed Anna's original plan to sell the store and return to Detroit.

Under Anna's management, Ace's Grocery Store changed the stock to meet the needs of the young people who frequented the Oven nearby. She equipped the store with provisions to which they would be attracted (116, 120). Determined to rise above the ignorance that permeated Ruby, she resisted the thought of conforming to the role of a minister's wife. Nevertheless, Anna accepted Rev. Misner's proposal of marriage on the condition that they remain in Ruby Oklahoma (212).

FLOOD, CHARITY [PA]. Charity Flood was the wife of Ace and mother of Anna. She was one of the women who tried to help Delia Best when she developed problems giving birth (197).

FLOOD, MINDY. *See* MORGAN, MINDY FLOOD [PA]

FLORENCE, AUNT. *See* AUNT FLORENCE [SS]

FLYING AFRICAN (SOLOMON, SHALIMAR) [SS]. Milkman learned that his great-grandfather was one of the "flying Africans" when he visited Shalimar, Virginia (322). According to the story told to Milkman by Susan Byrd, his maternal cousin, Jake (Macon Dead I) was actually dropped when traveling with his airborne father.

FONG, NINA [TB]. Ryk expressed a desire to marry Jadine Childs, but she wondered about his loyalty since he had once dated Nina Fong, a young woman that he was serious enough to take away for a weekend (48).

FONTAINE, JOAN (1971–) [TB]. As the young second wife of a wealthy man, Margaret was reminded by the sight of engraved bed linen of *Rebecca*, Alfred Hitchcock's award-winning movie of suspense and romance. Joan Fontaine played the role of the timid and frightened second wife of Maxim de Winters, whose first wife, Rebecca, had died mysteriously. Margaret Street, like Joan Fontaine's role in the movie was about a second wife's fear that the first wife's presence was dominating her marriage (58). The film won the 1940 Academy Award for best picture.

FOOLISH, FULLER [BE]. As an adolescent, Cholly Breedlove was curious about his real father's identity. In answer to Cholly's questions, his aunt recalled "Fuller Foolish" as the one who sired him. When pressed for Fuller Foolish's proper name, his aunt remembered Samson Fuller only as "Fuller Foolish" (133).

FORD, HENRY (1863–1947) [BE]. Mrs. MacTeer would always bring up Henry Ford—the pioneering automotive engineer, magnate, and billionaire—when she began to rant and rave about the struggles and constraints in her family's meager living conditions (25).

FORRESTER, MISS. *See* MISS FORRESTER [BE]

FOSTER, DR. *See* DR. FOSTER [SS]

FOSTER, ESSIE [BE]. It was rumored that Essie Foster, a friend of Cholly Breedlove's Great Aunt Jimmy, baked her the peach cobbler that caused her death (139).

FOUCALT, MARY THERESE [TB]. Mary Therese was the aunt of Gideon and servant of the Street family on the Isle des Chevaliers. Through letters to Gideon in the United States, Mary Therese lured him back to the island with promises of property that never existed (108). Together they worked for the Streets on the Isle des Chevaliers until Mary Therese's passion for apples resulted in theft and dismissal (109, 201). Mary Therese disliked Americans and would not even enter the Street's house to use the bathroom (110–11, 153). She adored Son (William Green), the chocolate eater, but eventually, she led him astray. Her relationship with Ondine, the woman who gave the orders at L'Arbe de la Croix, was unfriendly.

Nearly blind, but innately astute, Mary Therese used her prescience to discover the presence of Son on the island. In sympathy, she tried to leave him food (105, 153). A proud nurse woman, Mary Therese bragged about her magic breasts that still produced milk (154). Renaming people was also part of her charm; Ondine was "Machete-Head," Sydney was "Bow-tie," Jadine was "Fast ass," and Son was "Chocolate eating black man" (108, 107, 104).

FOUR LITTLE GIRLS [SS]. As the Sunday member of the Seven Days, Guitar Bains was responsible for avenging the death of the four little girls killed in a church bombing. The weight of this assignment was heavier for Guitar because, white or black, it involved children as victims of hate.

Addie Mae Collins (1949–1963), Carole Robertson (1951–1963), Cynthia Wesley (1949–1963), and Denise McNair (1949–1963) were the actual four little girls killed as they prepared for church services on the morning of September 15, 1963, in the Sixteenth Street Baptist Church in Birmingham, Alabama. The attack was meant to stop the growing civil rights activities in the South. However, it should be noted that just eighteen days prior to the bombing in Alabama, on August 28, 1963, 250,000 people—60,000 of whom were white—gathered in Washington, D.C., and listened attentively to Dr. Martin Luther King's monumental "I Have a Dream" speech in front of the Lincoln Memorial.

Robert "Dynamite Bob" Chambliss, a truck driver and member of the Klu Klux Klan was convicted of the bombing in 1977. In 1985, at the age of eighty-one, Chambliss died in prison.

On May 22, 2002, Bobby Frank Cherry, at age seventy-one, was convicted for his role in bombing the Birmingham Sixteenth Street Baptist Church. According to the *New York Times*, "an Alabama jury wrote the final page of one of the most heart-rending chapters in the United States civil rights history" (*NYT* 23 May 2002).

FOWLER WILLIAMS. *See* WILLIAMS, ADA & FOWLER [BE]

FOX, LEON [PA]. When Leon Fox was away from home, his wife Norma Keene, with the assistance of their driver, took advantage of his absence to solicit randomly young girls from the street for perverse recreation (137).

FOX, NORMA KEENE [PA]. Norma Keene Fox was the rich and eccentric woman who solicited the company of young girls for sexual entertainment during her husband's absences from home. She was generous to Seneca before dismissing her upon the news of her husband's return (136–38).

FRANCES MILLER. *See* MILLER, FRANCES [JZ]

FRANCINE GREEN. *See* GREEN, FRANCINE [TB]

FRANK. See CISSY & FRANK [TB]

FRANK ALBRIGHT. *See* ALBRIGHT, FRANK [PA]

FRANK GREEN. *See* GREEN, FRANK G. [TB]

FRANK WILLIAMS. *See* MR. FRANK & WILLIAMS, RHODA & FRANK [JZ]

FRANKIE ALBRIGHT. *See* ALBRIGHT, SALLY, FRANKIE, & BILLY JAMES [PA]

FRANKLIN G. GREEN. *See* GREEN, FRANKLIN G. (I.E., OLD MAN) [TB]

FRED GARNETT. *See* GARNETT, FRED [SS]

FREDDIE [SS]. To most people, jail was considered mandated confinement, but to Freddie, those cells were home. Born in a town without an orphanage to a mother who died after seeing a ghost appear as a white bull, Freddie was raised within locked doors. The ethereal circumstances surrounding his birth and his father's untimely death months prior, left no one brave enough to take the infant son of a woman who died after seeing a ghost (109–10).

As a young man, Freddie worked in Gerhardt's Department Store as a janitor/deliveryman, which allowed time for his passion of roaming around town spreading news. Considered a reliable messenger for the most successful Negro businessman in town, Freddy stopped short of taking credit for the renaming of Macon Dead II's son.

It was Freddie who christened young Macon Dead III with the name "Milkman." One day, after seeing Ruth Foster nurse her son long after infancy, Freddie labeled him a natural "milkman." The name stuck, and Macon Dead II, the father, never knew why (15).

Freddie was a human newspaper with a keen eye for news. The news of Mr. Smith's leap from the roof of "No Mercy Hospital" was a scoop for Macon Dead II, but not as newsworthy as the armed and drunken Henry Porter bellowing death threats from the window on the eve of rent-collection day (23, 25–26). It was also Freddie who made Milkman suspicious about his sister, First Corinthians, Henry Porter, and the Seven Days. No one else made the connection about the budding relationship between the tenant and the landlord's daughter, but Freddie did (112).

FREEDMEN'S BUREAU [SS]. It was during the mandatory registration of all ex-slaves by the Freedmen's Bureau that Jake's name mistakenly was changed to Macon Dead. An intoxicated Yankee interviewer recorded the information that Jake's father was dead and his place of birth was Macon into the name of Macon Dead. Illiterate, Jake—now Macon Dead—did not know to complain or attempt to rectify the situation. When Sing, his wife, discovered the error, together they decided the name would give them a new lease on life (53).

The Freedmen's Bureau was established in the War Department by an act of March 3, 1865. After an extensive study of the Freedmen's Bureau, W.E.B. DuBois wrote, "The Secretary of War could issue rations, clothing, and fuel to the destitute, and all abandoned property was placed in the hands of the Bureau for eventual lease and sale to ex-slaves in forty-acre parcels" (DuBois, 354–65). The bureau records were created and maintained by bureau headquarters, the assistant commissioners, and the state superintendents of education and included personnel records and a variety of standard reports.

FRIEDA MACTEER. *See* MACTEER, FRIEDA [BE]

FRISCO (I.E., SAN FRANCISCO) [TB]. As the story goes, it was the man named San Francisco who paid Son the "original dime" that he earned scouring a tub of fish. This cherished dime bought Son some smokes, a flavored soda pop, and a lifetime of storytelling (169). Frisco was very dear to Son, and it broke Son's heart when the tragic news of his friend's death in the gas fields was within days of the death of his wife, Cheyenne. On the lame for causing the death of his spouse, Son had to leave Eloe, Florida, swiftly before paying his respect at Frisco's funeral (169–70).

FULLER FOOLISH. *See* FOOLISH, FULLER [BE]

FULLER, SAMSON (I.E., FOOLISH FULLER) [BE]. Samson Fuller was the biological father of Cholly Breedlove. Great Aunt Jimmy considered him to be of low moral character. As Cholly Breedlove's guardian, Great Aunt Jimmy chose to ignore the biological link and named her ward after Charles Breedlove, her brother. When Cholly traveled to Macon, Georgia, to find his real father, Samson Fuller validated Great Aunt Jimmy's low opinion of him by cursing and humiliating the young boy. As Cholly was frightened away by the vulgarity, the father/son relationship between the two men was never revealed (156–57).

FULTON BEST. *See* BEST, FULTON & OLIVE [PA]

G

GABLE, CLARK (1901–1960) [BE]. Pauline Breedlove enjoyed watching the movies of Clark Gable, the popular romantic star of American motion pictures. He appeared in over seventy films, but was best known as Rhett Butler in *Gone with the Wind* (123).

GAINES MR. *See* MRS. GAINES [BE]

GALVESTON LONSHOREMEN'S STRIKE OF 1920 [JZ]. Living through the trauma of the Galveston Longshoremen's Strike was one of the many reasons Joe and Violet Trace looked forward to their new life up North (33). The labor dispute in Galveston, Texas, came to a head on March 12, 1920 when the longshoremen walked off the docks in protest. The steamship company of Mallory and Morgan attempted to curtail the effects of the strike by employing racial motivation tactics to divide the cultures. In addition, the availability of food and store chains like Armour, Swift, and Montgomery Ward were comprised with the employ of illegal immigrants from Mexico. Confusion reigned as the workers organized to gain bargaining power.

GARBO, GRETA (1905–1990) [BE]. Upon meeting the MacTeer sisters, Henry Washington likened the girls to Ginger Rogers and Greta Garbo

(16). Born in Sweden as Greta Lovisa Gustafsson, Greta Garbo was a silent-film movie star of the 1920s and 1930s.

GARLAND PRIMARY [SU]. Sula Peace and Nel Wright were both students at the Garland Primary School. Nel's mother looked down on the women in the Peace family and spoke disparagingly about them. Nel became independent in thought and action when she returned from the trip down South. She openly ignored her mother's prejudice against the Peaces and one day approached her classmate, Sula Peace at Garland Primary School in friendship (29).

GARNER, LILLIAN [BLV]. Lillian Garner was married to Mr. Garner, a man who dared to cultivate a special kind of slave (140). As Mrs. Garner, Lillian was equally as considerate and compassionate of their female counterparts. When Baby Suggs left Sweet Home after her son bought her freedom, Mrs. Garner willingly accepted young Sethe as her replacement. Mrs. Garner showed kindness to both women while in her employ (59).

When Baby Suggs arrived at Sweet Home with a shattered hip, Mrs. Garner was kind and considerate (139–41). When Sethe announced her desire to marry Halle Suggs, one of the Sweet Home men, Mrs. Garner expressed delight with good wishes and the gift of earnings (60). It was apparent that, as Garner's wife, she shared his philosophy of treating the slaves as human beings with some degree of respect.

GARNER, MR. *See* **MR. GARNER [BLV]**

GARNER, PAUL A. [BLV]. Paul A. Garner was one of the Sweet Home men beaten by Schoolteacher (197).

GARNER, PAUL D. [BLV]. Paul D. Garner was one of the five Sweet Home men and, after many years, lover of Sethe Suggs. After witnessing the emotional and physical demise of the two strongest slaves at Sweet Home, the shame of iron in his mouth and about his neck, the constraint of a chain gang, and eighteen years of reading trails as a fugitive slave on the run, Paul D. finds in a house haunted by a ghost the woman whom he has respected and adored for over twenty-five years. In the joy of seeing Sethe, he quickly realizes that Baby Suggs, Halle's mother, was dead, Sethe's two sons had run off, and neither daughter (living or dead) welcomed him into their lives (7–13).

Although Paul D. tried to intimidate the ghost with his loud masculine voice, he soon learned that it was futile. Paul D. had gone through a great deal in his life of slavery, managing to escape from bondage five times, but he was emotionally unprepared for the terror he found in

Sethe's home (268). The spirit appeared as the young woman, Beloved, and soon Paul D. had to vacate 124 Bluestone Road. In time, Stamp Paid showed Paul D. the newspaper clipping that revealed the details of Sethe's imprisonment for taking the life of her infant daughter. Although Paul D. had strong feelings for Sethe, he could not understand mother love that shed a child's blood (155–57, 187).

Paul D. grew up the youngest of three boys, all of whom had a different father. He always longed for the love and security of the family he never had (219). However, Stamp Paid explained that Sethe was only a desperate mother trying to safeguard her children from the horrors of Schoolteacher's brand of slavery. Then Paul D. realized that it was not insanity, but intolerance that overtook Sethe's heart and mind (270–73). Paul D. only returned to Sweet Home after assurance that Beloved was gone.

GARNER, PAUL F. [BLV]. As one of the five Sweet Home men, Paul F. worked and laughed with the rest of them. The others were saddened when he was the first slave sold after Mr. Garner died. As a widow, Mrs. Garner did not want to sell any of the men, but as a widow in charge of Sweet Home, she was concerned about lack of money to run the plantation (36).

GARNETT, FRED [SS]. Milkman had missed the ride back to Danville with Rev. Cooper's nephew, when Fred Garnett stopped to give him a lift into town. It was out of Garnett's way, but he agreed to give the tired walker a ride. Milkman visibly was fatigued and thirsty, and the sight of soda prompted him to make an offer for purchase. Garnett was a southern gentleman and did not accept Milkman's money. In hospitality, he generously offered his rider the soda.

After drinking the warm soda, Milkman repeated his offer to pay. Only, this time Garnett was offended by his northern passenger's insistence, and stated, "My name's Garnett. Fred Garnett. I ain't got much, but I can afford a Coke and a lift every now and then" (254–55).

GARVEY, MARCUS MOSIAH (1887–1940). *See* UNIA (UNIVERSAL NEGRO IMPROVEMENT ASSOCIATION) [JZ]

GENERAL LEE (HOG). *See* LEE, ROBERT E. [SS]

GEORGE [TB]. George was the man servant for the Street family of Philadelphia when Valerian was a child and long before Sydney Childs assumed the position. As a dutiful servant, George watched over young Valerian. George alerted the Street parents when he saw the child's bruised hands and feared young Valerian was being exploited by the washerwoman. George reported that the washerwoman was manipulating the child in doing her work. Little did George know that the washerwoman was a friend to a desperately lonely little boy. The washerwoman was let go after George reported what he saw to the Street family (142).

GERALDINE [BE]. Geraldine was a complex woman who denied her son and husband love and affection, which she instead reserved for her cat. When Junior blamed Pecola for hurting the beloved cat, Geraldine became very nasty and chased her away from the home. Characteristic of the "brown girl" mentality, Geraldine was precocious and self-centered. Mothering without tenderness, she raised her son to be a lonely and callous bully, and he later grew to hate her (86–91).

GERHARDT'S DEPARTMENT STORE [SS]. Magdalene called Lena and First Corinthians Dead made red velvet roses to be sold at Gerhardt's Department Store. Freddie, the janitor and courier for the store, alerted them when an additional supply of flowers were needed (10).

GIANT [BLV]. Sethe and Denver Suggs, accompanied by Paul D., enjoyed the antics of the Giant as he danced with the Midget at the carnival outside of Cincinnati, Ohio (48).

GIBBON, EDWARD (1737–1794) [BE]. The perseverance of a historian like Edward Gibbon escaped young Elihue Micah Whitcomb because he preferred strife over patience (169). His book, *The Rise and Fall of the Roman Empire*, is considered the most comprehensive history of the western Roman Empire, as it consists of seventy-one chapters with over one million words and nearly eight thousand footnotes. As an English historian and an extensive researcher of the Roman Empire, Gibbon believed that Christianity was responsible for the breakdown and decline of Rome because it undermined paganism, which, in turn, lessened the credibility of the state.

GIBSON, MANLEY [PA]. Gigi's father, Manley Gibson, was on death row until his sentence was reduced to life behind bars. One day, the daughter whom Manley Gibson had last seen as an adolescent, passed by his prison work site as a woman, now dressed for war (309–10).

GIDEON (I.E., YARDMAN) [TB]. The nephew of Mary Therese Foucalt, Gideon returned to his home in the Caribbean at his aunt's insistence via her many letters. Upon his return, however, he found that the property she bragged about was nonexistent, much like the success and wealth he boasted he'd found in America (108, 110). His failed marriage and his inability to make a fortune abroad prompted Gideon to remain in the Caribbean. He ultimately found work at Isle des Chevaliers with the Street family under the supervision of Ondine and Sydney Childs. Addressed only as "Yardman," Gideon was an invaluable worker for Ondine (41). Gideon was dutiful and hard working, but he knew to keep his ability to read from Ondine so that his chores would not increase (42, 154).

Gideon liked Son, the stranger who roamed about at night. The two men shared stories when Mr. Street asked Gideon to take Son into town for a haircut. The trust extended to a shared passport when Son left for New York (154–55).

GIDEON, THE GET AWAY MAN [TB]. Valerian Street called Gideon, his yardman, "Gideon, the Get Away Man" after he fired him and Mary Therese Foucalt for stealing apples (201).

GIGI. *See* GRACE [PA]

GISTAN [JZ]. Gistan was a protective buddy of Joe Trace who—with another friend, Stuck—decided to shield him from the embarrassment of knowing that his wife, Violet, had tried to steal a neighbor's baby (22). Gistan was a true friend because, when Joe needed a job, he was right there to help him find one (129).

GOBINEAU, JOSEPH ARTHUR, COMTE DE (1816–1882) [BE]. Soaphead Church found comfort in the philosophy of Joseph Arthur Comte de Gobineau, who promoted the thesis that the races are innately unequal and that the white Aryan (German) race is not only the purest, but also superior to all others. (168). According to this thesis, any race other than white was inferior. After studying the life of Gobineau, Michael D. Biddiss wrote, "Gobineau's writings prior to 1850 indicated a search for social order. He was convinced that without the sense of hierarchy and stability, which this implied, there could be no meaningful freedom (Biddiss, 156). Gobineau's writings were used by German Nazi theorists as justification for anti-Semitism.

GOLDEN GRAY. *See* GRAY, GOLDEN [JZ]

GOLIGHTLY, KATE HARPER [PA]. Daughter of Harper and Catherine Jury and half sister to Menus Jury (197), Kate sought an early marriage so that she could escape from the friction in her home under her father's dominance. As one of the local women in Ruby, Oklahoma, Kate Golightly played the organ and sang solos at social events (144, 155). It was

Kate and Anna Flood who washed the unsightly graffiti from the Oven wall (102–3).

GOOD (DOG) [PA]. Good was one of the two collie dogs owned by Steward Morgan. As alert Scottish watchdogs, collies require weekly brushing to keep their coats clean and free of matting. Biannually, K.D. brought the dogs into Ruby for a complete grooming. In a melodic rendition of soul music, K.D., serenaded the dogs with a tune designed just for them (54).

GOOD SHEPHERD BAPTIST CHURCH. *See* A.M.E & GOOD SHEPHERD BAPTIST CHURCHES [TB]

GOODROE, BIRDIE [PA]. Mother of Mavis and grandmother of deceased twins and Frankie and Billy James Albright, Birdie Goodroe was sympathetic to her daughter, but she did not approve of a mother fleeing from her children. She strongly felt that after the death of the twins, the remaining children needed their mother's care. When Mavis realized that her mother had telephoned her husband, she took what she wanted and headed west (30–33).

GOSHEN, VIRGINIA [JZ]. Joe Trace and his closest friend, Victory Williams, were happy to find work in Goshen, Virginia (175).

GRABLE, BETTY (1916–1973) [BE]. Maureen Peal commented to Pecola Breedlove how much she adored Betty Grable, the 1930s glamorous movie star who was famous for her pinup picture during World War II. Many of the soldiers fighting in battle were able to deal with the loneliness of war because Betty Grable smiled out at them from pinups on the barracks walls, far away from home (69).

GRACE (I.E., GIGI) [PA]. Before going to the Convent, Gigi lived the fast life. Socially bankrupt, she antagonized and humiliated all but a select few. At the Convent, Gigi liked Connie because Connie saw the loneliness and despair that fueled Gigi's negative behavior. If Gigi wasn't verbally bedeviling, she was acting out in other ways. At their first meeting, Mavis Albright was appalled by her nudity, but Gigi only agreed to put on clothes when Connie reassured her that, nude or dressed, she was still loved (75–76). As a woman who believed that self-hatred gave her the license to hurt others, Gigi exploited situations and people for fun. Frustrated because her boyfriend, Mikey Rood, was doing time and the meeting place for after his release was nonexistent, Gigi decided to take her grandfather's advice and head home (63–65).
    Bored on the train, she deliberately selected the slightly built man with

an earring for conversation. Feeling superior, she artfully fought for Dice's rights as a passenger and helped him get his suitcase from the overhead when the train reached his destination. Typical of Gigi, she later, in a disparaging manner, called him a "lying freak" (68). Ironically, though, it was Gigi who misrepresented to Dice the facts about her family's size and location. Her sole relative in Mississippi somehow became a host of relatives in California because it was too painful for her to disclose that her dad was sentenced to die in prison when she was only eleven and her mom, uncaring, was off somewhere (257, 310). Always pushing to see how far she could go, Gigi sexually toyed with K.D., the starry-eyed Ruby resident, until he struck her in anger. Later she jokingly mocked the size of his male organ (180, 256).

Gigi was crude and did not hesitate to ask Pallas if she was the daughter of a stripteaser, Seneca why she never bathed, and Mavis why she was sex starved (181, 256, 168). She was good at hurting, but she was still at the Convent the morning when the experts from Ruby came.

GRACE LONG. *See* **LONG, GRACE [SS]**

GRAFFITI ARTISTS [TB]. Arriving in New York City, Son looked for familiar sights, including the work of the Three Yard Boys (3YB), a graffiti crew from the 1970s (215). As a cultural medium, graffiti dates back to ancient Roman times, when Pompeii was recognized as a public space for artistic expression. Like so many others who grew to appreciate the creative spray paint expression, Son searched for the art forms of Pax, Stay High 149, Three Yard Boys 3YB, Teen, P-Komet, and Popeye within urban culture. Unique to each master is the coded tag name of authorship, and a "throw up" is a shortened form of that identity. In 1974, Norman Mailer illustrated certain graffiti artists in his book, *Faith of Graffiti*. According to Susan A. Phillips, "This type of graffiti is geared towards people who already understand the messages and may act to enhance group solidarity" (Phillips, 269).

GRAHAM, MICHAEL-MARY [SS]. Michael-Mary Graham was the poetess who employed First Corinthians Dead as a maid and later encouraged her to acquire clerical skills by taking typing lessons. A woman of some means and position, Michael-Mary was well known and respected within the literary community. First Corinthians hid her domestic position with Ms. Graham from her family, and, from Ms. Graham, she hid her four-year liberal training at Bryn Mawr. So when her maid understood the works of Steinbeck, Shakespeare, Browning, and other literate notables, Ms. Graham was pleased with herself for hiring someone worthy of boasting about in her bookish circle of friends (188–89).

GRANDFATHERS, THE [JZ]. Henry Les Tory/Lestory was named the "Hunters Hunter" by a group of older men called the "grandfathers." Their years of expert hunting was now compromised by age, but the old men still respected the skill in Mr. Henry. In turn, the Hunters Hunter was sensitive to how aging had limited their skills and went out of his way to protect their dignity (166–67).

GRANDMA BABY [BLV]. Denver Suggs loved to call her grandmother, Baby Suggs, "Grandma Baby" (35).

GRANDMOTHER STADT [TB]. As the Street family matriach, Grandmother Stadt promoted goodwill amongst their family business, Street Brothers Candy Company. She was also known within the family for her holiday bread making (52).

GRANT, ULYSSES S. [SS]. Old Macon Dead named his cow "Ulysses S. Grant" in honor of President Ulysses Simpson Grant, general and political leader of the nineteenth century (52). During the Civil War, General Grant was commanding officer of the Union army, and it was he who accepted the unconditional surrender of General Robert E. Lee, the commanding officer of the Confederate army at Appomattox Courthouse in April 1985. Grant later became president of the United States, serving two terms from 1869 to 1877.

GRAY, COLONEL WORDSWORTH [JZ]. Colonel Wordsworth Gray was the father of Vera Louise Gray. Hearing the news of his daughter's forthcoming birth of a mulatto grandchild was staggering for Colonel Gray, what with the seven racially mixed children already on his plantation(140–41).

GRAY, GOLDEN [JZ]. Golden Gray was the mulatto son of Henry Les Story/Lestory; a black man, and Vera Louise Gray, a white woman. Born with golden skin and sandy hair, Golden Gray received a fancy name and a charmed life instead being raised in the Catholic Foundling Home (139–40). Pampered by Vera Louise and True Belle, the maid servant who adored him, the young, mulatto son of a Colonel's daughter wanted for nothing. Upon maturity, armed with the truth about his bloodline and the whereabouts of his Negro father, he left home. In route to Vesper County, Virginia, Golden Gray encountered an unconscious, deranged and wounded pregnant woman in need of help. He was angry and insecure about meeting his father for the first time. When he found this injured black woman in the woods, Golden Gray went out of his way to help her to impress his father (143–48). It was only the appearance of chivalry that prompted him to put her in his carriage (143–48). Alone with the woman, the bitterness that he nursed for the father he never knew disintegrated. Upon meeting Henry Lestory, the Hunters Hunter, Golden Gray found a proud black man/father with principles that commanded and received respect (168–73).

GRAY, VERA LOUISE [JZ]. Vera Louise Gray was the daughter of Colonel and Mrs. Wordsworth Gray and mother of Golden Gray, a mulatto son. When sex with a black boy resulted in pregnancy, Vera Louise was cast out of the home in Virginia by infuriated parents (141). Only the appearance of an infant son with golden skin and hair cancelled her plans to put the child in a Catholic Foundling Home. Emotionally padded with money and the aid of her faithful servant, Vera Louise raised her son under the cloak of deception in the city of Baltimore, Maryland (139). Vera Louise lost her precious son when he found out the truth about his black roots, as he went in search of his father (143).

GREAT AUNT JIMMY [BE]. When Aunt Jimmy rescued her infant great-nephew, Cholly Breedlove, from the garbage heap, she disavowed the natural father (Samson Fuller) by naming the child for her dead brother, Charles Breedlove. She wanted to distance young Cholly from his biological father, who had an unsavory reputation. Great Aunt Jimmy's love for young Cholly was recognized openly within the family (140). When Great Aunt Jimmy became ill, many friends came to her bedside. According to rumor, it was a peach cobbler prepared by one of her well wishers that killed her (132–33).

GREATER SAINT MATTHEW [SU]. Greater Saint Mathew was the black church up in the Bottom of Medallion, Ohio (127).

GREEN, CHEYENNE BROWN. *See* **CHEYENNE [TB]**

GREEN, FRANCINE [TB]. Francine Green was the daughter of Franklin G. (Old Man) and sister of Son (William Green), Horace, and Porky Green. One day, after horsing around with her brother, Francine went dashing through the meadows and encountered trained canines on a criminal search. The animals had lost the original scent and turned on Francine. She was under attack for thirty seconds before she was rescued. From those few seconds Francine suffered extensive physical and psychological damage. The end result of the painful ordeal was Francine's confinement in a mental institution in Jacksonville, Florida. What happened to Francine was disheartening because she had been a fine sprinter with a future athletic career before the misfortune (247, 268).

GREEN, FRANK G. [TB]. Frank G. Green was the son of Franklin G. (Old Man) and brother of Son (William), Horace, Porky, and Francine. Frank G. died in Korea (247).

GREEN, FRANKLIN G. (I.E., OLD MAN) [TB]. Franklin G. Green was the father of Son (William), Francine, Frank, Horace, and Porky. Franklin G. Green had worn the label of "Old Man" since the age of seven. Later, when "Old Man" became a father, William, his first born became "Old Man's son." Then William became just "Son" when Frank, the second son was born.

Old Man was a prideful and protective parent who always tried to shield his children from pain. When Son got into trouble and had to leave town in a hurry, Old Man met him outside of town to give him comfort and money. When Son returned home after eight years on the lame, it was time for rejoicing. The two macho men spiritually embraced without touching. It was then that Son learned that the money he had sent home to his father was used sparingly to avoid any attention drawn to the family from the authorities or the mother of the wife whom Son had killed. Old Man needed the funds, but his first concern was for the well-being of his son.

When Old Man found out that Son's traveling companion was not his wife, he encouraged Son to take her to Aunt Rosa's instead, for lodging. Old Man believed that honesty strengthened character and accountability. A little embarrassed, Son attempted to defend his lady friend by bragging about her uniqueness, but Old Man simply countered with an indifferent "me too"—I am also unique—reply. Bold and loving, Old Man commanded and received respect (248–50).

GREEN, HORACE [TB]. Horace Green, who lived in Gainesville, Florida, was the son of Franklin G. (Old Man) and brother of Son (William), Porky, and Francine (247).

GREEN, PORKY [TB]. Porky Green was the youngest daughter of Franklin (Old Man) and baby sister of Son (William), Francine, and Horace. A runner like Francine, Porky earned educational funding to A&M University as a member of the track team. This enabled her to remain in Eloe while attending school (247).

GREEN, WILLIAM. *See* **SON [TB]**

GREENE, JUDE [SU]. Jude Greene was the husband of Nel Wright and father of three children. As one of eight children in a churchgoing family, Jude Green was popular and respected by the community. Working as a waiter, he longed to gain employment on the construction project for the new bridge. A failed attempt to secure a job more masculine than waiting on tables left Jude determined to validate his manhood through other means. The challenges of marriage gave him a partner and a purpose, so he proposed to Nel (80–83). Nel's best friend, Sula Peace, left town the night of the wedding, only to return ten years later to betray Nel by sleeping with her husband, which broke up the marriage (105–6).

GREENE, NEL WRIGHT [SU]. Nel Wright Greene was the daughter of Helene and Wiley Wright, granddaughter of Rochelle, great-granddaughter of Cecile Sabat, and best friend to Sula Peace. Nel's father was away a lot and her mother doted on her only child (18). When news came that her great-grandmother was ill, Helene, with young Nel in tow, headed south to New Orleans, Louisiana.

Upon their return, Nel discovered her uniqueness as a person (20–28). Secure in her "me-ness," Nel had the courage to disregard her mother's bias about the Peace women and approached Sula Peace in friendship (29). Nel and Sula were from totally different homes, but they shared many childhood experiences together. Nel's mother worked hard to cultivate her daughter and dispel the negative influence of her promiscuous Creole grandmother (26). Sula, on the other hand, lived in a home that lacked maternal controls. Sula loved the structure of Nel's home, and Nel appreciated the freedom of Sula's (29).

As children, the cultural imbalances strengthened Nel and Sula's bond of friendship, however, as adults, things drastically changed. Leaving Medallion the day of Nel's wedding (85), Sula returned ten years later, expert in the ability to hurt without conscience. The years had widened the gap between them, and Sula ultimately violated Nel's trust by sleeping with her husband (105). Only in the end, when Sula lay dying, did Nel realize that childhood friendships could not erase the pain of adulthood betrayal (144–45).

GREER, MAMA. *See* MAMA GREER [PA]

GREGORY, DICK (RICHARD CLAXTON) (1932–) [TB]. Michael Street had one of the few Dick Gregory. For President souvenir buttons (21). He admired Dick Gregory, the comedian, civil rights activist, nutritionist, and politician known for his ability to weave comedy into candor. Through a series of hunger strikes, platforms for social change, and his stand-up comedy routine, Dick Gregory has made an powerful imprint on American civil liberties. In 1968, Gregory ran for president as an independent on the Freedom and Peace Party with Mark Lane. He won 47,000 votes, primarily from California.

GRINNING HATTIE [BE]. Mrs. MacTeer and her lady friends included "grinning Hattie" on the list of the town's women who were rumored to be a little strange, like Della Jones and Aunti Julia (13).

GUITAR BAINS. *See* BAINS, GUITAR [SS]

H

HAGAR [SS]. Hagar was the Daughter of Reba and granddaughter of Pilate. Hagar was raised by two free-spirited women in an environment devoid of rules. Her mother and grandmother loved her, but they could not give Hagar a normal life with school, playmates, church, relatives, and social boundaries. Yet, as three cohabiting women, Hagar accepted her life as the norm. Pilate saw the void in Hagar's life and made a decision to find Macon Dead II, her long-lost brother. Hagar needed the security of family dynamics, and Pilate thought Macon could provide it (151). However, memories of the gold he sacrificed and the years apart had hardened Macon's heart, and he shunned his kin.

However, at age seventeen, Hagar met and began an affair with Milkman, her twelve-year-old first cousin. The affair lasted over eleven years (43, 45, 147, 99). What began as an innocent curiosity became an obsession. The adolescent lover grew into a man who no longer wanted or needed her. The letter Milkman wrote to end the relationship was painful, but seeing him with another woman was more than she could bear. On a monthly basis, Hagar began stalking him in an effort to take his life (118–19). She felt unloved and unattractive. Encouraged by Pilate and Reba to go on a spending spree for items that made her feel pretty, Hagar became disoriented. She later died.

HALLE SUGGS. *See* SUGGS, HALLE [BLV]

HAMLET [BE]. Before Soaphead Church changed his name, he was Elihue Micah Whitcomb, boy scholar. *Hamlet*, one of William Shakespeare's tragedies, graced his reading list (169). Hamlet, son of the deceased King Hamlet of Denmark, discovers from the ghost of his father that he was murdered by Hamlet's uncle, who is now married to Hamlet's mother. Hamlet loved Ophelia, but he rejects her when he learns of her betrayal. Hamlet reacted in a vicious manner toward his once-beloved Ophelia, often verbally and profoundly belittling her at will.

HAM'S SON [SU]. After finding the body of a colored child (Chicken Little), the racist bargeman contemplated the plight of the biblical Ham's son, Canaan, in the wake of liberal white people (63). For years, extremists have used these passages as biblical justification of slavery (Gen. 9: 20–27). According to biblical scripture, Noah left the ark to plant a vineyard. The sampling of too much wine made him fall asleep naked. Noah had three sons, Shem, Ham, and Japeth. Ham saw his father laying uncovered in the tent, and summoned his brothers to look for entertainment. Out of respect for their father, Shem and Japeth entered the tent backwards to avoid seeing him naked. When Noah awakened and learned of Ham's antics, he cursed Ham's son and his grandson, Canaan, vowing that he and his descendants would forever be slaves to his brothers. And he said, "Cursed be Canaan; a servant of servants shall he be unto his brethren" (Gen. 9:26).

HANNAH PEACE. *See* **PEACE, HANNAH [SU]**

HANSEL & GRETEL [SS]. Morrison referenced the apprehension of Hansel and Gretel, the brother and sister in the Grimm's nineteenth-century fairy tale, to describe Milkman's fear of entering the woods in search of the cave. As an adult, Milkman's anxiety equaled that of a child. The comparison was an excellent example of how fear transcends age and boundaries. Terror is an emotion that spans cultures, years, and seasons (219).

"Hansel and Gretel" is the classic story about a brother and a sister who are taken into the forest and left to starve at the suggestion of their mean stepmother. The children overheard the insidious plot to do away with them, and, secretly, they placed pebbles on the path to guide them back home. After a while, the brother and sister are again taken into the woods, only this time without an opportunity to leave a trail. However, an encounter with a mean witch, her death, and her pearls and jewels got them securely back home to find a joyful father in the absence of the stepmother.

HARD GOODS (HORSE) [PA]. The mare owned by Nathan DuPres, Hard Goods, advertently contributed to the naming of a little boy (K.D.) and the shaming of a little girl (Billie Delia Cato). The winner of the race organized by Ossie Beauchamp to celebrate the road to street naming, Hard Goods was instrumental in young Coffee Smith's winning the Purple Heart and being renamed K.D., for Kentucky Derby. When K.D., the son of Ruby Blackhorse Smith (the town's namesake and a Morgan nephew), rode the horse, there was pride and recognition. However, when little Billie Delia Cato rode him, she suffered shame and condemnation.

Nathan DuPres was quite generous to the children, and often came into town encouraging them to go for a ride on his horse, Hard Goods. One day, excited by the anticipation of riding on the horse, three-year-old Billie Delia Cato, daughter of Billy and Patricia, innocently stepped out of her panties to ride bareback. As Billie Delia was accustomed to riding in that manner, the act itself was insignificant. However, the reaction of onlookers was shock and condemnation. To make matters worse, in concert with the mood of the crowd, Billie Delia's mother spanked her on the spot. From that day on, the little girl's chastity and good name were in question (150).

HARLON RICKS. *See* RICKS, HARLON [JZ]

HARLOW, JEAN (1911–1937) [BE]. Pauline Breedlove loved to escape the dullness of her life by attending movies, and Jean Harlow was one of her favorite screen stars. Pauline fantasized about wearing her hair like this screen siren of the 1930s. One day, sitting in the theatre, Pauline broke her tooth on a piece of candy and realized the defeat of her fantasy (123).

HARPER JURY. *See* JURY, HARPER [PA]

HARRY [PA]. Seneca's self-mutilation began in Mama Greer's foster home, where she lived with Harry, another foster child. One day, while sexually molesting Seneca, Harry badly bruised her skin. Mama Greer was sympathetic to the injury until Seneca told her about Harry's sexual advances. Mama Greer reacted angrily about the two children having sex because it reflected poorly on her home as a safe haven for children. Harry was allowed to remain in the foster home, but Seneca was moved to another home. Both Harry and Mama Greer responded to the bruise, so Seneca continued using self-mutilation as a way to cope with the secret shame (260–61).

HATCHERS, THE [TB]. The Hatchers, neighbors of the Street family in the Carribean, hosted an extravagant weekend yuletide event (65).

HAVEN, OKLAHOMA [PA]. The Old Fathers—which represented the Blackhorse, Beauchamp, Morgan, Poole, Fleetwood, Cato, Flood, and two DuPres families—were forced to pick up their belongings and leave Fairly, Oklahoma. After days of aimless travel, someone appeared to lead the settlers to Haven, Oklahoma. As Oklahoma and Indian Territories joined in statehood, coexistence between whites, blacks, and Indians created friction once again forcing generations of New Fathers to resettle in a place they named Ruby, Oklahoma (188–89).

HAYDN, FRANZ JOSEF (1732–1809) [TB]. The plants in the greenhouse of L'Arbe de la Croix, the home of Valerian Street, were serenaded in the musical expression of Franz Josef Haydn (12). Famous for his compositions of string quartets, Haydn has been hailed as the "creator of chamber music." Valerian felt that his plants flourished when instrumental music played in the background.

HAZELNUT MAN [BLV]. For twelve years everyone in town shunned the gray and white house at 124 Bluestone Road. When Paul D. came, Denver called him the "hazelnut man" because of the medium brown coloring of the hazelnut. Denver did not like his hairy unshaven look or the fact that he came without gifts. Paul D. was either the "hazelnut man" or the "hazelnut stranger," but always someone who Denver envied for having a relationship with the father she never knew (13).

HEADLESS BRIDE [BLV]. Shortly after Paul D. arrived at 124, Sethe told him about the spirit residing in the home. Denver added that the spirit was her deceased sister. In an effort to relate, Paul D. then reminded Sethe of the headless bride that frightened everyone at Sweet Home by traveling through the forest at night (13).

HEATTER, GABRIEL (1890–1972) [SU]. In Nel Greene's shattered emotional state, she was still able to recognize the look of annoyance in the face of her husband, Jude, when she interrupted his intimacy with her best friend, Sula Mae Peace (105). She had seen the same look when their children dared to interrupt their father during one of Gabriel Heatter's radio broadcasts.

Famous for beginning his broadcast with, "Ah, there is good news tonight," Gabriel Heatter's powerful voice over the air was riveting, yet comforting to many Americans of all races during the 1940s. In Gabriel Heatter's March 31, 1972, *New York Times* obituary, it was written, "Mr. Heatter found silver linings that soothed his admirers and exasperated his critics during a radio career that spanned the Depression, World War II, Korea and the Cold War" (*NYT*, 31 March 1972). As a newscaster for various networks, Gabriel Heatter regularly communicated to the world, bringing vital information during a crucial period in American history.

HEDDY BYRD. *See* BYRD, HEDDY [SU]

HELEN BEAUCHAMP. *See* BEAUCHAMP, LUTHER [PA]

HELEN MOORE. *See* MOORE, HELEN [JZ]

HELENE SABAT WRIGHT. *See* WRIGHT, HELENE SABAT [SU]

HELMUT (DOG) [SS]. Helmut was one of the Weimaraner dogs owned by the Butler family (240).

HENRI MARTIN. *See* MARTIN, HENRI [SU]

HENRY, JOHN [TB]. A Negro gadabout of a steel miner, John Henry was famous for his large physical build and his ability to drive steel with precision and force. This character was compared to Son as one of the vagabond-type men who travel the globe running from trouble (166).

HENRY LES TORY/LESTORY. *See* LES TORY/LESTORY, HENRY [JZ]

HENRY PORTER. *See* PORTER, HENRY [SS]

HENRY WASHINGTON. *See* WASHINGTON, HENRY (I.E., MR. HENRY) [BE]

HERE BOY (DOG) [BLV]. The spirit that plagued the Suggs home damaged and badly hurt Here Boy, the Suggs pet dog. The yard became Here Boy's home because he was afraid to reenter the home after the assault (12). He only returned when he was sure that the angry spirit had departed. Paul D. saw Here Boy's return as a positive sign that Beloved had left them alone finally (263).

HI MAN [BLV]. Of the forty-six men on the chain gang in Alfred, Georgia, only Hi Man was permitted to speak, and he thus became the chain gang's communicator and savior. As the lead man in the chain gang, his "Hiii" signaled the end of the morning sadism, and, at dusk, his "Hooo" signalled the end of the day. Hi Man was the formal and informal leader who protected his fellow prisoners with insight and timing. When the rains brought freedom, it was Hi Man they trusted to lead the way out (108–9).

HIGH JOHN THE CONQUEROR [SU]. One of the herbs used by Ajax's mother was High John the Conqueror (126). In an article written by Rick Ansorge for the *Florida Times–Union*, Jacksonville, Florida, he quotes Yvonne Chireau, a religion professor at Pennsylvania Swarthmore College and a leading authority on African American folk medicine, "It [High John the Conqueror] was considered one of the most powerful herbs for healing and bringing good luck" (Ansorge, C1).

HODGES FUNERAL HOME [SU]. Shadrack did odd jobs for Hodges Funeral Home, the white-owned establishment that funeralized Sula Mae Peace (150, 157).

HODGES, MR. *See* MR. HODGES [SU]

HONOR [JZ]. Honor was the thirteen-year-old son of Patty who looked after the animals when Henry Les Tory/Lestory was away. Arriving one day to tend the animals, he found the cabin occupied by a slightly intoxicated "whiteman" and an unconscious pregnant woman. Curious and respectful, Honor gave any information asked for about the whereabouts of Mr. Les Tory/Lestory (Hunters Hunter) to the stranger he assumed was a "whiteman."

Honor was summoned by the stranger (Golden Gray) to the bedside of the wounded black woman, and subsequently he fetched water to wash the dried blood from her face. When Mr. Les Tory/Lestory returned home, Honor was eager to greet him with news of the two strangers inside his home (155– 57, 160, 168).

HONORE ISLAND [SS]. Honore Island was the beach community for prosperous black people that Macon Dead II and his family visited in the summer (33).

HORACE GREEN. *See* GREEN, HORACE [TB]

HORSES IN RACE (RUBY, OKLAHOMA) [PA]. In the all-black town of Ruby, Oklahoma, there was a horse race to mark the celebration of a road's transformation to a named street. Ossie Beauchamp organized the race to bring everyone together in recognition of the town's growth and even donated his Purple Heart medal as a prize to the winner. The ten horses in the race were Ossie's two-and-four-year-olds, Ace Flood's spotted horse, Miss Esther's featherweight, Nathan DuPres's four plow horses, an auburn mare named Hard Goods, and a half-broke pony (10).

HORST (DOG) [SS]. Horst was one of the Weimaraner dogs owned by the Butler family (240).

HOSPITAL TOMMY [SS]. Hospital Tommy was the joint owner with Railroad Tommy of the local barbershop. Hospital Tommy was the more eloquent of the two because he was known for using words that others did not comprehend (59). As a World War II veteran, he was disillusioned when he left the military service and came back to a country that mocked, humiliated, and lynched blacks. Hospital Tommy's membership in the Seven Days, a group of black men who avenged the death of their people, was personal. As a member of the 92nd Infantry during the war, he risked his life defending America on foreign soil and resented their betrayal by tolerating the racial abuse experienced by the veterans returning home (100–101).

HOT STEAM [JZ]. One of the pieces of mail correspondence that Sweetness stole, and his aunt, Malvonne Edwards, read, was a sexually explicit letter from "Hot Steam" to her neighbor/lover Daddy, aka Mr. Sage. She closed the erotic letter with "yours always, Hot Steam" (44).

HOWARD SUGGS. *See* SUGGS, HOWARD [BLV]

HUCK FINN. *See* FINN, HUCK [TB]

HUNTERS CAVE [SS]. Once intended as a base camp for tired hunters, the Hunters Cave became a graveyard. After young Macon Dead II buried his father, the body resurfaced after the rains. Later, fishermen recognized the body floating in the river and deposited him in Hunters Cave (244). Earlier, after leaving the protection of Circe, he took refuge in Hunters Cave, and, out of the confusion and the fear of being discovered, young Macon killed a weary hunter (169–71).

HUNTERS HUNTER [JZ]. Hunters Hunter was the name given to Henry Les Tory/Lestory, the black father of Golden Gray, by the older hunters, who were called the "grandfathers." His reputation as a skilled marksman and hunter was well known throughout Vesper County, Virginia (125, 167).

HUNTING PARTY [SS]. During his visit to Shalimar, Virginia, Milkman was asked to join a hunting party that included Omar, Luther Solomon, Calvin Breakstone, and Small Boy (269–71).

HURSTON [PA]. Hurston was the crooner at K.D. and Arnette's wedding (157).

HURSTON & CALINE POOLE. *See* POOLE, HURSTON & CALINE [PA]

I

IAGO [BE]. As an avid reader, young Elihue Micah Whitcomb (Soaphead Church) was familiar with the characters in *Othello*, the Shakespearean tragedy, of which Iago was a one (169). As a military aide to Othello—the Moorish general of Venice who is married to Desdemona, a Venetian lady—Iago schemes to undermine the marriage. Iago is successful in his deceptive plot, as Othello becomes convinced of her unfaithfulness and subsequently takes Desdemona's life.

IKE & TINA GIRL [PA]. Mavis Albright enjoyed the sounds of good music as she traveled back with the gas station attendant to her immobilized car. Ike and Tina Girl, the husband-and-wife rock and roll team of the 1950s, was one of the groups to which she listened. Born Anna Mae Bullock, Tina married Ike Turner and became the band's songstress. Later the band was renamed the "Ike and Tina Turner Review" (45).

INDIGO, THE [JZ]. Upset with the news of her husband's infidelity, Violet Trace imagined how Joe Trace might have taken Dorcas, his young lover, to the nightclub called the Indigo (95).

IRENE'S PALACE OF COSMETOLOGY [SU]. Irene's Palace of Cosmetology was a unisex beauty parlor slated for destruction in Medallion, Ohio (3).

IRON-EYED WOMAN [BLV]. When Sethe, at the age of sixteen, came to Sweet Home to replace Baby Suggs, the five young men on the plantation called her the "iron-eyed woman" (10).

ISALEY'S [BE]. The MacTeer girls and others frequented this ice cream parlor in Lorain, Ohio (68).

ISLE des CHEVALIERS [TB]. Isle des Chevaliers was the site of the elaborate winter residences in the scenic Caribbean (9). Valerian Street's L'Arbe de la Croix was located there (10). The island had no more than fourteen people, of which none were children (39).

ITUMBA MASK [TB]. Jadine Childs reveals her snobbery when she comments to Valerian Street, "Picasso is better than an Itumba mask. The fact that he was intrigued by them is proof of his genius, not the maskmakers' " (74). In essence, Jadine discounted the art of her African heritage in order to validate the works of her European neighbors. Jadine's snobbery ignored the obvious fact that Picasso replicated the African images in his art.

In Picasso's *Les demoiselle d'Avignon*, his first of what would be known as Cubist art, the influence of the Itumba masks he had seen in Africa is clearly apparent. The dominance of the bulging eyes and the elongated nose of the Itumba masks are reflected in the two right-hand figures in *Les demoiselle d'Avignon*. As part of the ethnographical tradition of the Babangi tribe of the French Congo, the Itumba masks represent the Etumbi village near Gaboon and French Congo. Leon Siroto wrote in a 1954 study that "Itumba is a variant of the place-name 'Etumbi' " (Siroto, 149).

IVY [BE]. Woman soloist in choir that sang "Precious Lord" with the "death-defying death" that Pauline experienced deep within her soul (113).

IVY [SU]. As her upstairs neighbor, Ivy joined Dessie behind Shadrack in his National Suicide Day parade after the death of Sula Mae Peace (158).

J

JACK [PA]. After Jean abandoned her daughter, Seneca, she married a man named Jack. He was unaware that, as a teenager, his wife had birthed a child (316).

JACK, BLUE [BE]. As the one the few males in the life of young Cholly Breedlove, Blue Jack played a pivotal role in his development. Although the two men were years apart in age, they spent many hours together working at the Feed and Grain Store. Blue Jack was a storyteller with many tales about life, love, and adventure to wile away the time. Cholly lived in a female-dominated home, and Blue Jack gave him exposure to masculine thought and behavior. When Blue Jack was given the heart of a watermelon at the Fourth of July picnic, he chose to share it with Cholly Breedlove (133–35).

As time passed, Blue Jack's aging and memories of events made him escape through the bottle more frequently. Cholly knew that, more and more often, Blue's moments of intoxication were more frequent than his moments of soberness. It was this knowledge that hindered Cholly's seeking the counsel of his old friend when white men threatened his manhood (151).

JACKSON, MRS. *See* MRS. JACKSON [SU]

JACKSON TILL. *See* TILL, JACKSON [BLV]

JADINE CHILDS. *See* CHILDS, JADINE (I.E., JADE) [TB]

JAKE [BE]. Jake was the distant cousin of Cholly Breedlove who escorted a girl by the name of Suky into the woods after Great Aunt Jimmy's funeral (144).

JAKE. *See* DEAD, MACON I [SS]

JANEY. *See* WAGON, JANEY [BLV]

JEAN [PA]. As a child birthing a child, Jean learned deception early in life. After giving birth to Seneca at the age of fourteen, Jean chose the role of sister instead of mother (127). Somehow the responsibilities of a mother far outweighed the responsibilities of a sister. When Jean abandoned her five-year-old daughter, she didn't look back until after her marriage. Somehow, having a new family, headed by a husband, brought home the guilt of abandonment. By then, however, it was too late to help Seneca (316).

JEFFERSON FLEETWOOD. *See* FLEETWOOD, JEFFERSON [PA]

JENNY WHITLOW. *See* WHITLOW, JENNY [BLV]

JEROME [PA]. Jerome was the son of Dee Dee and Milton Truelove and brother of Pallas (166).

JESUS [BLV]. Jesus is believed by Christians to be the Son of God. It was Jesus in Amy Denver who enabled her to help Sethe, a young pregnant and wounded black girl, in the woods. When Amy fully grasped the situation, after meeting Sethe and all during the encounter, Amy beckoned her "Jesus" (78–79). When Amy found the boat, she advised Sethe (who introduced herself as "Lu") that, "Jesus is looking after you," (83).

In a conversation with the newly arrived Beloved, Denver innocently asked her who she saw "down there": "You see Jesus? Baby Sugg?" (75). She did not realize that the spirit of Jesus is thought to be light and up, not dark and down.

JIGS (I.E., JIGABOOS) [TB]. The salesman advised the Street uncles that the Valerian candy was a bad investment because it was only bought by "Jigs" in the South (51). "Jigs" is short for "jigaboos," a racial insult to blacks. The use of the offensive and derogatory comment was accepted by the Street uncles. The racial slang sets the stage for understanding the environment in which young Valerian Street was raised. A careful look at other factors paints a picture of financial and social dominance supported by loyal servants of ethnic minorities. The Street Brothers Candy Company were loyal to their employees, who were "Swedish and German women" (52). Valerian Street enjoyed the services of his domestic staff (Ondine and Sydney), but dissuaded his lonely wife from fraternizing with them (59). Upon retirement, he bought a house on a Caribbean island, but chose not to associate with his diverse community of neighbors (14).

JOANNE [PA]. Joanne was a woman who worked as an executive secretary for Milton Truelove, father of Gigi (253).

JOE NATHAN. *See* NATHAN, JOE [BLV]

JOE TRACE. *See* TRACE, JOE (I.E., JOSEPH) [JZ]

JOHN. *See* ELLA & JOHN [BLV]

JOHN [SS]. Grace Long took delight in revealing to Milkman, Susan Byrd's northern guest, that John, one of the Byrd relatives, was denouncing his race by passing for white. Grace was firm in her convictions about John because she actually saw him in Mayville (290).

JOHN HENRY. *See* HENRY, JOHN [TB]

JOHN L. [SU]. Sula and Nel shared a joke about John L. and his foiled sexual encounter with a girl named Shirley. It seemed that John L. had a serious problem with anatomy (97).

JOHN SEAWRIGHT. *See* NEW FATHERS OF RUBY, OKLAHOMA

JOHNNIE, PRETTY. *See* TAR BABY [SU]

JOHNNY [BE]. Johnny was the gangster boyfriend of Miss Marie whom the Federal Bureau of Investigation (FBI) asked her to help apprehend. Miss Marie bragged about how well she was paid for the information that led to his capture (142).

JOHN SHILLITO'S [BLV]. John Shillito's was a neighborhood store that Sethe Suggs goes to buy notions, like ribbon, buttons, and lace (240).

JOHNSON, MRS. *See* MRS. JOHNSON [BE]

JONES, LADY. *See* LADY JONES [BLV]

JOSEPH LORDI. *See* LORDI, LENORA & JOSEPH [TB]

JOSHUA. *See* STAMP PAID [BLV]. "Joshua" was Stamp Paid's slave name before he left the plantation because he could not tolerate the sexual abuse of his wife, Vashti (232).

JUDD, WINNIE RUTH (1905–1998) [SS]. The men in Tommy's Barbershop would spin tales about Winnie Ruth Judd on the loose when a murder of a white person occurred in the South. Known as the "Trunk Murderess," Winnie Ruth Judd was a white woman in one of the most shocking murder trials of the 1930s. She was committed to an insane asylum in the state of Arizona from 1933–1971 for at least one murder and the dismemberment of two women on October 31, 1931. The story began on October 18, 1931, when young Ruth arrived at the Los Angeles Union Station with two pieces of luggage dripping with the bloody remains of Agnes Anne LeRoi, thirty-two, and Hedvig "Sammy" Samuelson, twenty-four, both of whom had been cut into pieces. Ruth was convicted and sentenced in the Phoenix courts. Instead of the death penalty, she was confined to the Arizona State Hospital for the Insane. The national outcry for mercy included the voice of Eleanor Roosevelt, wife of President Roosevelt.

Somehow, Winnie Ruth Judd managed to escape two or three times a year. Once she was gone for almost seven years before she was caught and returned to the hospital (99–100).

JUDE GREENE. *See* GREENE, JUDE [SU]

JUDY [BLV]. Paul D. asked everyone about Judy, the woman who worked in the slaughterhouse and lived on Plank Street (231–32).

JULIA, AUNTI. *See* AUNTI JULIA [BE]

JULY [PA]. July was the woman employed as a secretary for Deacon Morgan in the bank (114).

JUNE [PA]. June was a female journalist sent to the Albright home to cover the story about the death of their infant twins (22–23).

JUNIE BUG [BE]. One of the four schoolboys who taunted Pecola Breedlove in the schoolyard. In cowardly gang fashion, the group encircled Pecola and chanted cruel catchphrases (65).

JUNIOR (I.E., LOUIS JR.) [BE]. Only son of Geraldine and Louis, Louis Jr. competed unsuccessfully with a cat for his mother's love and attention (86). Longing for dominance over some area of his life, Louis Jr. ruled the playground next door to his home. His mother was unemotional, yet controlling, as Louis Jr. was allowed to play only with white children (87). Ralph Nisensky was boring and lethargic, which made him the perfect playmate for Junior. This stance was not so much to protect her son, but to maintain her elitist status. Louis Jr. hated his mother's cat and wanted to get ride of the animal. He enticed Pecola Breedlove into his home and used her as an instrument to satisfy his sadistic revenge on the animal (89–93).

JUPE CATO. *See* CATO, JUPE [PA]

JURY, CATHERINE BLACKHORSE [PA]. Second wife of Harper Jury and mother of Kate Golightly and stepmother of Menus Jury. Pat Best Cato was grateful to Catherine because she was one of the women in the town of Ruby, Oklahoma, that tried to help when pregnancy threatened her mother's life (43, 197, 215).

JURY, HARPER [PA]. Harper Jury was married twice; first to Martha Stone, mother of Menus, and then to Catherine Blackhorse, mother of Kate Golightly. As one of the New Fathers of Ruby, Oklahoma, Harper Jury was known to side with the Morgan twins on key issues. It was rumored that his first wife had been unfaithful and thereby heightened Harper's distrust of women (197). When his son, Menus, returned from Vietnam in love with a young woman of questionable character, Harper's fatherly advice was to abandon the notion of marriage and terminate the relationship.

Harper ruled the roost and the lives of his second wife and daughter, who were also affected negatively by his fixation with the evil of loose women. The assault on the Convent was tailor-made for Harper to enact revenge on the opposite sex (278).

JURY, MENUS [PA]. Menus Harper was the son of Harper Jury and Martha Stone and half sister to Kate Golightly. The war in Vietnam was hell for Menus, but so was returning to Ruby, Oklahoma, with the sandy-haired girl whom he wanted to marry and who was scorned by his father and the town. Starry-eyed, Menus found the promise of love and happiness short-lived. His intended bride had pale skin which signaled racial tampering and thus was frowned upon in Ruby, Oklahoma (195). Menus cowarded under the pressure of family and public opinion, so the life he longed for was abandoned and alcoholic despair became his badge of failure.

Cloaked in self-pity and despair, Menus disregarded the kindness of the Convent women who took care of him during one of his drunken stupors. The women cleaned up after Menus defecated on himself, and their mothering shamed and weakened him (165). In an effort to regain his manhood, he rallied with the other eight men in the raid upon the Convent. Menus suffered great emotional and physical injury (277). Ironically, the damage done to his shoulder at the Convent ended his business as a barber in Anna Flood's store (126, 299).

JUVENAL DUPRES. *See* **DUPRES, JUVENAL [PA]**

K

KATE GOLIGHTLY. *See* GOLIGHTLY, KATE [PA]

K.D. (I.E., COFFEE SMITH) [PA]. K.D., short for "Kentucky Derby," was born Coffee Smith, the only son of the town's namesake, Ruby Morgan Smith, and the nephew of Deacon and Steward Morgan and husband of Arnette Fleetwood. As the only heir to the Morgan lineage, K.D. was protected by his uncles. When he gets into trouble, his uncles rally around to support him. However, in defiance of their authority, he got involved with one of the women living at the Convent. His passion for adventure soured when the women at the Convent chased him away (256). Ultimately, the invitation to join the men going to the Convent for reprisal was accepted willingly by the rejected suitor (278).

KEANE, PRIVATE. *See* PRIVATE KEANE [BLV]

KEEPING ROOM [BLV]. Two pieces of furniture and a patchwork cover constituted the room in 124 Bluestone that the Suggs women used for serious conversations with spiritual forces, both living and dead. Baby Suggs started the tradition in her home and Sethe and Denver Suggs followed suit (38–39, 43, 55).

   It was Denver's sight of a white dress in prayer beside her mother,

Sethe that signaled a purposeful spirit abound. The keeping room provided the sanctity for petitions to God on a daily basis (35).

KENNEDY, ROBERT (1925–1968) [SS]. Robert Kennedy, attorney general, was appointed in 1960 in President John Kennedy's administration. Guitar Bains told Milkman that any white man would join a lynching party if given an opportunity, even Kennedy (156).

As attorney general, Robert Kennedy was instrumental in protecting the rights of black people. In 1962, he ordered the US marshals and troops into Oxford, Mississippi, to enforce a federal order admitting the first African American student to the University of Mississippi. He worked closely with his brother, President Kennedy, to advance civil rights, and tragically, both Kennedy brothers were assassinated while in office.

KENTUCKY WONDERS [SU]. Hannah Peace prepared dinner by snapping "Kentucky Wonders," an extremely long and flavorful pole bean popular in the American South (68).

KING (CAT) [JZ]. True Belle's cat was named "King" because a masculine name for a feline appealed to her (152).

KING, DEWEY [SU]. Three young boys came to Eva Peace with individual names. They were all renamed "Dewey," and the name of "Dewey King" was given to all three when they started school (39).

KING EDWARD. *See* EDWARD, KING [SS]

KING EDWARD'S GAS STATION [SS]. No longer equipped with the pumps and air hoses for a gas station, King Edward's gas station became a meeting place for friends. When Milkman was invited to go hunting, he was told to meet at King Edward's at dusk. The memorabilia of King Edward's career as star pitcher adorned the walls and served to spark hours of conversation amongst the men (271).

KING, MARTIN LUTHER, JR. *See* DR. MARTIN LUTHER KING JR. [PA]

KING OF THE MOUNTAIN [SS]. "King of the Mountain" was Milkman's name for his father in the wake of his mother's meekness (75).

KING SOLOMON [PA]. The music of King Solomon (Solomon Burke) (1936–) filled the air as Mavis rode back to the Convent to get her disabled car. Known as "King of Rock and Soul," this Memphis soul pioneer is still a great showman on the stage today (45).

KINGFISH [TB]. Margaret Street poked fun at her husband, Valerian Street, for his reliance on his servants, Sydney and Ondine Childs. Disparagingly, she called them Scared "Kingfish" and "Beulah," two characters in television comedies. Kingfish was a character in the *Amos n' Andy* series that was first broadcasted over Daily News the WMAQ radio station in the "Scared Kingfish" on March 19, 1929. Later on June 28, 1951, it became the television show featuring an all-black cast. Kingfish was the egotistical and selfish man who tried to look after his brother (31).

L

LADY BUTTON EYES [BLV]. Amy Denver sang the song that she learned from her mother about Lady Button Eyes (81).

LADY IN RED [BE]. China made a wisecrack to Miss Marie about comparing herself to the Lady in Red in the story of how she aided the FBI to capture her boyfriend, Johnny (54).

Anna Sage, a madame in whose brothel John Herbert Dillinger had spent the night, was the authentic "Lady in Red," who wore red to help the FBI identify and capture the notorious criminal. The couple was followed to the Biography Theatre, where, after watching *Manhattan Melodrama* on July 22, 1934, Dillinger was gunned down by the FBI agents.

LADY JONES [BLV]. A home school teacher, Lady Jones was a neighborhood woman in Cincinnati, Ohio, who used her inclusive advantages as a mulatto to help the disadvantaged children of color. Side by side, Lady Jones taught her offspring as well as the children in the community. Her children went on to Wilberforce College, but their educational beginnings were taught at home alongside of those less fortunate. A nickel was the tuition and the Bible was the textbook (102). When Denver braved the world outside of 124 Bluestone in search of food and assistance, she sought it first from Lady Jones, the kind woman who taught her the beauty of the letters in her name (246–47).

LAKE SHORE PARK [BE]. Pecola's mother worked for the Fishers, whose house was in front of Lake Shore Drive, the white-only city park. In search of Pecola, who was with her mother at work, Claudia and Frieda went to the restricted area (105–6).

LAMARR, HEDY (1913–2000) [BE]. Movie star of the early 1930s whose hairstyle was referenced by a young black girl named Audrey in a story told by Maureen Peal (69).

LANGSTON UNIVERSITY [PA]. Despite an unwanted pregnancy with her then boyfriend, K.D.'s child, Arnette Fleetwood was making plans to attend Langston University, one of Oklahoma's historical land grant colleges. She was not going to let her condition interrupt her plans for Langston, so she went to the Convent for the purpose of performing an abortion on herself (54).

Langston University was founded in March 1897 by House Bill 151 as the Colored Agricultural and Normal University. In a study of development of the Negro public college, Rufus B. Atwood wrote, "If there has been no Civil War, there may never have been a Negro college since the concept of this college was not crystallized until the days of the upheaval and the uncertain years following emancipation" (Atwood, 240). One of the stipulations in the original design for the college was that the land on which the college would be built would have to be purchased by the citizens. Picnics, auctions, and bake sales were held to raise money, and the land was purchased within a year by black settlers in the all-black town of Langston, Oklahoma, who were determined to provide higher education to their children.

LAURA [SU]. When Sula Peace returns to Medallion, she fires Laura, her grandmother's (Eva Peace) cook/housekeeper because she is uncomfortable when the woman is in the home (99–100).

L'ARBE DE LA CROIX [TB]. Valerian Street bought and retired to L'Arbe de la Croix. His home was one of the most prestigious houses on the Isle des Chevaliers (11).

LEE, ROBERT E. (1807–1870) [SS]. Old Macon Dead named his hog "General Lee" after Robert E. Lee, a notable southern general. As a military man, General Lee was recognized many times, but his greatest accomplishment was the Battle of Chancellorsville in May 1863. The Civil War ended on April 9, 1865, when many other generals followed General Lee's lead in his surrender at Appomattox Court House.

LENORA & JOSEPH LORDI. *See* LORDI, LENORA & JOSEPH [TB]

LEON FOX. *See* **Fox, Leon [PA]**

LEONARD [TB]. As a good friend of Jadine Childs, Leonard gave Son a job tending bar at a fashion affair. During the few-hour stint, Son managed to foul up the orders. Leonard was thrilled when he left (224).

LES TORY/LESTORY, HENRY [JZ]. Henry Les Tory/Lestory was the black teenage lover of Vera Louise Gray who fathered Golden Gray. Living in Vienna (Vesper County), Virginia, and unaware of his son's existence, Henry Les Tory/Lestory's reputation for skillful hunting earned him the name of "Hunters Hunter." As young men, Joe Trace and Victory Williams had benefitted from his counsel about hunting in the woods (125–26).

Mr. Les Tory/Lestory was acquainted with the woman whom he named "Wild," but he did not expect to find her in his home with a mulatto claiming to be his son when he returned (176–77). As Golden Gray met the father he had never known, the interaction between the two men was interesting as respect replaced Golden's anger (167–73).

LICKING RIVER [BLV]. It was in the Licking River that Stamp Paid found the red ribbon that reminded him of how cruel slavery had been and could be to children. Once Stamp Paid found the red ribbon, it became a keepsake, thereby attaching the importance of the ribbon to his soul. In remembrance and love, he never left home without it, carrying the ribbon in his pocket at all times. At times, he fingered the ribbon during stressful conversations (180).

LILA SPENCER. *See* **SPENCER, LILA [JZ]**

LILAH [SS]. Lilah was one of Susan Byrd's cousins whom Grace Long reported was now shunning her race by passing for a white woman (290).

LI'L JUNE [BE]. Li'l June was the little girl who went to the store for the black thread requested by the critically ill Great Aunt Jimmy, but she returned after Great Aunt Jimmy's death (141).

LILLIAN GARNER. *See* **GARNER, LILLIAN [BLV]**

LILY [SS]. Lily, owner of Lily's Beauty Parlor, could not do Hagar's hair when she came to the salon without an appointment, but Marcelline could. However, the time slot given to Hagar was never filled (312).

LINCOLN, ABRAHAM (1809–1865) [SS]. Old Macon Dead named his plow horse President Lincoln and his farm Lincoln's Heaven after the man who issued the Emancipation Proclamation in 1863 (52). Abraham Lincoln was a native Kentuckian who became the sixteenth president of the United States. Initially none of the slaves were set free, but it changed the Civil War. Black men joined the fight in the Union Army as defenders of their right to be free.

LINCOLN, MARY TODD [SS]. Old Macon Dead named the foal of his plow horse, President Lincoln, "Mary Todd." Mary Todd (1812–1882) was the wife of President Abraham Lincoln and first lady of the United States. Daughter of Eliza Parker and Robert Smith Todd, she met and married young Lincoln in 1842. During their union four children were born: Robert, Edward, William, and Thomas. Mary Todd lived seventeen years after the assassination of her husband (52).

LINCOLN'S HEAVEN [SS]. Old Macon Dead could not read or write, but, out of respect for the national leader, he named his plow horse "Abraham Lincoln" and his farm "Lincoln's Heaven" in honor of Abraham Lincoln, the sixteenth president of the United States. The farm, which took Old Macon Dead many years of hard labor to cultivate before yielding a good crop, cost him his life. Lincoln's Heaven was over a 150 acres, with a large percentage of natural resources. There were ponds and valuable forestry, which might have heightened the greed of the Butlers. The mountains shielded the streams with plenty of wildlife for hunting. The fruit trees stretched for miles above the Susquehanna (51).

LINDA SANDS. *See* SANDS, LINDA [PA]

LINDEN CHAPEL FUNERAL HOME [SS]. Ruth Foster got the money for her husband to take care of the funeral arrangements for Hagar's last rites. The services were held in Linden Chapel Funeral Home (316).

LISZT, FRANZ (1811–1886) [TB]. Valerian Street believed that the music of Franz Liszt promoted the budding of his plants. As the composer of many piano compositions, Valerian trusted the musical talents of Liszt to mutate the growing cycle of his cherished plants (12).

LITTLE CAESAR. *See* SWEETNESS (I.E., WILLIAM YOUNGER) [JZ]

LITTLE FISHER GIRL. *See* FISHER GIRL [BE]

LITTLE, MALCOLM. *See* RED HEADED NEGRO NAMED X (I.E., MALCOLM X) [SS]

LITTLE PRINCE **[TB].** Valerian Street recommended this world-famous book by Antone de Saint-Exupery to Jadine Childs, telling her to look beyond the words for the profound meaning within (73). *Little Prince* was published in 1943, one year after Saint-Exupery's death. Originally written in French, *Little Prince* has been translated into many languages. Written in riddles, the book is filled with philosophical and poetic meanings as the little prince discovers the secret of what is important in life. In the story the fox tells the little prince his secret: "It is only with the heart that one can see rightly; what is essential is invisible to the eye" (de Saint-Exupery, 87).

LONE DUPRES. *See* **DUPRES, LONE [PA]**

LONG, GRACE [SS]. A nosey neighbor visiting Susan Byrd when Milkman—as an out-of-towner—comes looking for information about his family, Grace Long was a busybody, and her presence greatly stifled the conversation between Milkman and Susan. Susan Byrd knew that information overheard by Grace one day would be town gossip the next. Ms. Long admired Milkman's watch and asked him to take it off for a closer look. She failed to return the watch and later claimed it as her own (287–92, 324–25).

LORAIN, OHIO [BE]. Lorain, Ohio, hometown of Toni Morrison, was also the hometown of the Breedloves, the MacTeers, Maureen Peal, Soaphead Church, and all of the characters in *The Bluest Eye* (34, 171).

LORD NELSON. *See* **NELSON, LORD [BLV]**

LORDI EXTENDED FAMILY [TB]. The Buffalo great-aunts, Celestina, and Alicia, came to town to validate young Margaret's glowing tresses when the question of sleeping arrangements came into play. Adolphe, Campi, Estella, Cesare, Nick, Nuzzio, and Mickelena were only a few of the Lordi relatives who came into mind as possible lodging options (56).

LORDI, LENORA & JOSEPH [TB]. Lenora and Joseph were the parents of Margaret, the wife of Valerian Street. When their daughter was born, the Lordis were so astonished and frightened by her beauty. The child's features were unlike those of the other children, and they emotionally withdrew from her. There was the fear of gossip from neighbors and family about the authenticity of birth. So the Lordis summoned the great twin aunts from Buffalo to confirm the unusual features in the child (55–57). Margaret was starved for affection as her parents reacted with disdain and confusion toward her. The marriage of their teenaged daughter to Valerian Street was opposed by the Lordis, but it gave Margaret an exit from a family in which she never really was a part of (82).

LORDI, MARGARET. *See* **STREET, MARGARET (MARGARETTE) LENORA LORDI**

LOST FAMILY [PA]. Driving a car with Arkansas license plates, a white couple with a sick child lost their way and arrived in Ruby, Oklahoma. Only the husband entered Ace's Grocery Store looking for medicine and a doctor. Rev. Misner went and got aspirin for the sick child. The wife was apprehensive and refused to bring the children into the store and out of the cold. The white family left, ignoring words of caution about the forthcoming storm, the blizzard that eventually took all of their lives (121–22).

LOT'S WIFE [BLV]. Paul D. feared the fate of Lot's wife if he allowed his eyes to divert from their fixed gaze as he tried to resist Beloved's seductive advances (117). In the book of Genesis, it is written that God told Lot to take his family and leave the sin city of Sodom. They were instructed not to look back when leaving the city, but Lot's wife disobeyed and was turned into a pillar of salt. She could not resist a final glance back at her worldly possessions (Gen. 19:1–38). Edith Deen who has studied all the women of the bible, writes, "Fifteen words in the Old Testament tell the story of Lot's wife. This one brief, dramatic record has placed her among the well-known women of the world" (Deen, 1955). In the New Testament, Jesus is speaking to his disciples about his second coming and preparedness for judgment, so he cautions them to "Remember Lot's wife" (Luke 17: 32). This biblical woman, without a given name, is so well known, that the Flemish baroque artist Peter Paul Ruebens (1577–1640) dramatically captured Lot's wife's dilemma in his 1625 *Flight of Lot* painting, which depicts angels whispering to her as demons fly overhead.

LOUIS [BE]. Louis was the husband of Geraldine and father of Louis Jr. Louis provided the financial support for his family (86–87).

LOUIS JORDAN (1908–1975) & HIS TYMPANY FIVE [PA]. Music played at the celebration horse race was that of Louis Jordan and his Tympany Five. Louis Jordan, born in Arkansas, was the dean of jump blues in the late 1940s and one of the most popular rhythm and blues artist of the post–World War II period. In 1938, he formed the Tympany Five (though the group always had more than five members). Some of his songs were "I'm Gonna Move to the Outskirts of Town," "Caldonia," "Let the Good Times Roll" and "Is You Is, or Is You Ain't Ma Baby" (10).

LOUIS JR. *See* JUNIOR [BE]

LOUIS MANFRED. *See* MANFRED, LOUIS [JZ]

LOUIS STOVER. *See* STOVER, LOUIS [TB]

LU [BLV]. After escaping, Sethe Suggs was found pregnant, hungry, and wounded in the woods by Amy Denver, a young white girl. For fear of being captured and sent back to Sweet Home, Sethe wanted to remain anonymous, so when queried for a name, she chose Lu (33).

LUBBOCK, TEXAS [PA]. In search of Lubbock, Texas, the white family with Arkansas automobile license plates wandered into Ruby, Oklahoma. The husband entered Ace's Grocery Store, but the woman did not. His need for medicine for sick children was remedied as Rev. Misner went to get them medicine. The family discounted the warning of a coming blizzard and was later found lifeless in their car (122).

LUCILLE M. WILLIAMS. *See* WILLIAMS, LUCILLE M. [BLV]

LUKE ANGELINO. *See* ANGELINO, LUKE [BE]

LUTHER BEAUCHAMP. *See* BEAUCHAMP, LUTHER [PA]

LUTHER SOLOMON. *See* SOLOMON, LUTHER [SS]

M

MA'AM [BLV]. The "cooing women" were all called "ma'am." They were responsible for taking care of the slave children of mothers working in the field (30).

MABLE FLEETWOOD. *See* FLEETWOOD, MABLE [PA]

MACDONALD, JEANETTE (1903–1965) [TB]. The fancy hats worn by Janette MacDonald, a movie star, plagued Jadine Child's dreams. She associated the big hats with the sadness of her mother's funeral (166).

MACHETE-HEAD [TB]. Therese Foucalt is a servant for the Streets and boasted about disliking Americans. She made fun of them by making up names behind their backs. Ondine Childs, her boss at the Street home, wore her hair in braids across her head, so she became "Machete-Head" (34, 108).

MACON DEAD I. *See* DEAD MACON I (I.E., OLD JAKE) [SS]

MACON DEAD II. *See* DEAD, MACON II [SS]

MACON DEAD III. *See* DEAD, MACON DEAD III (I.E., MILKMAN) [SS]

MACON DEAD'S HEARSE [SS]. The name given to the Packard owned and driven only on Sundays by Macon Dead II. The car had virtually no life as it was used only once a week and never traveled more than twenty miles an hour (33).

MACON, GEORGIA [BE]. Young Cholly Breedlove traveled alone to Macon, Georgia, in search of Samson Fuller, his biological father, after the embarrassing incident in the woods with Darlene (152–56).

MACTEER, CLAUDIA [BE]. Nine-year-old sister of Frieda and daughter of Mr. and Mrs. MacTeer, Claudia MacTeer narrated the story of Pecola's life. As a typical young girl, she viewed grown-ups as authority figures who demanded and received respect. Comfortable in her family's love, she experienced life paired with her sister in mischief and curiosity. Claudia hated the blue-eyed, yellow-haired, pink-skinned dolls she received at Christmas, but loved the warmth and smell of her grand-mother's kitchen. She desperately wanted input into Christmas gift decisions so she could express her desire for an experience, not an example of what other girls her age wanted. Claudia was always jealous of Frieda's older-sister status, so when told of Mr. Henry's advances toward her sister, she felt slighted.

MACTEER, FRIEDA [BE]. Frieda MacTeer was the ten-year-old sister of Claudia and daughter of Mr. and Mrs. MacTeer. Many of the lines of the novel begin with "Frieda and I" or "Frieda and me," as the two sisters spent a great deal of time together and were inseparable. However, Frieda clearly bespoke leadership and maturity when Pecola came into "womanhood." She took charge of the situation by protecting Pecola and commanding Claudia to get water from the kitchen.

When Frieda was abused sexually by Mr. Henry, the roomer in her parent's home, she immediately told her mother, who, together with the father, chased him away. Believing Miss Dunion's claim of ruination at the touch of Henry Washington, together, the girls set about finding a cure (100–1).

MACTEER, MR. See MACTEER, MR. [BE]

MACTEER, MRS. See MACTEER, MRS. [BE]

MADGDALENE DEAD CALLED LENA. See DEAD, MAGDALENE CALLED LENA [SS]

MAGDALENE, MARY [BE]. Young Elihue Micah Whitcomb (later Soap-head Church) had difficulty understanding Christ's adoration for one of his faithful followers, Mary Magdalene, (169). Mary Magdalene was a woman in the Bible, raised in Magdala, a large city on the Sea of Galilee. After being freed of seven demons, she became a devoted follower of Christ (Luke 8:2–3). Mary Magdalene witnessed Jesus' crucifixion and was one of the first to record visually His resurrection (Mark 15:40; 16: 9).

MAGINOT LINE. *See* MISS MARIE [BE]

MALCOLM LITTLE. RED HEADED NEGRO NAMED X (I.E., MALCOLM X) [SS]

MALCOLM X. *See* RED HEADED NEGRO NAMED X (I.E., MALCOLM LITTLE) [SS]

MALVONNE EDWARDS. *See* EDWARDS, MALVONNE [JZ]

MAMA GREER [PA]. Mama Greer was the foster mother of Seneca and Harry. One day Harry seduced Seneca, and, when Mama Greer was told, she became upset because the incident reflected negatively on her home as a safe place for foster children. Seneca was moved to another home, whereas Harry remained with Mama Greer (260–61).

MAMA MAY. *See* DOWNING, MAY [TB]

MANFRED, ALICE [JZ]. Alice Manfred became a surrogate parent for a young niece, Dorcas, who lost both parents within a few days in the riots of East St. Louis. She tried hard to overcome the trauma sustained and raise Dorcas with good moral values. However, unresolved grief, emotional upheaval, and peer pressure could not deter a young girl's curiosity for fast living (67).

Alice could not have known that a chance meeting in her home would lead to secrecy, adultery, deceit, and death. She never thought Joe Trace would disrespect the confines of a neighborhood to seduce her niece (73). The child who had suffered the death of both parents was murdered by Joe, a lover/neighbor whom she had respected. Then his crazy wife, Violet, disrupted the funeral with a knife aimed at the coffin (75). As if that wasn't enough of the Traces, Violet begged to visit Alice to discuss her dead niece. Ironically, the two women do form a bond that transcended suffering. Looking back in her life, Alice Manfred remembers a deceased husband, a choice he made to continue an affair and destroy a marriage, and the pain of a broken heart. Alice Manfred commiserated with Violet Trace in sincerity and sisterhood (86–87).

MANFRED, DORCAS [JZ]. The grief of losing both of her parents within days of each other drastically colored Dorcas Manfred's young life. As a child, Dorcas was too shocked to show emotion, so her silence masked her grief. The family and friends around her never saw her emotional disturbance (57). In the mourning of her dolls, Dorcas managed to deal with a small degree of the pain that accompanied the death of her parents, but not enough to become a healthy, well-adjusted teenager.

Life with Aunt Alice Manfred on Clifton Place in New York City came with social restrictions that hampered Dorcas' yearning for acceptance. Starved for affection, Dorcas wanted the validation of the opposite sex. In Felice, she found an ally and a friend, but not the love and attention she craved. The attention of an older man came after the rejection of the young ones (67).

However, the excitement of clandestine meetings with Joe Trace, the "sample caseman" (13), could not survive the lure of Acton, a popular young man interested in Dorcas.

Dorcas Manfred was brutal in her rejection of Joe Trace and in some ways she might have anticipated her fate (192). It is possible that after the loss of her parents, Dorcas simply orchestrated her life in a way to join them.

MANFRED, LOUIS [JZ]. Louis Manfred was the philandering husband of Alice Manfred who disrespected his marital vows. Alice Manfred could relate easily to Violet Trace's pain as she too longed to do physical damage to the woman who wrecked her home. Louis chose the pleasures of an adulterous relationship, and, within a few months, death chose him. Long in the grave, Alice Manfred continued to nurse the pain of her husband's betrayal (76, 86).

MANLEY GIBSON. *See* GIBSON, MANLEY [PA]

MARCELLINE [SS]. When Hagar wandered into the beauty parlor asking to get her hair done, it was Marcelline who agreed to accommodate her. Marcelline's reasons for offering to do her hair were twofold; first, she knew Hagar had tried to kill her lover/cousin, and did not want to upset her for fear of reprisals; and second, she did not want any trouble from Pilate, Hagar's grandmother. Hagar did not keep the appointment (312).

MARGARET (MARGARETTE) LENORA LORDI STREET. *See* STREET, MARGARET (MARGARETTE) LENORA LORDI [TB]

MARIE APPOLONAIRE. *See* APPOLONAIRE, MARIE [BE]

MARIE, MISS. *See* MISS MARIE [BE]

MARSHALL PLAN [TB]. As the young and unworldly Mrs. Valerian Street, Margaret knew nothing about many things discussed in her presence, of which the Marshall Plan was one (58). She was unaware of the economic and physical destruction of Europe after World War II that required a recovery plan for America to help the nations of Europe help themselves. The plan was later known as the "Marshall Plan," named for Secretary of State George C. Marshall (1880–1959), who was instrumental in its design and implementation. In recognition of Secretary Marshall's efforts, he was awarded the Nobel Peace Prize in 1953.

MARSHALL, THURGOOD (1908–1993) [PA]. Dovey Morgan knew that her husband, Steward, was a radical who opposed all racial protests. He had labeled Thurgood Marshall a "troublemaking Negro" for getting involved in the NAACP segregation case against the law school of the State University of Norman. Some thought Marshall a savior, not a troublemaker, but Steward was on target about Marshall's involvement in the Norman segregation case. As a New York representative of the NAACP, Marshall not only served as one of the lawyers trying the case, but also devised the plans deliberately to challenge the "separate but equal doctrine in the state of Oklahoma (82).

Marshall needed a black Oklahoman qualified and willing to become the plaintiff in his segregation suit. According to Ada Lois Sipuel Fisher's autobiography, the first choice of the local NAACP organizers was Lemuel, the son of Travis B. and Martha Bell Sipuel, but he declined because of personal educational goals after his stint in the Army (Fisher 77). Ada Lois Sipuel, his sister, instead applied for admission—knowing that admission would be denied—to Oklahoma Law School, the only institution in the state offering instruction in law. *Sipuel v. Board of Regents of University of Oklahoma et al.* was filed in the Supreme Court of Oklahoma. In 1947, the court found that Sipuel was entitled to a comparable legal education to white students, but the "separate but equal" education doctrine in Oklahoma was lawful and nondiscriminatory.

The Oklahoma Board of Regents resisted and would not admit Miss Sipuel. In order to comply with the ruling, they set up a separate facility just for Miss Sipuel, in a separate section of Oklahoma City's state capital, with three teachers assigned to her. Marshall was outraged and, in 1948, he went back before the justices to argue that separate facilities did not provide an equal educational opportunity for Sipuel.

The seven-to-two decision ruled against Marshall, and Ada Lois Sipuel received her law school education alone. Thurgood Marshall went on to become one of the most well-known figures in the history of American civil rights and the first black Supreme Court justice (82).

MARTHA STONE. *See* JURY, HARPER; STONE, MARTHA [PA]

MARTIN [JZ]. Martin was a classmate of Dorcas who, at a party, asked Dorcas to dance. It was very apparent to Dorcas that Martin was better at twirling around the dance floor than studying his speech lessons (66).

MARTIN, HENRI [SU]. Henri Martin was the neighbor of Cecile Sabat's in New Orleans, Louisiana, who telephoned Cecile's granddaughter, Helene Wright in Medallion, Ohio, with news of her illness (19).

MARTIN LUTHER KING JR. *See* KING, MARTIN LUTHER, JR. [PR]

MARY [SS]. *See* BYRD, MARY [SS]

MARY JANE (CANDY) [BE]. Pecola Breedlove found the image on the Mary Jane candy wrapper appealing because the little white girl appeared happy, and she wasn't. Living within a dysfunctional family, Pecola longed for the feeling of contentment and bliss that graced the yellow symbol (49–50).

In the lives of many children across America, the Mary Jane candy has a rich and impressive history. In 1884, the Charles N. Miller Company began a small business making and selling homemade candy and 19 North Square in Boston, Massachusetts, the former home of Paul Revere (1734–1818), was their headquarters. The production of the molasses and peanut butter candy called Mary Jane began in 1914 and was so named in honor of Charles N. Miller's aunt.

MARY MAGDALENE. *See* MAGDALENE, MARY [BE]

MARY MAGNA. *See* SISTER MAGNA, MARY (I.E., REVEREND MOTHER) [PA]

MARY THERESE FOUCALT. *See* FOUCALT, MARY THERESE [TB]

MARY TODD (YOUNG HORSE). *See* LINCOLN, MARY TODD [SS]

MARYS [TB]. In the Caribbean many of the baptized women had Mary interwoven into their names (40). So the members of Valerian Street's household always referenced the woman/women as "a Mary." Developing a relationship with the servants on the island was just not important. Once, when Sydney was told to dismiss Mary Therese Foucalt because of her surly attitude, Mary Therese returned to work in a few days introduced as a different Mary (153).

MATTIE [PA]. Mattie was the woman who prepared meals in the home of Norma Keene and Leon Fox (137).

MAUREEN PEAL. *See* **PEAL, MAUREEN [BE]**

MAVIS ALBRIGHT. *See* **ALBRIGHT, MAVIS [PA]**

MAY [JZ]. Daughter of True Belle and sister of Rose Dear, May was only ten-years-old when True Belle left for Baltimore, Maryland, with Miss Vera Louise Gray, the white woman for whom she worked (141).

MAY DOWING. *See* **DOWING, MAY [TB]**

MCQUEEN, BUTTERFLY (1911–1995) [SS]. Pilate's planned entrance into the police station was compared to Louise Beavers and Butterfly McQueen, two black film stars of the 1920s and 1930s. She deliberately appeared dumb witted and slow at comprehending the seriousness of the situation. The characterization was compared to the negative roles played by McQueen as a film actress, not for her personally. McQueen's most famous role was as Prissy, the slow-witted slave in the film *Gone With The Wind.* In McQueen's biography, Darlene Clark Hine noted, "In fairness to McQueen, however, it is important to note that she herself regarded Prissy as backward and that, on the set, she resisted offensive characterizations and situations (Hine, 778).

M'DEAR [BE]. M'Dear was the neighborhood midwife and healer on whom everyone relied for unconventional remedies during ailments. When M'Dear visited the bedside of Great Aunt Jimmy, young Cholly Breedlove was surprised to find a woman so tall and impressive in height. She prescribed pot fluids and a slop jar under the bed to alleviate Great Aunt Jimmy's condition. M'Dear predicted that Great Aunt Jimmy would soon recover from her ailments, but later, after briefly feeling better, she died (136–37).

MEDALLION CITY GOLF COURSE [SU]. Medallion City Golf Course was the new construction project in Medallion, Ohio, where the Bottom once stood (3).

MEDALLION, OHIO [SU]. Medallion is the town in which the novel *Sula* is set; where Shadrack marches in the National Suicide Day parade (8); the home of three generations of Peace women (30); the high school where Nel and Sula bond as friends (29); and where Chicken Little fell to his death (61).

MELBA'S BOY [BE]. There were two initial questions when Cholly Breedlove met Samson Fuller, his biological father: "Who sent you ?" and "You Melba's boy?" (155).

MENUS JURY. *See* JURY, MENUS [PA]

MERCY HOSPITAL [SS]. It was from the roof of Mercy Hospital that Mr. Robert Smith, the insurance man, chose to emulate the eagle and end his life. The long history of denying blacks medical treatment was reversed on the day that Smith attempted to fly, when Ruth Foster was admitted to give birth to a son. Mercy Hospital was known as "No Mercy Hospital" within the black community because of their racially restrictive policies (5–9).

MERLE ALBRIGHT. *See* ALBRIGHT, MERLE & PEARL [PA]

MEXICO [JZ]. Dorcas begged Joe Trace to take her to Mexico, the night-club with circular tables, seductive lighting, and sultry music (40). In their attempts to be discreet, the married man and his young lover were still seen by ladies in the beauty parlor (202).

MICHAEL-MARY GRAHAM. *See* GRAHAM, MICHAEL-MARY [SS]

MICHAEL STREET. *See* STREET, MICHAEL [TB]

MICHELENA [BE]. Michelena was a girl Pecola Breedlove mentioned when she attempted to measure the blueness of her eyes. Actually, Pecola has been duped by Soaphead Church and does not have blue eyes (202).

MICHELIN, DR. ROBERT. *See* DR. ROBERT MICHELIN [TB]

MICKEY [SU]. As an infant, Mickey was one of Nel and Jude Greene's children who had difficulty nursing (104).

MICKEY ROOD. *See* ROOD, MICKEY [PA]

MIDGET [BLV]. As one of the leading acts at the carnival, Midget danced on stage with Giant. The crowd reacted with glee at seeing someone so large dance with someone so tiny (48).

MIKELL'S [TB]. When Son (William Green) left Jadine Childs and went to New York City from Valerian Sweet's home on Isle des Chevaliers, he briefly made reference to Mikell's, once a Manhattan jazz club at Columbus Avenue and 97th Street (216). Owned and operated by Mike Mikell, it was the haunt of many black musical and literary notables. In the obituary of David Baldwin, who worked there, James Campbell wrote about how James Baldwin, his world famous brother spent a lot of time in Mikell's during the 1960s and 1970s. "During this period, his brother

Jimmy was living in France, and Mikell's functioned as his social HQ when he visited New York" (Campbell, 19).

MILDRED [BE]. When asked by Claudia how she knew that "ministratin" meant that a girl could have a baby, Frieda credited Mildred and her mother (28).

MILKMAN. *See* DEAD, MACON III [SS]

MILLER, FRANCES [JZ]. Frances Miller was the sister of Neola. As the Miller sister with two good arms, Frances was the more straitlaced of the two. Frances did not seem to have the emotional problems her sister had (62).

MILLER, NEOLA [JZ]. Neola was the sister of Frances. Handicapped with only one arm, Neola had emotional scars that surfaced when Frances was not around. Whenever the opportunity presented itself, Neola took advantage of her young after-school audience to vent the disappointments of her life. Normally she read biblical scriptures to the children, but, as soon as her sister disappeared, Neola entertained the children with tales of past passions and betrayals. Paralyzed in limb and sensibilities, Neola spun stories of sin's power to overcome the minds of the young and foolish (62–63).

MILLER SISTERS [JZ]. *See* MILLER, FRANCES; MILLER, NEOLA [JZ]

MILTON TRUELOVE. *See* TRUELOVE, MILTON [PA]

MINDY FLOOD MORGAN. *See* MORGAN, MINDY FLOOD [PA]

MINDY RIVERS. *See* RIVERS, MINDY [PA]

MING FLEETWOOD. *See* FLEETWOOD, MING [PA]

MINNIE [JZ]. Minnie was the beautician who gave Joe Trace personal information about Dorcas (131).

MISNER, RICHARD. *See* REVEREND RICHARD MISNER [PA]

MISS ALICE [BE]. Miss Alice was a dear Christian friend of young Cholly Breedlove's Great Aunt Jimmy. During Great Aunt Jimmy's illness, Miss Alice was a great comfort as she sat by her bedside and read passages from the Bible. There were other sympathetic and comforting friends, but nothing touched Aunt Jimmy as deeply as the personal letters of the apostle Paul, found in First Corinthians, read to her by her closest friend (136).

MISS CHINA [BE]. Miss China was one of the three prostitutes who lived above the Breedlove apartment. Realistic and clever, China prodded and teased Miss Marie as Pecola looked on in amazement. Curling her hair busied her hands as she sprinkled conversations with spirited comments that evoked laughter (51–58).

MISS DELLA JONES [BE]. Mrs. MacTeer, Henry Washington's, new land-lady, gossiped with her friends about Della Jones, his former landlady, who was known to have emotional problems. The story was that Mr. Jones, Della's husband, ran off with another woman because he preferred a "virtue less woman" to one who smelled of violet water (12–14).

MISS DUNION [BE]. Miss Dunion was the neighbor of the MacTeer family who said Frieda might be "ruined" after Henry Washington's sexual advances. The remark was dismissed by Mrs. MacTeer, but it sent waves of fear through the hearts and minds of her daughters, Claudia and Frieda. Miss Dunion's reference to being ruined sent the girls on a frantic search for a remedy to nullify her prediction (101).

MISS ERKMEISTER [BE]. The elementary gym teacher, Miss Erkmeister, criticized Maureen Peal for wearing shorts in class. Maureen hated wear-ing bloomers so she was envious and resented her teacher's freedom of choice in attire (68).

MISS ESTHER. *See* **FLEETWOOD, ESTHER [PA]**

MISS FORRESTER [BE]. Frieda MacTeer was furious with Bay Boy and his friends for picking on Pecola Breedlove. She commented to Claudia, her sister, that Miss Forrester, their teacher, even thought that Bay Boy was "incorrigival" (67).

MISS MARIE (MAGINOT LINE) [BE]. Of the three prostitutes whom Pecola visited, Miss Marie is the more notorious. She had cavorted with gang-sters and, on occasion, served, as an informant for the FBI (53). However, the religious influence from her childhood clearly was evidenced in her behavior. Miss Marie reserved her respect for church ladies, but she be-came angry and hurt when confronted with their negative opinion of her. In fact, the church ladies blatantly labeled her as a "ruined woman" within the gossip circles.

Obedient to the wishes of her mother, Miss Marie was careful to avoid profanity in her speech. She imprecated with "whoa Jesus" and a number of others when the urge to curse came upon her (54). Understanding the loneliness of a little girl, Miss Marie often entertained Pecola with tales of adventure and shared laughter.

MISS MARY [SS]. Miss Mary was part owner in the most popular bar and grill in the Blood Bank District. Flashy in dress and makeup, she ran one of the communities strongholds. In her establishment, she catered to everyone's distinct needs for entertainment and socialization. United in their need to escape the mundane facets of their daily lives, the housewife, drunk, whore, and teenager alike found acceptance and fun at Mary's (83).

MISS MINDY. *See* **MORGAN, MINDY FLOOD [PA]**

MISS POLAND [BE]. Miss Poland was the licentious roommate of Miss Marie and Miss China, living in the apartment above the Breedloves. Pecola likes to hear her sing the blues as she irons (52).

MISS TYLER [TB]. Son had three choices for piano access in Eloe, Florida: the two churches or the home of his friend's aunt, Miss Tyler, who finally consented to give him lessons. His buddies playfully suspected that he had ulterior motives that involved romance with Andrew's aunt. After a while, they witnessed Son's mastery of the piano and all rumors were dispelled (136).

MISSY RIVERS [PA]. Patricia Best pondered the relationship of Missy Rivers to Thomas Blackhorse as she worked on the genealogy of Ruby, Oklahoma (187).

MISTER (CHICKEN) [BLV]. Paul D. rescued a baby chick whose mother had abandoned him for dead. After naming him "Mister," Paul D. watched the chick grow into a fierce rooster that commanded his territory. As a slave, Paul D. envied the emancipation and arrogance that Mister took for granted (71–72).

MONTOUR COUNTY [SS]. Lincoln's Heaven, the 150-acre farm owned by Old Macon Dead, was nestled in Montour County (51).

MOON [SS]. It was Guitar Bains and Moon who wrestled the knife away from Hagar when she came into the bar after Milkman, her ex-lover/ cousin (119).

MOORE, HELEN [JZ]. One of the stolen letters Malvonne Edward found and read was addressed to Helen Moore (42).

MORGAN, BECK [PA]. Beck Morgan was the wife of Rector and mother of twins, Deacon and Steward; Ruby; and Elder.

MORGAN, DEACON [PA]. Twin brother of Steward, son of Rector and Beck, husband of Soane, and grandson of Zechariah, Deacon shared his brother's love and pride of family and community, but they differed in expression. Steward was short sighted, controlling, and explosive, whereas Deacon tempered his resistance to change with historical reasoning. At times, Deacon was able to laugh at himself (107).

In the Fleetwood home dispute, Deacon was the mediator and Steward was the hothead (59–62). At the meeting with the young people to discuss the renaming of the inscription on the Oven, Deacon resisted change with an explanation of historical relevance (85–86), but Steward simply threatened to shoot anyone who altered the wording (87). The twins had shared memories, but from different perspectives. It is interesting that Deacon's memories were often of trips, family, and adventure (108–10), but Steward recalled the anger and shame of past events (95–99). The recollections made Steward obstinate, whereas Deacon grew in optimism. Deacon was the stronger twin, but his pride precluded questioning his brother's authority until it was too late.

Deacon knew that he had married a virtuous woman and he shared Soane's pain for the loss of their two sons. He denied her nothing, but he did question Soane's friendship with Connie at the Convent. His guilt about the affair with Connie however, limited his interference to sarcastic remarks (105–7). Deacon believed the tales and feared the influence of the Convent women on the town, but he also had a personal stake in their wellbeing. Steeped in denial, Deacon followed his twin into the Convent like a unthinking warrior (4). It was not until after the gunshots and carnage that Deacon faced his shortcomings and the belittling influence of his brother (291–92). There was an interchangeable link in expression, that often caused Deacon to function more like Steward than himself. As one of the nine men who invaded the Convent, this turning point alienated the twin brothers beyond repair.

Deacon found his conscience and his voice, but at a price that weighed heavy on his heart. Only then did he dare oppose his brother with the conviction of truth. Deacon's trip to see Rev. Misner sparked a change in his life that required an honest look at himself, his twin, and their motives for dominance in Ruby, Oklahoma (291, 301–3).

MORGAN, DOVEY BLACKHORSE [PA]. Dovey Blackhorse Morgan was the sister of Soane and wife of Steward Morgan. As a devoted wife, she often disagreed with her husband, but always supported him (87). Dovey knew that their inability to have children was a great disappointment to her husband (95, 112). Helpless to alter his behavior, Dovey knew that

Steward's hatred and anger affected his physical and emotional well-being.

Staying in Menus Jury's old house in town gave Dovey some relief from Steward's discontent. It was also there that she could see and talk to the Stranger who wandered aimlessly through her yard (90–93).

MORGAN, EASTER [PA]. Easter Morgan son of Deacon and Soane and brother of Scout. The Morgan brothers spent a lot of time together. Easter was there when the car flipped over and Scout almost died (224–25). Both brothers joined the military and both brothers gave their lives serving their country (112).

MORGAN, ELDER [PA]. Son of Zechariah and Beck, husband of Susannah Smith, and father of six children, Elder rushed to defend a Negro street woman being assaulted by white men in New York City. Outnumbered, he disregarded the odds in the wake of his rage. From that day forward, he was unable to escape the image of the white fist smashing into the black skin. Elder was so moved by the incident, he insisted on being buried in the tattered uniform he wore in defense of the woman's honor (94–95).

MORGAN, MINDY FLOOD [PA]. Mindy Flood Morgan was wife of Zechariah "Big Papa" Morgan and mother of nine children (191).

MORGAN, RECTOR. *See* BIG DADDY [PA]

MORGAN, SCOUT [PA]. Scout was the son of Sloane and Deacon Morgan and Easter's brother. Curious as a teenager, Scout and his brother, Easter, shared many adventures. One day after an automobile accident near the Convent, Scout's life was saved by Connie Sosa and Lone DuPres (244–45). A few years later, both brothers joined the military and both ultimately lost their lives serving their country (112).

MORGAN, SOANE BLACKHORSE [PA]. Soane Blackhorse Morgan was the wife of Deacon, sister of Dovey, mother of Scout and Easter, and sister-in-law of Steward. Soane was a caring wife, sister, mother, and friend. Sharing a life with Deacon, Soane had comfort and status. After suffering the loss of her sons in a war she did not understand, Soane was devastated as she searched for meaning in the futility of living without her children (112–15).

All areas of Soane's life revealed caring, commitment, and compassion. When Deacon voiced opposition to her friendship with Connie, Soane stood her ground. She easily could have denounced Connie as a friend, but she chose not to (105). The hurt of her husband's betrayal with Connie had been dealt with by Soane and the two women had forged a spiritual bond with mutual concern for one child lost and another child saved (246, 288).

Soane also enjoyed the continuity and comfort of having Dovey as a sister/friend, even though marriage to the twin brothers was as complicated as the men themselves (81–82). As the wedge between Deacon and Steward broadened, so did the discord between the two sisters, forced to take sides as wives of two totally different brothers (292, 300).

MORGAN, STEWARD [PA]. Steward Morgan was the son of Rector and Beck, brother of Elder, twin brother of Deacon, sister of Ruby, and grandson of Zechariah and Mindy Flood Morgan. The Morgans were a prestigious and controlling family in Ruby, Oklahoma. Steward's grandfather, Zechariah Morgan, was one of the ex-slaves and one of the original Fathers who fought the odds to forge a new life in Fairly, Oklahoma. The stories were told and retold from generation to generation about their trials, tribulations, and triumphs. Steward's hero-worship of his grandfather was the foundation for his views on pride, self-reliance, and prosperity (13).

As twins, Steward and Deacon shared Morgan pride, birthdays, military service, love for Blackhorse women, ancestral pride, and family, but little else. Steward was the irate and more intolerant of the two, stubborn on many issues. His views on matters of right and wrong were fused with ancestral pride because he dwelled in the yesterdays of his grandfather's era (16).

Compromise was foreign to Steward Morgan, as differences of opinion were not tolerated. As a Mount Calvary Baptist Church parishioner, Steward resisted the changes that came with the new, young, progressive minister. Rev. Misner publicly sided with the young people on changing the inscription on the Oven, was mediator for the discourse with the Fleetwoods to chastise his only nephew, championed civil rights causes, and opposed adults in order to give the young people a voice in community matters. Steward fretted because he knew that Rev. Misner was unimpressed with Morgan prestige and domination (94).

As his wife, Dovey sensed Steward's unhappiness and watched him suffer because of material gain. As he gained material possessions, he lost spiritual ones. The inability to sire a Morgan heir was also a disappointment that contributed to his bitterness (82).

Steward disliked everyone and everything that challenged his authority. The two brothers communicated without words and every expression in the one was matched by a corresponding expression in the other. However, Deacon had cause to distrust the Convent women because he blamed Connie for his weakness in the affair, but he did not hate them. On the other hand, Steward felt that the women in the Convent were different, threatening, independent, and, therefore, expendable. Most of the men went to the Convent the night of the raid because of Steward's encouragement and influence (19). Steward was also the first to fire his weapon. Steeped in the past, Steward wanted revenge, and the Convent women became his target.

MORGAN, SUSANNAH SMITH [PA]. Susannah Smith was the wife of Elder and mother of six children. In defense of a Negro prostitute, her husband had fought white men in the street. During the struggle, his military uniform was ripped badly. Elder was proud of his actions in aiding the fallen woman and requested to be buried in the torn and dirtied uniform worn in the fight. Elder Morgan wanted his coffin to showcase his valor.

As a wife, Susannah wanted her husband outfitted in more presentable attire. However, matrimonial rights took a back seat to Morgan's pride as his brothers demanded that Elder's request be honored (95).

MORGAN, ZECHARIAH (I.E., BIG PAPA; COFFEE SMITH) [PA]. Zechariah Morgan was the husband of Mindy Flood; twin brother of Tea; father of Rector, Pryor, Shepherd, Loving, Ella, Selanie, Governor, Queen, and Scout; and grandfather of Ruby, Elder, Steward, and Deacon. Born Coffee Smith, he renamed himself "Zechariah Morgan" to seek a political position, and was called "Big PaPa" fondly by his family. In choosing the names "Steward" and "Deacon" for his twin grandsons, Zechariah endowed them with authority (55). As a proud and arrogant man, his actions often affected his family. When he failed in the roles of lieutenant governor and banker, those he loved suffered financial hardships (84).

Zechariah (Coffee) never invited his twin brother to join the families leaving Fairly, Oklahoma, for a new life. The problems between them began when the twins were approached and taunted by white men requesting them to dance on the spot. Zechariah (Coffee) and his pride chose to take the consequences of denying their request (a bullet in the foot), but he could not forgive Tea for choosing compliance over crippling (302).

After the "walking man" had led them to their new settlement, it was Zechariah's idea to build the Oven as a symbol of strength and unity. As a way to protect their women from the fear of redress and undress by the masters, fieldwork was always preferred over housework. Now as ex-slaves, the Oven became a communal cooking place that brought men, women, and children together in security, socialization, and harmony. The wording on the front of the Oven was also Zechariah's idea, and he did everything possible to minimize the weakening of their force. "Together we stand, separated we are victimized" was his doctrine against failure. "Scattering" was one of his greatest fears, as he witnessed the assault on blacks who shared their race, but not their hue (194).

Steward and Deacon, the twin grandsons whom he named, remained loyal to his memory and often made decisions based on what Big PaPa would have done.

MOSS DUPRES. *See* DUPRES, MOSS [PA]

MOTHER SUPERIOR [PA]. Sister Mary Magna was graced with the position of Mother Superior during her stay at the Convent (11). Her wish when she died was to be near the place that shared her name—Superior.

MOUNT KILIMANJARO [TB]. Michael Street retained his foot locker of his youth. The key was known to be at the top of Mount Kilimanjaro, which translated as "nonexistence." Mount Kilimanjaro is located inside the Kilimanjaro National Park in Tanzania. It is the highest mountain in Africa and the tallest free-standing mountain on earth (21).

MR. ARMOUR. *See* GALVESTON LONGSHOREMEN'S STRIKE OF 1920 [JZ]

MR. BOJANGLES (I.E., BILL ROBINSON, 1878–1949) [BE]. Claudia MacTeer disliked Shirley Temple, the white child movie star, because she dared to dance with Mr. Bojangles, her idol (19).

As a vaudeville dancer and film star, Bill 'Bojangles' Robinson was a hoofer at a young age. He was talented, graceful, and creative as he danced his way into America's heart. According to James Haskins and N. R. Mitgang, for a black actor to play with Shirley Temple in *The Little Colonel*, "They needed an actor who knew his place but had a little dignity. Bill Robinson seemed to fit the part" (Haskins and Mitgang, 224). In a well-written article Ann duCille discusses the Temple/Robinson scene in *The Little Colonel*, "The famous stair dance that follows [putting Shirley Temple to bed] is actually the black butler's tricksterlike way of luring the resistant white child up to bed" (duCille, 17).

As an actor/dancer, Bill Robinson appeared in four movies with Shirley Temple: *The Little Colonel* (1935), *The Littlest Rebel* (1935), *Rebecca of Sunny Brook Farm* (1938), and *Just Around the Corner* (1938).

MR. BRADEE [SS]. Macon Dead II was making a repair at the home of Mr. Bradee, one of his tenants, when he received the news of his father-in-law's (Dr. Foster) death (73).

MR. BROUGHTON [TB]. Jadine Childs and Margaret Street spent time gossiping about the strange love life of their neighbor, Mr. Broughton (84).

MR. BUDDY [BLV]. The memories of Mr. Buddy, the plantation overseer back home, came to mind when Amy Denver saw the brutality of School-teacher's nephews. Lu's (Sethe's) back was so badly butchered, it resembled a tree with welts akin to branches. Amy recalled the beatings received from Mr. Buddy, but they were not nearly as gruesome as what Lu (Sethe) experienced. Amy told Sethe (Lu) about the rumor she heard about Mr. Buddy being her daddy, but she refused to believe it (79–80).

MR. BUFORD [BE]. Mr. Buford was the neighbor of the MacTeers who offered his loaded gun to the outraged parents when Mr. Henry Washington touched their daughter, young Frieda, improperly. Mrs. MacTeer refused the weapon, but Mr. MacTeer grabbed it and chased the villain from the yard (100).

MR. FINLEY [SU]. Mr. Finley was the neighbor rumored to have died from sucking a chicken bone after seeing the notorious Sula Peace (114).

MR. FRANK [JZ]. Taken in as an infant into the Williams family, Joe Trace never missed having a father because Mr. Frank (Williams) gave him love and attention (125).

MR. GARNER [BLV]. Mr. Garner was not a typical slaveowner because his home was called Sweet Home, and for his slaves, Paul D., Paul F., and Paul A. Garner, Baby and Halle Suggs, and Sixo and later young Sethe, it was just that. As a secure and defiant Kentucky slaveowner who enjoyed life, Mr. Garner was independent and defiant in the manner of treating his slaves. He also was married to a woman who shared his compassion for those in human bondage. Under his charge, the slaves were treated with respect and allowed privileges unknown to many others. When Halle wanted to buy his mother's freedom, Mr. Garner agreed and, after the debt was paid, arranged for her lodging as a free woman with the Bodwins, friends of his friends up north in Ohio (141–47).

As the master of Sweet Home, Mr. Garner's compassion for human life brought destruction and despair after his death (36).

MR. HENRY. *See* WASHINGTON, HENRY [BE]

MR. HODGES [SU]. Owner of Hodges Funeral Home, Mr. Hodges hired Shadrack to do odd jobs (157).

MR. MACTEER [BE]. Mr. MacTeer was the father of Claudia and Freida and husband of Mrs. MacTeer. Strong, silent and fatherly he counsels his family on the preservation of heat during the winter. Working night and day, he provided for his family with love and affection. However, when Henry Washington improperly touched Freida, Mr. MacTeer became enraged and chased him away with Mr. Buford's gun (100).

MR. MALLORY. *See* GALVESTON LONGSHOREMEN'S STRIKE OF 1920. [JZ]

MR. MONTGOMERY WARD. *See* GALVESTON LONGSHOREMEN'S STRIKE OF 1920 [JZ]

MR. PERSON [PA]. Mr. Person rented a cornfield that the Sisters at the Convent owned. Mavis Albright complained because the money coming into the Convent was low and nothing was coming in from his rental for a couple of months (258).

MR. SAWYER [BLV]. The Bodwins were able to get Sethe a job at Sawyer's Restaurant as a cook after she was released from jail for killing her infant. In the beginning, Mr. Sawyer was a considerate employer, but his sentiment toward Sethe changed after the death of his son. Mr. Sawyer became critical and hard to please, eventually letting Sethe go for tardiness (191, 204).

MR. SEALSKIN [TB]. As Jadine prepared to leave for France, Ondine asked if she was going to marry Mr. Sealskin. The sealskin coat given to Jadine Childs by Ryk, her European boyfriend, gave Ondine license to rename him "Mr. Sealskin" (91, 277).

MR. SHEEK [TB]. Impressed with an invitation to dinner after being discovered hiding in the bedroom closet of Mrs. Margaret Street, Son (William Green) addressed Valerian Street as "Mr. Sheek" (144). There are many variations of the word *sheek*, and in Arab countries it is a title of respect for the "sheik" or "sheikh," someone that heads a family or tribe having complete authority over the house.

MR. SOLOMON [SS]. Mr. Solomon was the husband whom Pilate created in her story to the police about why she carried around a dead man's bones. She lied for Guitar and Milkman, saying that they simply were joking with an elderly woman when they broke into her home to steal. Embellishing and quoting scripture as she went along, Pilate told the tale of Mr. Solomon, a stately black man who had been lynched in Mississippi, and how the authorities would not allow her, his lawful wife, to cut down the body. Without money for funeral expenses, Pilate said she returned to collect her husband's bones so they could be buried together and ascend into heaven as man and wife. Pilate was so convincing, the police released Milkman and Guitar from jail (206–7).

MR. SWIFT. *See* GALVESTON LONGSHOREMEN'S STRIKE OF 1920 [JZ]

MR. WHITLOW [BLV]. Mr. Whitlow was the slaveholder who sold Baby Suggs and her son to Mr. Garner (14). After Baby Suggs gained her freedom, she had the minister write letters back to Mr. Whitlow to inquire about the whereabouts of her children (147).

MR. YACABOWSKI [BE]. Mr. Yacabowski was the white immigrant shopkeeper who looked at young Pecola Breedlove with disdain as she came into his store and attempted to purchase candy. Mr. Yacabowski was awkward in the company of this shy little black girl, and his behavior was one of indifference and social disregard. Pecola felt uncomfortable, and internalized Yacabowski's ignorance as self-doubt and evidence of her unworthiness (48).

MRS. BAINS [SS]. The accidental death of her son and the flight of a daughter-in-law too hurt to cope in her husband's absence left Mrs. Bains responsible for the well-being of her grandchildren (21). Times were hard, but Mrs. Bains was assisted by her family. Aunt Florence invited the Bains children South in the summer and Uncle Billy relocated from Florida to lend a hand (85, 179).

On public assistance and with limited funds, Mrs. Bains tried to shield the children from the shame of poverty. However, young Guitar and his brothers witnessed their grandmother's pleas to Macon Dead II, the Negro landlord who shared their culture but not their plight. As curious children, they watched as he vowed to evict the family because they could not pay rent (21–22).

MRS. BUDDY [BLV]. Mrs. Buddy was the wife of Mr. Buddy, Amy Denver's plantation boss. In conversation Amy Denver compared Sethe (Lu) to another black slave girl without schooling, who had a mastery of sewing delicate fabrics for Mrs. Buddy (80).

MRS. BUTLER [SS]. Mrs. Butler lived a life of luxury as a wife and mother in a family of white landowners in Virginia. The Butlers were well known throughout Virginia and credited with the brutal death of Macon Dead I, a neighboring black landowner. Through the years, the economy shifted as drastically as their social status. Unable to cope with poverty as the surviving Butler, left alone in a mansion with only Circe, her servant, Mrs. Butler committed suicide (242).

MRS. CAIN [BE]. Mrs. Cain was Woodrow's mother. In a rather gossipy manner, Mrs. Cain shared personal information with Mrs. MacTeer about Woodrow's bed-wetting problem. Frieda MacTeer, Woodrow's classmate, overheard the conversation. Later, Frieda threatened Woodrow with disclosure of his secret if his taunting of Pecola Breedlove did not cease. Woodrow backed off for fear of disclosure (80).

MRS. ESTHER COOPER [SS]. As the wife of Rev. Cooper, Mrs. Cooper was cordial and hospitable. As a hostess, Mrs. Cooper entertained her guests with traditionally cooked southern meals. When Milkman arrived from Michigan, he was unaccustomed to down-home food and had trouble digesting her meals (253).

MRS. GAINES [BE]. Together with Miss Alice, another close friend, Mrs. Gaines visited young Cholly Breedlove's Great Aunt Jimmy during her illness. The three women were close in age and had shared life's experiences. Chatting with friends who understood the problems of growing old was comforting to Great Aunt Jimmy as she struggled with poor health (137).

MRS. JACKSON [SU]. Kind neighbor of Eva Peace with a passion for eating ice. Mrs. Jackson was considerate and supplied milk for the children after BoyBoy Peace left his family (32).

MRS. JOHNSON [BE]. Frieda MacTeer repeated a comment to Claudia, her sister, that she overheard Mrs. Johnson say about how it would take a miracle for poor Pecola Breedlove's baby to live (191).

MRS. MACTEER [BE]. Mrs. MacTeer was the mother of Claudia and Frieda and wife of Mr. MacTeer. Even though Morrison chose not to give her a first name, Mrs. MacTeer represents the strongest female character in the novel. As a mother/wife, she filled the kitchen with song, enjoyed gossip with her church sisters, fussed over her daughters, nurtured a little girl without a home, scolded when necessary, and strongly criticized a man who dared to hurt his family (11, 13, 23–25). Mrs. MacTeer was the kind of mother whose peace and happiness were linked directly to the well-being of her family. She became upset and annoyed when Claudia and Frieda were affected by illness, cold weather, pain, or any adverse circumstances. As their maternal defender, Mrs. MacTeer verbally attacked frigid temperatures, childhood carelessness, clogged nostrils, and depleting milk supplies in an effort to protect her family and maintain her emotional equilibrium.

Illness always was conquered in the MacTeer home because Mrs. MacTeer had "the hands that do not want [them] die" (12). Mrs. MacTeer's disciplinary traits extended beyond her family to chastisement of irresponsible fathers (Cholly Breedlove), loose women (Miss Marie), and repulsive tenants (Henry Washington). As a caring mother, Mrs. MacTeer's love extended to Pecola, a little girl confused and battered by circumstances beyond her control. Mrs. MacTeer found an outlet for daily frustrations in song, which communicated her strength and unity in the wake of life's problems.

Emotionally distraught but secure in her mother's love, Freida was quick to forgive her mother when a rush to judgment resulted in an undeserved spanking. Mrs. MacTeer did not realize that her daughters were ushering young Pecola Breedlove into womanhood as Pecola's menstrual cycle began (31).

MRS. RAYFORD [SU]. After the pain of finding her best friend, Sula Mae Peace, and her husband, Jude, together, Nel Wright checked on the lilacs in her backyard and was disappointed that the flowers were not in bloom. She takes comfort, however, in the realization that the lilacs of her neighbor, Mrs. Rayford, had not flowered either (109).

MRS. REED [SU]. Mrs. Reed was the woman who took the three Dewey boys to school for registration their first day. The boys were seven, five, and four, but they all were enrolled as six-year-old cousins under the name of "Dewey King" (39).

MRS. RHODA [JZ]. Joe Trace affectionately called the mother of his adopted family "Mrs Rhoda." Within the Williams family, he was given the name of "Joseph," after Mrs. Rhoda's brother (123).

MRS. SUGGS [SU]. Eva Peace left her children in the care of Mrs. Suggs when she left town to find a solution to her economic woes.

MRS. TURTLE [PA]. Eddie Turtle's mother, Mrs. Turtle, listened attentively when Seneca came with news of her son's incarceration. Money was Eddie's motive for sending Seneca to his mother, but misery was the message. Mrs. Turtle was upset, but not about to contribute to her son's defense. In sincerity and seniority, she cautioned Seneca about the manipulation behind her son's actions. Mrs. Turtle accepted motherhood with complete honesty and regret. Overcome with shame and disappointment, she managed to reserve any display of her grief until the foolish young messenger had cleared the door (133–34).

MRS. WILKENS [SU]. Sula Peace tired of the antics of her grandmother, Eva, and signed the old woman into a white-managed assisted living facility. Nel Wright Greene was horrified when she learned what Sula had done. Nel commented that only people like Mrs. Wilkens—someone bereft of money, sanity, or relatives—went into establishments like that. Nel chastised her friend for being so cruel and thoughtless (100).

MY PARROT [JZ]. "My Parrot" was the name of Violet Trace's pet parrot. "Love you" was the chant of My Parrot, who ate soul food and was discarded after six years by a disoriented Violet Trace (28, 93).

N

NAN [BLV]. Nan was one of the cooing slave women who stopped Sethe from climbing into a pile of dead bodies to search for her mother's mark. Nan had one good arm and one that ended at the elbow. Handicapped, she had a repository of words larger than most and a genuine fondness for children, especially Sethe. Nan wanted Sethe to know that her mother loved her. She had known Sethe's mother, and told the story of her babies being discarded at birth because they were born of of rape. Nan explained that Sethe was the only baby allowed to live because she was sired by a black man. In the story of her birth, Nan gave Sethe an emotional bond to a mother she never really knew (62).

NANADINE. *See* **CHILDS, ONDINE [TB]**. As a child, Jadine tried to pronounce "Aunt Ondine," but it came out "Nanadine" (38).

NATHAN DUPRES. *See* **DUPRES, NATHAN [PA]**

NATHAN, JOE [BLV]. Joe Nathan was the man who told Amy Denver that Mr. Buddy was her father (80).

NATIONAL SUICIDE DAY [SU]. Shadrack created National Suicide Day, and for many years, he was the sole marcher in the National Suicide Day parade. In 1917, the horrors of war engulfed Shadrack's life with fear.

Shadrack needed to control the anxiety that threatened his existence, so he designated the third day in January as National Suicide Day. It took Shadrack twelve days to devise a plan that would pinpoint one day for self-destruction or murder to free the other 364 from panic (7, 14–15).

On the first National Suicide Day, in 1920, Shadrack's marching and ringing would have rivaled any Fourth of July celebration. The only difference was that Shadrack needed no crowd control, as he strutted alone.

Initially, the Bottom residents resisted National Suicide Day as a symbol of Shadrack's insanity, but in time the day became interwoven throughout the tapestry of their lives. Ironically, after the death of the notorious Sula Peace, Shadrack was joined in his National Suicide Day celebration by some of the townspeople (159).

NEL WRIGHT GREENE. *See* **GREENE, NEL WRIGHT [SU]**

NELSON, LORD [BLV]. Lord Nelson was a classmate of Denver Suggs in Lady Jones' house/school. Curious, as most children are, Lord Nelson harmlessly asked Denver a question about her mother's imprisonment, which evoked shame and withdrawal from the book-learning sessions she loved (104). Unsure of the answer, Denver became very apprehensive around Sethe, and eventually came to the conclusion that her brothers were not driven away from their home by an angry spirit, but by the terror of a potential slaughter from their mother's hands.

NEOLA MILLER. *See* **MILLER, NEOLA [JZ]**

NEPHEW [SS]. When Rev. Cooper's job prevented him from taking Milkman to the farm, he enlisted the help of his thirteen-year-old nephew named "Nephew" to drive him. Milkman saw how impressed Nephew was with his clothing and gave the young boy a shirt (237).

NEPHEWS, THE [BLV]. The nephews were the two young boys who came to Sweet Home with schoolteacher when Mr. Garner died. The two boys called Schoolteacher "Onkai," so it was understood they were his nephews. Sadistic in manner, it was under his watchful eye that one nephew held the pregnant Sethe down, while the other stole her milk. Sethe was beaten brutally when Mrs. Garner was told about the milking incident (36).

NERO BROWN. *See* **BROWN, NERO [SS]**

NEW FATHERS OF RUBY, OKLAHOMA [PA]. The New Fathers of Ruby, Oklahoma, were Deacon and Steward Morgan, William Cato, Ace Flood, Aaron Poole, Nathan DuPres, Arnold Fleetwood, Ossie Beauchamp, Harper Jury, Sargeant Person, John Seawright, Edward Sands, and Roger Best (194–95).

NEW HAVEN, OKLAHOMA [PA]. The New Fathers called their new home New Haven for three years, until Ruby Morgan Smith died and the town was renamed "Ruby" in honor one of their own (17).

NEW RIVER ROAD [SU]. Tar Baby was jailed because, intoxicated, he caused a politician's daughter to have a car accident on New River Road (132).

NIGGER JIM [TB]. One of the literary characters that depicts the cavalier behavior of Son (William Green) on the lame from Eloe, Florida, was Nigger Jim, a runaway slave in Mark Twain's (Samuel L. Clemens [1835–1910]) *The Adventures of Huckleberry Finn.* Jim's character is that of a principled slave, and is one of the moral foundations of the book. Huck Finn was his friend, and, as a slave, Jim risked his life and his potential freedom to safeguard that bond (166).

NIGHT (HORSE) [PA]. Night was the horse that Steward Morgan liked to ride around his ranch from sunup to sundown (99).

NIGHT MOVES CAFÉ [TB]. Son had a job at the Night Moves Café. Jadine Childs remarked that the quality of time Son spent in the Night Moves Café was lesser than that she spent studying for educational advancement (264).

NIGHT VISITORS [PA]. Mavis Albright had sexual allusions that came to her in her sleep. She labeled them "night visitors" because her illusionary lovers were both of human and animal form. Connie counseled her to ignore them, but need was too great (171–72).

NIGHT WOMEN [TB]. As an international model and world traveler, Jadine Childs was unimpressed with visiting Eloe, a small town in Florida, with Son. Leaving abruptly after a short stay, she returned to New York City alone. However, being away from Son, her lover, was difficult and summoned dreams of Night Women who plagued her sleep. She believed that the Night Women—Cheyenne, Son's deceased wife, whom she had never met; Aunt Rosa, Son's aunt, who didn't like out-of-towners sleeping nude; Nanadine, her aunt at L'Arbe de la Croix, who dared to judge her; Francine, Son's mentally challenged sister, who was confined to an institution; and Mama, her mother, who left her alone at age twelve—were all harlots down in Eloe, Florida, enticing Son. Jadine feared that the attention of the Night Women was preventing Son from returning to New York.

In Jadine's mind, it was the lack of sophistication that united the Night Women, whereas, she relied heavily on her elegance and glamor to fend off the pain of loneliness. In a sense, Jadine relived the trauma of being spat at by the African woman in the market. Once again, feelings of inadequacy were heightened and distressing. Emotionally directing her anger toward the Night Women allowed Jadine to gain some sense of stability (261).

NINA FONG. *See* **FONG, NINA [TB]**

NINE MEN WHO INVADED THE CONVENT [PA]. The nine men who invaded the Convent were Harper and Menus Jury, Arnold and Jefferson Fleetwood, Steward and Deacon Morgan, Coffee "K.D." Smith, Wisdom Poole, and Sergeant Person (274–80).

NINE ORIGINAL FAMILIES [PA]. There were nine original families tossed out of Fairly, Oklahoma, to later find a home in Haven: Blackhorse, Morgan, Poole, Fleetwood, Beauchamp, Cato, Flood, and both DuPres families (188).

92nd INFANTRY DIVISION [SS]. Hospital Tommy was proud of his stint in the army as a member of the 92nd Infantry Division, a military unit of black men from the southern states (101). According to Robert W. Kesting, "On October 24, 1917, the 92nd Infantry Division was organized. Its insignia became the black buffalo" (Kesting, 2). Reactivated for duty in World War II on October 15, 1942, the men of the 92nd Infantry Division received rudimentary stateside training before deployment overseas. Many of the men were unable to read and write, but were valiant nevertheless in fighting for their country. Heroism abroad, however, did not convert to hero worship back home. After researching the Negro soldiers, Rufus E. Clement wrote, "The returning Negro soldiers found themselves demobilized in a land which had become the creditor nation of the world" (Clement, 534).

NISENSKY, RALPH [BE]. Two years younger in age than Junior (Louis Jr.), Ralph was white and the only playmate of whom Junior's mother approved (87).

NO MERCY HOSPITAL [SS]. "No Mercy Hospital" was the name given to Mercy Hospital for its failure to provide medical services to black people. The day that Mr. Robert Smith, the insurance salesman, leaped from the roof, a black child was born at No Mercy (4–5).

NOAH FLEETWOOD. *See* FLEETWOOD, NOAH [PA]

NOMMO [TB]. In New York City, a female with a clean head and a filthy mouth is not all that uncommon. So, perhaps it was the ring in Nommo's nose that held Son's attention as he watched her hurl obscenities at her male companion. Passersby saw disrespect and boldness in her actions, but Son saw vulnerability and fear common to both of his sisters (Francine and Porky). Son gave Nommo the reassurance she needed in a bear hug, which included an invitation for a night's lodging. After an evening of conversation, the morning came and Nommo was gone, along with the cash on the table, which did not belong to her (227–28).

NORMA KEENE FOX. *See* FOX, NORMA KEENE [PA]

NORTHPOINT BANK & RAILROAD COMPANY [BLV]. After a year and half of basking in the luxury of the woman from Wilmington who provided him with a real bed with real linen, Paul D. was sold to the Northpoint Bank and Railroad Company (131).

NUMBER 7 CARPENTER'S ROAD [SU]. Number 7 Carpenter's Road was the address of the house built by Eva Peace (139).

O

OAKLAND, CALIFORNIA [PA]. Gigi and Mickey Rood were caught up in the mayhem of the Oakland, California, riots. The image of a wounded and defenseless little boy during the riots remained with Gi Gi for a long time (170).

OGLETHORPE, JAMES EDWARD (1696–1785) [BLV]. In the same vein that the Cherokees extended kindness to General James Edward Oglethorpe, the Indians reached out to help Paul D. and the forty-five fugitives who wandered into their camp in chains (102).

As founder of the colony of Georgia, General Oglethorpe communicated with the Indians in trust and respect after years of their being exploited by the Spanish and the French. He viewed the Indians as political partners in the well-being of Georgia.

In 1739 and 1752, Oglethorpe devised treaties that joined Georgia and the Indians in a pact to coexist in harmony. About Oglethorpe, Phinizy Spalding wrote, "Through the patient and considerate leadership, his concern for the welfare of the native population, and his unobtrusive empathy with Indian ways and wants, he made lasting impression upon the tribes and gained many loyal red friends" (Spalding, 94).

In 1835 Oglethorpe University was chartered in the state of Georgia in honor of James Edward Oglethorpe, the founder of Georgia.

O'HARA, SCARLETT [SS]. Guitar Bains references Scarltett O'Hara, the main female character in the 1939 movie, *Gone with the Wind*, when he offhandedly discusses the problems of black men making advances toward white women (81).

OHIO RIVER [BLV]. Crossing the Ohio River signaled freedom for the runaway slaves traveling north (147).

OKLAHOMA [PA]. Zechariah Morgan and the Old Fathers settled in Haven, Oklahoma, and later, the Morgan twin grandsons, and the New Fathers resettled in Ruby, Oklahoma. Although the towns are fictional, an understanding of the rich history of African American migration to the state of Oklahoma is important to the storyline in Morrison's *Paradise*. During the land run of the late 1800s, many Negroes joined white settlers in going west. Many Indian tribes were already inhabitants there. At one time, in addition to Oklahoma having the largest population of Indians, it was also once the most populated state with all Negro towns. After an intensive study on the subject, Murray R. Wickett writes about the migration of blacks to Oklahoma. "They sought a place where they would no longer be obliged to be reminded on a daily basis that they were second hand citizens" (Wickett, 33).

The diversity between the whites, Indians, and Negro cultures co-existing within the sate of Oklahoma created much disharmony and cultural friction. Many blacks went to Oklahoma for an opportunity for a better life. In researching this social movement, Mozell C. Hill wrote: "The development of all Negro communities in Oklahoma was an integral part of the Great Western Movement in this country during the late nineteenth and early twentieth centuries" (Hill, 254).

OLD BLUE. *See* JACK, BLUE [BE]

OLD HONEY (DOG) [BE]. Old Honey was the hunting dog of the white men who embarrassed Cholly Breedlove and Darlene during sex in the woods (148).

OLD JAKE. *See* DEAD MACON I [SS]

OLD MACON DEAD. *See* DEAD, MACON I (I.E., OLD JAKE) [SS]

OLD MAN. *See* FRANKLIN G. GREEN [TB]

OLD QUEEN HOTEL [TB]. On arrival back in the Caribbean from New York City, Jadine Childs waited patiently at the Old Queen Hotel for a ride to L'Arbe de la Croix (274–75).

OLD SLACK BESSIE[BE]. Mrs. MacTeer and her friends were discussing Peggy, the woman who ran off with Delia Jones' husband, when Old Slack Bessie's name came up. It was noted that Peggy was one of Old Slack Bessie's girls. It was common knowledge that Old Slack Bessie ran some sort of brothel (13).

OLD WILLY FIELDS. *See* FIELDS, WILLY [SU]

OLIVE BEST. *See* BEST, FULTON & OLIVE [PA]

OMAR [SS]. Omar was one of the men who invited Milkman on a hunt. Milkman soon found out that Omar was an experienced hunter, as well as a jovial kind of guy (269, 281).

ONDINE CHILDS. *See* CHILDS, ONDINE (I.E., NANADINE) [TB]

"ONE DROP LAW" [PA]. When Roger Best married Delia, a woman with mulatto features, he was criticized by the men of Ruby, Oklahoma. The child born of this union, Patricia Best (Cato), was also frowned upon because of the "one drop" (195). Normally, it was whites that imposed these cultural restrictions, but in Ruby, Oklahoma, it was the blacks that frowned on the mixing of races. Basically, the law states that if anyone has a black ancestor, no matter how fair in complexion, he/she is considered black and must adhere to that racial category. It is obvious that the "one drop law" is a convenient tool for racists to discourage interracial relationships. Blood composition was also important for the Indians. Murray B. Wickett devoted a chapter to the "One Drop Rule" in his book entitled *Contested Territory*, and in it he writes, "The tribes were afraid that blacks who intermarried with Indians would try to claim citizenship in the tribe, just as intermarried whites could do" (Wickett, 35).

ONE-TON LADY [BLV]. The One-Ton Lady was one of the eight acts at the carnival outside of Cincinnati visited by Sethe, Denver, and Paul D. (48).

124 BLUESTONE ROAD [BLV]. As an address, the gray-and-white house was designated as 124 Bluestone Road. Eventually the address dominated the residence, as 124 became an entity unto itself. When Mr. Garner told Baby Suggs about her lodging arrangements in Ohio, he united 124 to a spiritual force by stating, "These two angels got a house for you" (145). Angels and house—this divine relationship at the onset was clear evidence of the spiritual force and empowerment directly associated to the well-being of the Suggs family in 124. Under the threat of harm from angry spirits who appeared as less negative forces, deity played a significant role in the engagement of support, stamina, and survival within 124.

The Bodwins owned 124, deplored slavery, and were pleased to exchange housing for domestic services in the advancement of Baby Suggs, a free woman (145). At 124, Baby Suggs welcomed the children of the son who had worked so diligently to set her free. Later, a daughter-in-law she had never met arrived with an infant escaping the horrors of slavery. As their lives changed, so did 124 (147). Some people live quiet and private lives within their homes, but not the folks in 124. The house became a mirrored image of its residents. The joy and fellowship brought to the townspeople at the Clearing was ministered to them by the kind old woman in 124. So, when a granddaughter's death and a daughter-in-law's imprisonment broke Baby Suggs' heart, it directly halted religious services. In retaliation, 124 Bluestone Road was shunned by the townspeople as though it were a wicked foe.

When the ghost first arrived at 124, Sethe was surrounded by Baby Suggs, Howard, Buglar, and Denver. The spirit's presence in the home forced Sethe's sons, Howard and Buglar, too soon into a world hostile to blacks. Paul D. came along filled with love and admiration for Sethe and he, too, eventually was forced out of 124, and into the barn. So the haunt of 124 124 Bluestone Road was jealous and vindictive as it weakened the forces around Sethe to extract retribution.

As time and events evolved, 124 was consumed with the evil and demonic force of Beloved's empowerment over Sethe, and Denver had to leave the residence in search of help. The angelic spirit aligned with the Bodwin's gift to Baby Suggs, was the same divine force who reclaimed 124 through Denver and the women of the town. The house at 124 took on physical characteristics with spite and anger prevailing, and its exorcism came through the love and compassion of the town. The house at 124 Bluestone symbolized humanity with and without God.

ONKA [BLV]. The nephews of Schoolteacher called him "Onka," an ebonic variation of the word "uncle" (36).

OPHELIA [BE]. Little Elihue Micah Whitcomb's *literary selections* included Shakespearean tragedies. Ophelia is the daughter of Polonius in William Shakespeare's *Hamlet*. She is obedient to her father, who instructs her to stay away from Hamlet, the son of the late King Hamlet of Denmark and nephew to Claudius, the reigning king. Hamlet loved Ophelia, but under the influence of King Claudius, she betrayed him. Hamlet retaliates by mistreating Ophelia, as revealed in his famous "To be or not to be" soliloquy (*Hamlet*, 3.1.156). Hamlet later sarcastically instructs Ophelia to, "Get thee to a nunnery, why waltzed thou be a breeder of sinners?" (*Hamlet*, 3.1.124). Determined to hurt Ophelia, he belittled her by proclaiming that, "if thou wilt needs marry, marry a fool, for wise men know well enough what monsters you make of them."

OPPORTUNITY: A JOURNAL OF NEGRO LIFE [JZ]. Malvonne Edwards attached an article from the *Opportunity* magazine before forwarding Hot Steam's letter to Daddy Sage (44).

A magazine about the life of the Negro that began with its first issue on January 19, 1923, *Opportunity: A Journal of Negro Life* was promoted by John T. Clark, but Charles S. Johnson, director of research and investigations for the Urban League, was the first editor. In a study of African American periodicals, Michael Fultz writes of the official publication of the National Urban League, "its name (*Opportunity*) was taken from that organization's motto, 'Not Alms, But Opportunity.' In essence the magazine's naming strongly promoted 'chances for Negroes over charity for Negroes' " (Fultz, 101). The main emphasis of *Opportunity* was to combat inferiority by bringing positive news to and about black people (44). The strong editorial appeal for poetry made Langston Hughes one of the journal's frequent contributors.

OSSIE BEAUCHAMP. *See* BEAUCHAMP, OSSIE [PA]

OTHELLO [BE]. Elihue Micah Whitcomb (Soaphead Church) had a literary appetite that included the works of William Shakespeare (169). The plot in the Shakespearean tragedy *Othello* evolves when Othello, the Moorish general in the service of the Venetian army, elopes with Desdemona, the daughter of Senator Brabantio. The play's protagonist, Iago, is a military aide to Othello and is filled with jealousy. He schemes to undermine Othello through feigned loyalty and friendship. Iago is very successful in his endeavors, as the Moor believes that his wife has been unfaithful and murders her. Othello's emotional investment rendered him the sole believer of Iago's allegations of Desdemona's infidelity. Roderigo, Cassio, and Emilia (Iago's wife) all dismissed Iago's lies.

OTIS REDDING. *See* BROTHER OTIS [PA]

OUT THERE [PA]. The Old Fathers used the term "out there" to identify elements that threatened their survival. They felt that as long as they stayed together, their families were protected from the prejudice and hatred of the white man and unfriendly black men. The evil forces that destroyed the lives of black people and created havoc were outside of their homes: out there. As men, it was their responsibility to protect their wives and children from the elements out there (18).

O.V., UNCLE. *See* UNCLE O.V. [BE]

OVEN, THE [PA]. Zechariah Morgan had the original idea for building an oven as a communal cooking place, and an oven became *the* "Oven." During slavery, fieldwork was preferable to kitchen work because the men believed that their women were susceptible to the white man's salacious desires within the house (99). The Oven's original intention was shared cooking, but it took on meaning that implied idolatry.

The Oven was dismantled in Haven and transported to Ruby (103). During the trip, the women voiced their resentment for the sacrifice of room in the wagon to accommodate the Oven. They resented not having space for other necessities. As the Oven became a shrine for the elders, the young people could not understand the relevance of its engraved message. Against any and all opposition, the New Fathers diligently fought to assure the sanctity of the Oven's place in their lives. The Oven also served as a meeting place for the nine men who planned the assault on the Convent women (84–85).

P

PADREW, FATHER. *See* FATHER PADREW [SS]

PALESTINE, VIRGINIA [JZ]. Joe Trace searched for his mother, the woman called "Wild" in Palestine, Virginia (175–76).

PALLAS. *See* TRUELOVE, PALLAS [PA]

PAT CATO BEST. *See* BEST, PATRICIA (CATO) [PA]

PATRICIA BEST CATO. *See* BEST, PATRICIA (CATO) [PA]

PATSY [SU]. Patsy was the mother of Rudy and friend of Hannah Peace. In the discussion of parenting, Hannah remarked to Patsy that she loved Sula, her daughter, but she did not like her (57). Later, in a conversation about Sula,, Patsy bore witness to Hannah's daughter's strange behavior patterns (115).

PATSY (I.E., THIRTY-MILE WOMAN) [BLV]. Patsy was Sixo's woman. The fourteen-year-old slave woman snuck away into the woods to meet him. Their time was brief together because of the confusion about the meeting place. So gallant was Sixo, he equipped her with a viable excuse for tardiness and carefully charted her way back home for her (24–25). A child had been conceived and, out of love and protection, Sixo defended Patsy and his unborn baby as he prepared to die (219).

PATTY [JZ]. Patty was the mother of Honor, the young boy who did chores for the Hunters Hunter when he was away. Les Tory/Lestory referred to him as "Patty's boy" (168).

PAUL A. *See* GARNER, PAUL A. [BLV]

PAUL D. *See* GARNER, PAUL D. [BLV]

PAUL, ERNIE [TB]. Ernie Paul was an old friend of Son (William Green). When Jadine Childs was fed up with visiting Eloe, Florida, Son's hometown, she insisted on leaving. Son could not accompany her because his old friend Ernie Paul had sacrificed wages to drive down from Montgomery, Alabama, to see him (256, 260).

PAUL F. *See* GARNER, PAUL F. [BLV]

PAULINE WILLIAMS BREEDLOVE. *See* BREEDLOVE, PAULINE WILLIAMS [BE]

PAX. *See* GRAFFITI ARTISTS [TB]

PEACE, BOYBOY. *See* BOYBOY [SU]

PEACE, EVA [SU]. Eva Peace was the wife of Boyboy, mother of Hannah, Eva (Pearl), and Ralph (Plum); and grandmother of Sula. Marriage to Boyboy made life tough, especially when he left her with three small children and no money (31, 34). After trying to survive with the help of neighbors, Eva left her children with Mrs. Suggs and went in search of financial solutions. She returned almost two years later with money, but only one leg (34). Upon Eva's return to town, she built a home to her specifications. When Boyboy dropped by for a visit, his presence awakened the hatred of poverty and pain that Eva had buried (36).

Physically limited but orally astute, Eva manipulated and controlled everyone within her sight. She took in three very different little boys and renamed each of them "Dewey" (37–38). Eva called Pretty Johnnie "Tar Baby" because she was amused by the contradictions in his pale-colored skin (39). Intolerant of her son Plum's display of weakness after the horrors of war through drug addiction, Eva took his life by setting him on fire (45–48).

In an effort to understand her mother killing her brother, Hannah interrogated Eva about the existence of maternal love (43). The communication was shallow and fruitless.

When Eva Peace was left alone without money and three children to feed, the doctrine of survival took precedence over emotion and displays of affection. Eva did not realize that Hannah's questions were about life and death. However, when Eva looked out of her window and saw Hannah in the yard engulfed in flames, she risked her life to save her, but it was too late (75).

Years later, when Sula returned home, Eva lost her freedom when a disgruntled granddaughter signed her into a nursing home (100–101).

PEACE, EVA (CALLED PEARL) [SU]. Eva (called Pearl) was the daughter of Eva Peace, sister of Hannah and Plum, and aunt of Sula Mae Peace. Eva (called Pearl) married as a teenager and moved away from her family (41).

PEACE, HANNAH [SU]. Hannah was the Daughter of Eva, sister of Eva (Pearl) and Ralph (Plum), widow of Rekus, and mother of Sula. Hannah was raised by a mother who promoted man-love instead of self-love (41).

Hannah's marriage to Rekus was short-lived, as he died when Sula was quite young (41). Desperate for the affection and attention of the opposite sex, Hannah ignored social and moral boundaries to seduce husbands of friends and neighbors (42). Her mother was not capable of expressing the kind of love that Hannah wanted and needed, and, subsequently, Hannah emotionally starved her own daughter.

The emotional deprivation from the absence of maternal love and bonding created personalities nurtured by superficial sexual relationships. One day, Sula overheard Hannah say to one of her friends, "You love her like I love Sula. I just don't like her. That's the difference" (57). Later, the issue of maternal love resurfaced when Hannah asked her mother, "Mama, did you ever love us?" (67). Hannah was disturbed by Eva's self-righteous response. It was obvious that she was unable to deal with the anguish that bedeviled her heart. Shortly thereafter, Hannah was burned to death in a yard fire (75–78). Eva tried to save her daughter, but it was too late.

PEACE, RALPH (I.E., PLUM) [SU]. Ralph "Plum" Peace was the son of Eva and BoyBoy Peace and brother of Hannah and Eva (Pearl). As a child, Plum had bouts of constipation that required drastic measures (34). Pampered by a mother who saw him as the heir to the family fortune, Plum succumbed under the pressure to take over (45). Military duty added more stress, and he returned home a drug-addicted and disheartened young man. Plum stole from his family in order to maintain his drug habit.

One day his mother entered his room determined to free him from mental and social ruin. As Plum basked in the warmth of his mother's embrace, Eva lit the match that set him ablaze. In his incoherent state, Plum was incapable of resisting the painful death that engulfed him (46–48).

PEACE, SULA MAE [SU]. Daughter of Hannah and Rekus (who had no last name), granddaughter of Eva Peace, and best childhood friend of Nel Wright, Sula was a lonely, but adventurous young girl with a pronounced facial birthmark that resembled either a stemmed rose (52) or a tadpole (156), depending on whose commentary you preferred. Nel and Sula were inseparable and experienced many childhood adventures together. Morrison says they were like, "Daughters of distant mothers and incomprehensible fathers (Sula's because he was dead; Nel's because he wasn't), they found in each other's eyes the intimacy they were looking for" (52). Sula lived in a female-dominated home where man-love was more important than self-love (41). Sula saw her mother in bed with a man (44) and also overheard her say that she loved, but did not like her (57). Sula's friendship with Nel was comforting, but she was affected deeply by the unhappiness of her home life. Sula was tough and once sliced off the top of her finger to intimidate bullies (54). In a playful act, Sula accidently caused Chicken Little's death (59–64).

Upon her return to Medallion, Ohio, Sula's affair with Ajax was short-lived and filled with misrepresentation. As a Peace woman, Sula disregarded friendship boundaries in seeking sexual satisfaction from a man, so Nel's husband was fair game (105–6). Even as she lay dying, she was unable to grasp the seriousness of how she had hurt her childhood friend (144–45).

PEAL, MAUREEN [BE]. Maureen Peal was the new classmate of the MacTeer sisters whom just happened to be a well-off mulatto. The MacTeer sisters were united in their dislike of her clothes, racial tone, and snootiness. In search of a flaw, the MacTeer sisters found a birth defect and nicknamed her "Six-finger-dog-tooth-Meringue Pie." Maureen later deliberately hurt Pecola which gave credibility to Claudia and Freida's slander (62).

PEARL ALBRIGHT. *See* ALBRIGHT, MERLE & PEARL [PA]

PEARL PEACE. *See* PEACE, EVA (CALLED PEARL) [SU]

PECOLA. *See* BREEDLOVE, PECOLA [BE]

PEG [PA]. Peg was the neighbor of Mavis Albright who displayed sympathy at the funeral of her twins, Merle and Pearl. Mavis stopped at Peg's home in the early hours of the morning before leaving town, but she dared not knock on the door at that time in the morning (27).

PEGGY [BE]. Peggy, who was from Elyria, was a woman of loose character who seduced Della Jones' husband (13).

PENNEY. *See* CLARISSA & PENNEY [PA]

PEOLA [BE]. Upon introduction to Pecola Breedlove, Maureen Peal relates Pecola to Peola, a female character in the movie *Imitation of Life*. Even when Pecola Breedlove hears how pretty Peola was, she was detached emotionally from the world of glamour and movie stars.

The 1934 film, starring Claudette Colbert under the direction of John M. Stahl, was adapted from Fannie Hurst's novel of the same name. Peola Johnson was the mulatto daughter of Delilah Johnson, the Negro maid who befriends a white actress and her daughter. Still breaking her mother's heart by passing for white, Peola was renamed "Sarah Jane" for the modernized 1959 version of *Imitation of Life* (67).

PERSON, MR. *See* MR. PERSON [PA]

PETER BLACKHORSE. *See* BLACKHORSE, PETER [PA]

PHILADELPHIA, PENNSYLVANIA [TB]. As the "City of Brotherly Love," Philadelphia, Pennsylvania is rich in American history because it is where the First Continental Congress met, the Declaration of Independence was adopted, and the Constitution was framed. Valerian Street and Sydney Childs were both very proud of their hometown (82).

PHILLY [JZ]. Philly was the infant who Violet Trace took from a carriage. Violet was on her way home with her confiscated child to meet her husband, Joe. The baby's guilt-ridden sisters, who were responsible for babysitting, spotted Violet on the corner with the baby and ran to her. As she turned over the child to his sisters Violet responded with amusement at all the attention (20–21).

PHYLLIS, AUNT. *See* AUNT PHYLLIS [BLV]

PICASSO, PABLO (1881–1973) [TB]. Jadine Childs' comment about preferring a Picasso over the Itumba mask was a sign of her elitism. After a trip to Africa, Picasso's work was influenced notably by African art history. In a pompous manner, Jadine was saying that she preferred

African art filtered through the talent of Picasso's Italian influence over its native form (74). In Picasso's *Les demoiselle d'Avignon*, the influence of the Itumba masks is unmistakable.

PIE LADIES [TB]. The Pie Ladies were the Southern women whom Son (William Green) remembered fondly for giving out pie at the Good Shepherd Church festivities in his hometown of Eloe, Florida. They were his Aunt Rosa; Soldier's mom, May Downing, affectionately known as "Mama May"; Drake's grandmother, Winnie Boon; Miss Tyler; Beatrice; and Ellen (295, 299).

PIE WILLIAMS. *See* WILLIAMS, PIE [BE]

PIEDADE [PA]. Connie told Seneca, Pallas, Mavis, and Gigi all about Piedade and her magic. Piedade was a Portuguese singer whose haunting and passionate rendition of her homeland's melancholic musical tradition, known as "fado," brought her international fame, film stardom, and the Grand Cross of the Order of Santiago, Portugal's highest honor (284–85).

PIKE [BLV]. Amy Denver told Sethe about the pike (turnpike) that she would take on into Boston (82).

PIKE, REVEREND. *See* REVEREND PIKE [BLV]

PIKE, WILLIE [BLV]. Stamp Paid cited Willie Pike as one of the hospitable townspeople who would board Paul D. after leaving the home of Sethe Suggs at 124 Bluestone (232).

When Baby Suggs arrived at 124, a free woman, she engaged Reverend Pike to write letters to the Whitlowes back in the Carolinas to inquire about her seven children sold into slavery (146).

PILATE DEAD. *See* DEAD, PILATE [SS]

PIOUS DUPRES. *See* DUPRES, PIOUS [PA]

P-KOMET (I.E., P-COMET). *See* GRAFFITI ARTISTS [TB]

P.L. [BE]. P.L. was a classmate of Pecola Breedlove who was regarded by Geraldine as an unacceptable playmate for her son Junior (Louis), as she set high standards for her son (87).

PLUM. *See* PEACE, RALPH [SS]

POLAND, MISS. *See* **MISS POLAND [BE]**

POLLY [BE]. "Polly" was the nickname given to Pauline Breedlove by the Fishers, the family that employed her for domestic services (108).

POOLE, AARON [PA]. Aaron Poole was the husband of Sally Blackhorse and father of thirteen children. Together, Pious and Lone DuPres went to the home of Aaron Poole to encourage him to join their efforts to stop the threat of violence at the Convent. It is not clear if Aaron knew that his son, Wisdom, was one of the invaders (284).

POOLE, APOLLO [PA]. One of thirteen children of Sally Blackhorse and Aaron Poole, Apollo Poole and his brother Brood both were infatuated with Billie Delia Cato. After Billie Delia fought with her mother, it was Apollo who took Billie Delia to the Convent. Their infatuation led to a shooting that almost destroyed a family (202–3, 215, 277).

POOLE, BROOD [PA]. Brood was one of the thirteen children of Sally Blackhorse and Aaron Poole. Billie Delia Cato was the cause of tension between him and his brother. The situation got out of hand when his brother, Apollo, banished a weapon to settle their disagreement. Things cooled down when Billie Delia left town (202–3, 215, 277).

POOLE, BROOD, SR. [PA]. Brood Poole Sr. was the father of Aaron Poole and one of the Old Fathers leaving Fairly, Oklahoma (190).

POOLE, DEEPER [PA]. Deeper Poole was one of Sally Blackhorse and Aaron Poole's thirteen children (197).

POOLE, DINA [PA]. Daughter of Sally Blackhorse and Aaron Poole and one of thirteen children including (Apollo and Brood). Dina was the sister of Apollo and Brood, two brothers both in love with her teacher's daughter. Pat Best Cato did not like the Poole brothers' attention to her daughter, Billie Delia, because they were really distant cousins (197). When Dina commented about seeing Christmas lights outside of town, Pat Best Cato became suspicious and jumped to conclusions. Dina's innocent comments incited feelings of outrage for Pat Best Cato because she felt the Brood boy(s) were really visiting Billie Delia in Demby, which substantiated her daughter's clandestine relationship with one or both of the brothers (202).

POOLE, HURSTON & CALINE [PA]. Hurston and Caline Poole were two of the young people who attended the meeting at Mount Calvary Baptist Church to discuss the meaning of the motto on the Oven (85).

POOLE, SALLY BLACKHORSE [PA]. Sally Blackhorse Poole was the wife of Aaron Poole and mother of thirteen children, two of whom were Apollo and Brood, who rivaled each other for the affection of Billie Delia (197).

POOLE, WISDOM [PA]. Wisdom Poole was one of the thirteen children of Sally Blackhorse and Aaron Poole. His brothers Aaron and Brood were behaving foolishly over Billie Delia Cato. Both brothers were interested romantically in her and ignored all warnings to put an end to their sibling rivalry. Wisdom was older and felt responsible for the disgrace his younger brothers brought to the family. When he found out that one of them had taken Billie Delia to the Convent, he immediately embraced a hatred for the women living there (277). The news that the men of Ruby were determined to go to the Convent and run the women out of town emancipated his anger (281). At first, Wisdom was an eager participant, but after the violence and death he realized the shame of what had taken place. Wisdom knew that the guilt he lived with could only be absolved by God (277).

POPEYE. *See* GRAFFITI ARTISTS [TB]

PORKY GREEN. *See* GREEN, PORKY [TB]

PORTER, HENRY [SS]. Loneliness laced with intoxication rendered Henry Porter an exhibitionist and a fool as he threatened suicide from the attic window. When Freddie told Macon Dead I, the landlord, about Henry Porter, Macon went running to get the rent money before his tenant killed himself (25–26).

Porter knew who First Corinthians was when he first spied her on the bus and soon realized that her loneliness matched his. After a respectful surveillance period, he approached her with friendship. Hesitant at first, the two were uncomfortable forging a relationship. First Corinthians was responsive to the charm of her fellow bus rider because, at the age of forty-two, there had been no other suitor. Porter was not the caliber of man the Dead family would approve of for their oldest daughter. However, First Corinthians realized that an opportunity for romance and happiness rebuffed clan accreditation.

Milkman became alarmed when he realized that his sister, First Corinthians, was getting rides home from work with Henry Porter, a member of the Seven Days.

PORTER'S LANDING [SU]. Porter's Landing was the town on the other side of Medallion and was connected by a bridge (81). The man who found Chicken Little's body reported it to the authorities in Porter's

Landing. There were no black families in that town, so they deduced that the child lived in the town of Medallion (64).

PRAISE COMPTON. *See* COMPTON, PRAISE [PA]

PRECIOUS JEWEL [BE]. Soaphead Church had a strange habit of collecting things that people discarded. In his letter to God, he mentioned that one of his prized possessions was a blue ribbon that belonged to a little girl named Precious Jewel. The fact that Soaphead had the ribbon and knew her name presupposes that she was probably a victim of some perverted activity while in his company (183).

PRESIDENT LINCOLN (PLOW HORSE). *See* LINCOLN, ABRAHAM [SS]

PRETTY JOHNNIE. *See* TAR BABY [SU]

PRINCE, DEWEY [BE]. Dewey Prince was one of Miss Marie's lovers in the stories told to Pecola Breedlove (54).

PRINCESS [BLV]. Edward Bodwin was slightly annoyed as he traveled to pick up Denver at 124 Bluestone Road because she was not riding Princess, his preferred horse (259).

PRINCIPAL BEAUTY OF MAINE [TB]. "Principal Beauty of Maine" was the name given to the winner of the Miss Maine contest by the relative of a rival who did not win (54). Ondine Childs, the housekeeper, was seething with her guarded secret about Margaret Street, the Principal Beauty of Maine, and, one day in an outburst, she stated, "The Principal Beauty of Maine is the main bitch of the prince" (35).

PRIVATE KEANE [BLV]. The end of the war found Paul D. in the company of two soldiers of his hue. One of them, Private Keane, complained about the difference in pay for white and black soldiers. Paul D. could not understand his gripe, as he found hope in the prospects of getting money to fight in battle (269).

PRIVATE SMITH. *See* SMITH, COFFEE [PA]

PROVIDENCE [PA]. Providence was the eagle-eyed housekeeper and cook in Milton Truelove's home (166, 255).

PUERTO LIMON [PA]. Two of the three children rescued from the streets were put into an orphanage when Sister Mary Magna arrived in Puerto Limon, in eastern Costa Rica, a major seaport on the Caribbean Sea.

PULASKI COUNTY, KENTUCKY [BLV]. Paul D. believed there were three places of misfortune for black men that rivaled each other: Baltimore; Pulaski County, Kentucky; and Alfred, Georgia (66).

PULLIAM, ALICE. *See* AUNT ALICE [PA]

PULLIAM, SENIOR. *See* REVEREND SENIOR PULLIAM [PA]

PURPLE HEART [PA]. As the oldest military award given to the enlisted man, the Purple Heart has a rich history in American culture. First established by General George Washington during the American Revolution in 1782, the Purple Heart served to honor soldiers who exhibited outstanding gallantry, fidelity, and service during military exercises. Ossie Beauchamp's decision to donate his Purple Heart to the winner of the horse race symbolizes love and respect for the people in his community (10). The medal is heart shaped, and below the Washington family coat of arms is a superimposed picture of George Washington on a purple center. The words "For Military Merit" are engraved on the back, and the medal hangs from a purple ribbon.

Q

QUEEN OF FRANCE [TB]. Queen of France was a seaport town near the Isle des Chevaliers where Margaret Street and Jadine Childs went shopping (7, 9).

R

RAGGEDY ANN [PA]. Mavis Albright compared herself to a life-size Raggedy Ann doll during sex with her husband. The lack of penetration and physical contact rendered her lifeless. In essence, Mavis compared herself to a big floppy doll that just moved at will. Raggedy Ann is the world's best-known rag doll and was created and patented by Johnny Gruelle in 1915 (26).

RAILROAD TOMMY [SS]. Railroad Tommy was the co-owner of the barbershop where the local men gathered. When Guitar Bains and Milkman wandered into their establishment complaining about not being served a beer in Feather's Pool Hall, Railroad Tommy made fun of their situation by citing a long list of other desires they would be denied. As black men, they might want, but not get, handcrafted furniture, servants who attended to their needs on command, money to buy any real estate desired, breakfast trays adorned with flowers, four stars pinned on their chests even after risking life and limb for their country, stately lodging, and fancy deserts. Railroad Tommy ended the lecture balancing what they would never have with what they were sure to have, which was plenty of sorrow and senseless behavior throughout their lives (59–61). As a member of the Seven Days, a secret society of black men who avenged the death of their people by taking the lives of innocent whites, Railroad Tommy was commited to revenge (210–11).

RALPH NISENSKY. *See* NISENSKY, RALPH [BE]

RALPH PEACE. *See* PEACE, RALPH (I.E., PLUM) [SU]

RAMPAL'S RONDO IN D [TB]. Valerian Street had a greenhouse with plants that thrived on the music of Jean-Pierre Rampal (1922–2000), a world renowned flutist and conductor (12). Rampal promoted flute playing for a wide variety of music, including Indian and Japanese. According to the *New Harvard Dictionary of Music*, Rondo "is a multi-sectional form, movement, or composition based on the principles of multiple recurrence of a theme or section in the tonic key" (Randel, 717).

RAYFORD, MRS. *See* MRS. RAYFORD [SU]

READJUSTER PARTY [JZ]. On one of his infrequent visits to see his family, Violet Trace's father revealed that he was involved with the Readjuster Party, a group of black and white farmers demanding economic consideration in lower taxes during the 1870s. According to James T. Moore, the black participants received little recognition: "Oddly enough, however, scholars have almost totally ignored the activities of the black Readjusters. Most accounts described them as meer pawns in the political game, a cogs in the Mahone (leader of revolt) machine" (Moore, 167).

REBA (I.E., REBECCA) [SS]. Reba was the daughter of Pilate Dead and mother of Hagar. Reba was born to a teenager who experienced the painful separation and loss of family early in life and whose efforts to replace that bond of love and security were thwarted by ignorance and distrust. Consequently, young Reba's belief system about herself and societal norms was greatly distorted (140–147). She was raised by an eccentric and unconventional woman whose intellectual capacity and love of humanity contradicted her living. Reba's transition into adulthood was nonexistent, which resulted in a lifelong childlike personality. The social fabric of Reba's life was restrictive since survival for the two women came with behavior, dress, and rules, that differed with those of everyone else.

Living in isolation, without other children or adults as reference points, Reba considered Pilate's concept of right and wrong to be law. Family was Pilate and Pilate was family. As a child with only her mother's controlling obsession, in the face of losing loved ones early in life, Reba was emotionally and socially limited (150). Reba used sex and men for validation and socialization, which was a learned behavior from her mother, who also used relationships to compensate for emotional paucity.

Reba was a child when she gave birth to her daughter, Hagar. The rapture of motherhood as well as the responsibilities of parenthood were taken over by Pilate. Hagar and Reba shared a sisterly relationship because Pilate ruled their lives. Hagar called her grandmother "Mama," not her biological mother (93). Reba's uncanny ability to win raffles and games complimented her existence, but the trait was unrelated to the development of her emotional or psychological well-being. Often she did not understand the nature of what she won or what to do with it (45–47). The scene in which Pilate threatened Reba's boyfriend's life because he assaulted Reba clearly illustrates Pilate's dominance as head of household (94–95).

REBA'S GRILL [SU]. Reba's Grill was a restaurant in Bottom that was slated for destruction. The quality of food was ensured with the owner/cook's wearing of a hat (3).

REBECCA. *See* **FONTAINE, JOAN [TB]**

REBECCA. *See* **REBA [SS]**

RECTOR (BIG DADDY) MORGAN. *See* **MORGAN, RECTOR (BIG DADDY) [PA]**

RED CORA [BLV]. Sethe blamed a woman named Red Cora for disfiguring Buglar's hand when he tried to drink the milk in the parlor (160).

RED-HEADED NEGRO NAMED X (I.E., MALCOLM X; MALCOLM LITTLE) [SS]. Milkman compared the militancy of his friend, Guitar Bains, to that of the "red-headed Negro named X," who was really Malcolm Little, known as Malcolm X (1925–1965). Milkman challenged Guitar to adopt the name "Guitar X" and publicly claim his hostility toward white people (160).

Incarcerated at the age of twenty for burglary, young Malcolm Little adopted the Muslim philosophy, denounced his "slave name," added "X," and became "Malcolm X." This practice of renaming was common among Nation of Islam followers. When he was released from jail at age twenty-seven, he was a Muslim within the sect of the Nation of Islam under the teachings of Elijah Muhammad.

Like Guitar Bains, Malcolm X spoke of the grave injustices toward black people in America at the hands of their white brothers. Malcolm X believed that the "American Negro never can be blamed for his racial animosities because he is reacting to four hundred years of the conscious racism of American whites" (Malcolm X, 339–342). As Malcolm X continued to speak about the problems of the black man, his followers grew in numbers. There was a power struggle within the Nation of Islam as

Malcolm's popularity soared. On February 21, 1965, Malcolm X was assassinated as he delivered a lecture in Manhattan's Audubon Ballroom. The following year, Talmadge Hayer, Norman 3X Butler, and Thomas 15X Johnson were convicted of killing him.

REDDING, OTIS. *See* **BROTHER OTIS [PA]**

REDMEN PRESENCE [BLV]. Redmen Presence was a deserted cave that belonged to the Redmen that Sixo, one of the five slaves, discovered one night wandering outside of Sweet Home. In respect, he asked the Redmen if he could bring his girl there for a meeting. The response was affirmative and Sixo arranged the rendevous with his Patsy, Thirty-Mile Woman (24).

REED, BUCKLAND [SU]. Buckland Reed was the flamboyant neighbor and friend of Eva Peace (55). Buckland Reed ran numbers and joined Shadrack in the National Suicide Day parade after Sula Peace died (159).

REED, MRS. *See* **MRS. REED [SU]**

REESE, BERTHA [BE]. Storekeeper, landlady, and owner of a pet dog named "Bob." She rented a room to Soaphead Church, who hated her dog. One day, he tricked Pecola Breedlove into poisoning the dog by promising the little girl she would get blue eyes if Bob died (171).

REKUS [SU]. Rekus was the husband of Hannah and father of Sula. Remembered as a happy fellow, he died when Sula was only three-years old (41).

REN BEAUCHAMP. *See* **BEAUCHAMP, REN [PA]**

REVEREND COLES [SS]. In answer to Magdalene called Lena's comments about no black people being able to afford a beach house, First Corinthians stated that Rev. Coles and Dr. Singletary had the financial stability for such a luxury (33).

REVEREND COOPER (I.E., COOP) [SS]. When Milkman arrived in Danville, Pennsylvania, he made inquiries about a woman named "Circa" and was directed to Rev. Cooper's house. There he found hospitality, lodging, and kind people with fond memories of his kin. During the many talks that Milkman had with Rev. Cooper, he was shocked to learn that everyone had the knowledge that the Butler family had killed Old Macon Dead, his grandfather, yet nothing was done about the crime (232). Rev. Cooper felt badly, and, in defense of his honor as a proud and responsible black man, he wanted Milkman to know that he was not a coward. The large lump behind his ear, which he received in Philadelphia during an Armistice Day parade, validated he courage. Rev. Cooper told Milkman the story of how the marchers had taken every legal precaution to remain within the confines of the law and they were still beaten and abused (232).

Reverend Cooper opened his home to other townspeople who were eager to meet the Deads' son and grandson. Milkman and Reverend Cooper swapped stories about the bravery and success of the Dead men as neighbors looked on in admiration.

REVEREND DEAL [SU]. Reverend Deal was the local minister in Medallion, Ohio, who officiated at the funeral of Chicken Little, the little boy found dead in the river (65).

REVEREND MOTHER. *See* **SISTER MAGNA, MARY [PA]**

REVEREND PIKE [BLV]. Reverend Pike officiated at the funeral of Sethe's slain child. Sethe heard Rev. Pike say "Dearly Beloved," and, out of guilt, confusion, and anguish, she put "Beloved" on her child's tombstone (5, 184).

REVEREND RICHARD MISNER [PA]. Reverend Richard Misner was the minister of the Mount Calvary Baptist Church. As the handsome new minister of the most populated church in Ruby, Oklahoma, Richard Misner was popular with the ladies and young people, but often at odds with the New Fathers. Progressive in his thinking, he often served as mediator in controversial discussions. When the Fleetwoods and the Morgans were at odds, Misner was right in the middle (54–62). The sit-ins of the civil rights movement taught him that young people needed a voice in matters of civil concern. In Ruby, Oklahoma, it was unpopular to take the side of those under twenty-five, but Misner did just that (143, 206).

The changing of the words on the Oven was an explosive topic, but Misner stood his ground, insisting that everyone, especially the young, be heard. When the Oven was defaced in a youthful attempt to update the town's views on civil rights, Rev. Misner publicly supported their need to voice their opinions.

Steward Morgan resented Rev. Misner and his influence upon the youth in town (94). Richard Misner thought Steward Morgan was an explosive bully who wanted his own way (123). Rev. Misner recognized the opposition to his cause, but, as a religious leader, he felt compelled to work with the community as a whole, including, not excluding, the young (304). Romantically interested in Anna Flood, he eventually asked for her hand in marriage with hopes of settling down permanently in Ruby (304).

Rev. Misner was furious at Rev. Pulliam for his inappropriate remarks at the Arnette and K.D. wedding. Misner was right: St. Augustine of Hippo definitely would not have approved of such an arrogant display of religious authority. Rev. Misner chose the cross as a rebuttal and reminder of humility and perseverance (141).

Lone DuPres needed the counsel of Rev. Misner the night the men raided the Convent, but he and Anna were out of town (280).

REVEREND SENIOR PULLIAM [PA]. Reverend Senior Pulliam was the husband of Alice and the Methodist minister of New Zion church. As the minister of New Zion Methodist Church in Ruby, Oklahoma, Rev. Senior had seniority, but his colleague Rev. Misner at Mount Calvary Baptist Church, had the largest congregation, which included the Morgan families. This imbalance in prestige and spiritual following annoyed Rev. Pulliam. Rev. Misner was younger and more charismatic to the point that he openly encouraged the youth of Ruby to take an active role in civic matters. At the meeting to discuss the motto on the Oven, Rev. Pulliam interpreted the youthful energy as disrespectful yammering (85).

Rev. Pulliam had a packed audience and, filled with jealousy, he overstepped his boundaries at Arnette Fleetwood and Coffee "K.D." Smith's wedding. Invited as a guest minister, he went beyond his pastoral responsibilities by publicly challenging Rev. Misner's ability to function as a minister. Pulliam's comments were so inappropriate, it left the wedding attendees searching for relevancy. The irony lies in the fact that Rev. Pulliam began the wedding ceremony with a personal tirade that redefined God's love and entitlement. As clergy, he should have known that God's love makes no exception because His grace is sufficient. Pulliam's spite-propelled jealously told the congregation that, "God is not interested in you" (141–43).

Rev. Pulliam once again contradicted his religious doctrine when the women from the Convent came to the wedding reception. His intolerance of those less fortunate was evident in how he took the upper hand in censuring their conduct. The Convent women were yoked with Rev. Misner in Rev. Pulliam's indictment of behavior and social misconduct. Determined to limit the spread of their evil influence, Rev. Pulliam joined Steward Morgan in banishing the women from the wedding (144–47).

Rev. Pulliam gained knowledge of the raid on the Convent after it had begun. He was instrumental in transporting the injured to the hospital in Demby.

REVEREND SIMON CARY [PA]. Reverend Simon Cary was the husband of Lily; parents of Hope, Chastity, Lovely, and Pure Cary; and pastor of

Holy Redeemer, the Pentecostal church in Ruby, Oklahoma (102). As pastor one of the three churches in town, Rev. Cary took an active role in the community. The Pentecostal congregation of Holy Redeemer was not as large as the Baptist congregation of Mount Calvary, but Rev. Cary's sermons about the sacrifices one makes for a good life were well received (274). Both he and his wife often were called upon to sing duets at social functions (156).

RHODA WILLIAMS. *See* **MRS. RHODA** *and* **WILLIAMS, RHODA & FRANK [JZ]**

RICHARD [PA]. If the unborn child expected by Delia Best had been a boy, he was to be named "Richard" after Roger Best's brother. Unfortunately, Uncle Richard never received the honor as Delia died in childbirth with her daughter (198).

RICHARD MISNER. *See* **REVEREND RICHARD MISNER [PA]**

RICKS, HARLON [JZ]. Together, Joe and Violet Trace worked the land of Harlon Ricks after their marriage (126).

RICKY DJVORAK. *See* **DJVORAK, RICKY [SS]**

RITTER, TEX (1905–1974) [SU]. The young people of Medallion, Ohio, enjoyed watching Tex Ritter, the singing cowboy of the 1930s and 1940s, on the movie screen (154).

RIVER RAT [TB]. In anger, Jadine Childs called William "Son" Green, the outcast hiding in Margaret Street's closet, a "river rat." Jadine was outraged when Valerian Street gave the fugitive free run of the house (159).

RIVERS, MISSY. *See* **MISSY RIVERS [PA]**

ROAD TO PERDITION [PA]. Connie tires of the aimlessness of the four women (Seneca, Pallas, Gigi, and Mavis) who have taken up residence in the Convent. She is aware of their foolish antics and feels that their lives lack purpose. Connie knows that they are at risk of losing their souls. To be on the "road to perdition" means one is headed toward spiritual destruction and, basically, going to hell (222).

ROBERT MICHELIN, M.D. *See* **DR. ROBERT MICHELIN [TB]**

ROBERT SMITH. *See* **SMITH, ROBERT [SS]**

ROCHELLE. *See* DOLLS [JZ]

ROCHELLE [SU]. Rochelle was the Creole daughter of Cecile Sabat, mother of Helene, and grandmother of Nel. When Helene was born, Rochelle was working as a prostitute in the Sundown House (17). On a trip down south to New Orleans, Nel was introduced to Rochelle. The conversation between the women was strained because Rochelle, Helene, and Nel simply did not know each other (25–26).

ROCHESTER [BLV]. When Beloved appeared after the day at the carnival, Paul D. did not press her for information about the past because he remembered the four frightened women in Rochester. Alone with fourteen children after all the men of varied ages had been killed, the women searched for DeVore Street. They were told that there one could find a minister who gave aid and comfort to those in need (52).

ROGER BEST. *See* BEST, ROGER [PA]

ROGERS, GINGER (1911–1995) [BE]. Born Virginia McMath, Ginger Rogers was an actress best remembered for her musicals with Fred Astaire. When the MacTeer sisters met Henry Washington, he flattered them by comparing them to Greta Garbo and Ginger Rogers (16).

ROME, VIRGINIA [JZ]. The black families of Rome, Virginia, were kind to Rose Dear and her children when the family was without home, furnishings, and food (138).

ROOD, MICKEY [PA]. Mickey Rood was the boyfriend of Grace (Gigi) who sent her in search of an erotic monument. During the riots of Oakland, California, Mickey Rood was jailed (63–64).

ROOSEVELT, ANNA ELEANOR (1884–1962) [SS]. Guitar Bains and Milkman debated the sincerity of prominent people and their commitments to the plight of the black race. When Eleanor Roosevelt, wife of President Franklin Delano Roosevelt, was mentioned, at first Guitar was not as adamant about her lack of consciousness because she was a woman. However, he then remembered the contempt he felt when he saw white mothers hoisting their infants up high to get a good look at a lynching (156).

Eleanor Roosevelt, the notable and respected political activist, was far removed from that kind of ignorance. During her life she championed the cause of blacks, women, young people, old people, and the unemployed. History records her as one of the most ambitious and influential first ladies of the White House. Eleanor Roosevelt's entire life was devoted to serving others, and many black male and female leaders were counted among her friends. As the wife of a president, Eleanor Roosevelt was quite opinionated and outspoken. In a 1942 article for the *New Republic* she wrote: "It seems trite to say to the Negro, you must have patience, when he has had patience so long; you must not expect miracles overnight, when he can look back to the years of slavery and say how many" (Roosevelt, 136).

Eleanor Roosevelt wrote four books: *This is My Story* (1937), *This I Remember* (1950), *On My Own* (1958), and *Tomorrow Is Now* (published in 1963 after her death).

ROOSEVELT, FRANKLIN DELANO (I.E., FDR) (1882–1945) [SS]. Milkman related to FDR because he too had physical problems that restricted his gait (63). President from 1933 to 1945, FDR suffered with poliomyelitis, which confined him to a wheelchair.

ROOSEVELT, THEODORE (1858–1919) [JZ]. During his term of office as president of the United States from 1901 to 1909, Theodore Roosevelt caused a stir in the South by inviting Booker T. Washington, a prominent black leader, to sup with him in the White House on March 21, 1901 (127). Roosevelt respected Booker T. Washington and had long admired his work, and, in spite of the prejudice of many whites, he sought Washington's counsel in racial matters. Washington founded the Tuskegee Institute on July 4, 1881, and, according to William H. Walcott Sr., "Theodore Roosevelt served as a Trustee throughout his term in the White House and the years [that] followed to his death" (Walcott, 37).

ROSA, AUNT. *See* AUNT ROSA [TB]

ROSE DEAR. *See* DEAR, ROSE [JZ]

ROSEMARY VILLANUCCI. *See* VILLANUCCI, ROSEMARY [BE]

ROSSITER, SERGEANT. *See* SERGEANT ROSSITER [BLV]

ROYAL BEAUCHAMP. *See* BEAUCHAMP, ROYAL & DESTRY [PA]

RUBY MORGAN SMITH. *See* SMITH, RUBY MORGAN [PA]

RUBY, OKLAHOMA [PA]. Ruby, Oklahoma, was the town named for Ruby Morgan Smith that had three churches, a bank, and two grocery-type stores, but did not have a place to eat out, a place that housed the law, a place to get gas for a car, a place to watch a movie, a place for the sick or a phone booth to call out (12).

RUTH FOSTER DEAD. *See* **DEAD, RUTH FOSTER [SS]**

RYK [TB]. Jadine Childs' boyfriend in Paris, Ryk, gifted her with the seal-skin coat of which she was so proud. Ondine Childs questioned Ryk's weekly letters to her niece at L'Arbe de la Croix. Jadine did not divulge too much information about Ryk's proposal of marriage because she knew that her aunt did not approve of her relationship with the white European man (48, 88).

RYNA [SS]. Wife of Solomon (Shalimar), Ryna was left with twenty-one children when her husband took flight. After watching him fly away with her youngest son in tow, her screams became the legend of a tormented woman's pain and death (274).

RYNA'S GULCH [SS]. Ryna was the wife of Solomon, the Flying African, and the mother of twenty-one children (all boys). When her husband took off to fly back to Africa with their youngest son in tow, Ryna suffered a mental breakdown. Ryna's Gulch was a ravine that echoed the cries of the distraught woman when the wind shifted (322).

S

SABAT, CECILE [SU]. Cecile Sabat was the mother of Rochelle, grand-mother of Helene Sabat Wright, and great-grandmother of Nel. As a proud woman, Cecile Sabat worked hard to raise Helene in a home that fostered self-respect and love (15).

SABAT, ROCHELLE. *See* ROCHELLE [SU]

SAC & FOX MEN [PA]. The Sac & Fox men warned Big Daddy about entering Pura Sangre (153). In researching the Sac Indians, R. David Edmunds found that, "Sawk, Sauk, or Sak, also spelled Sac belong to the Algonquian language group of the North American Eastern Woodlands tribes" (Edmunds, 163). The Fox were close relatives of the Sacs, and the two cultures became one. The two tribes originally joined forces together in the 1700s to battle the Ojibwe, another Indian tribe that had formed an alliance with the French. The Sac & Fox people believed that long ago the Great Spirit chose a fertile valley and surrounding land for their home. While the two tribes thought of themselves as brothers, each would have their own sacred customs. As a point of reference, Jim Thorpe (1887–1953), the first and only person in American history to win both the Penthalon and Decathlon medals, was a Native America from the Sac & Fox tribe in Oklahoma. He represented the Sac & Fox Nation and the United States at the 1912 Olylmpic games in Stockholm, Sweden.

SAGE, ANNA. *See* LADY IN RED [BE]

SAINT AUGUSTINE, BISHOP OF HIPPO. *See* AUGUSTINE, SAINT, BISHOP OF HIPPO [PA]

SAINT CATHERINE OF SIENA (1347–1380) [PA]. Roaming around the Convent, Gigi stumbled upon the plaque of St. Catherine of Siena, a nun well known for serving the poor and those afflicted with repulsive disease, and for working diligently at the conversion of sinners. As a religious and feminine pioneer, she was the first woman to write and publish in Italian dialect. She symbolized the feminine perspective on issues during her era. St. Catherine believed in God as truth and love, and that the realization of God's truth in us is God's glory (174).

SALLY ALBRIGHT. *See* ALBRIGHT, SALLY, FRANKIE, & BILLY JAMES [PA]

SALLY BLACKHORSE POOLE. *See* POOLE, SALLY BLACKHORSE [PA]

SALLY BROWN. *See* BROWN, SALLY [TB]

SAMMY BREEDLOVE. *See* BREEDLOVE, SAMMY [BE]

SAMPSON. *See* CHIPPER & SAMPSON [BLV]

SAMSON FULLER. *See* FULLER, SAMSON (I.E., FOOLISH FULLER) [BE]

SAN FRANCISCO. *See* FRISCO

SANDRA. *See* DUSTY [PA]

SANDS, DEED [PA]. In addition to Luther and Ren Beauchamp and Aaron Poole, Deed Sands was enlisted by Pious DuPres to go to the Covent to stop the men determined to hurt the women (284).

SANDS, LINDA [PA]. When the young people of Ruby, Oklahoma, met at Mount Calvary Baptist Church to discuss the meaning behind the motto printed on the Oven, Linda Sands sat in the audience. Publicly, she had little to say, but was in attendance to show support for her peers, Royal and Destry Beauchamp (85).

SARGEANT PERSON. *See* NEW FATHERS AT RUBY, OKLAHOMA [PA]

SATURDAY GIRL [BLV]. Sethe commented that, without work, she almost became a Saturday Girl (someone who sold her body for money) (204).

SAUL [SS]. In Shalimar, Virginia, Milkman's keen interest in the women of the town and his total disinterest in the men created a hostile situation. Milkman was interested in men only for a means to identify the women. The men resented his show of prosperity in the wake of their poverty as he locked up one car while discussing the ability to purchase another.

As struggling black southern farmers, most of the men felt disrespected by Milkman's arrogance, and Saul was the spokesperson to defend their honor. He antagonized Milkman until a fight broke out. As the men egged him on, Saul banished a knife in an effort to even the score with this uppity well-dressed northerner (267–68).

SAVE-MARIE FLEETWOOD. *See* FLEETWOOD, SAVE-MARIE [PA]

SAWYER, MR. *See* MR. SAWYER [BLV]

"SCARED KINGFISH" [TB]. *See* KINGFISH

SCARLETT O'HARA. *See* O'HARA, SCARLETT [SS]

SCHOOLTEACHER [BLV]. Schoolteacher was Mr. Garner's brother-in-law who came to take control of Sweet Home about two years after Mr. Garner's death (36). Sweet Home soured quickly when a controlling racist came with his two nephews and sadistic ways. Once considered men, the Sweet Home men were now specimens to be watched and studied for the enjoyment of Schoolteacher's nephews (37). The atmosphere around Sweet Home became hostile and threatening. Paul F. had been sold and Paul A. was beaten and demeaned, which signaled trouble for the slaves that remained at Sweet Home. Sixo had learned of the Underground Railroad, and, he thought, escape was just a song away. Before Sethe could escape, under Schoolteacher's watchful eye, she was milked like a cow and savagely beaten (16–17).

Ultimately, it was the pain and horror of Schoolteacher and his nephew's brutality that set in motion Sethe's plan to kill her children. As a mother, she felt that she had to prevent them from ever going back to Sweet Home (148–49).

SCHWEITZER, ALBERT. *See* DR. ALBERT SCHWEITZER [SS]

SCOUT MORGAN. *See* MORGAN, SCOUT [PA]

SCRIPTURE WOODRUFF. *See* WOODRUFF, SCRIPTURE [BLV]

SEABIRD II [TB]. *Seabird II* was a fifty-six-foot Palaos owned by neighbors of the Streets in the Caribbean (14). Son (William Green) stowed away aboard the *Seabird II* after leaving the *Stor Konigsgaarten* (5–7).

SEALSKIN, MR. *See* **MR. SEALSKIN [TB]**

SEIN de VIELLES [TB]. Valerian Street's Isle des Chevaliers retirement home was near a densely fogged swamp the Haitians called Sein de Vielles (10).

SENECA [PA]. Seneca was a young women who arrived at the Convent in the company of a disoriented Sweetie Fleetwood. Seneca was sensitive to the pain of others because she was abandoned by her sister at the age of five and spent her early years in foster homes. The tearful woman walking aimlessly down the road reminded Seneca of the "crying woman" whom as a deserted child she had seen while waiting patiently for the sister, who was actually her mother, to return to the apartment (127–28).

   In the foster home of Mama Greer, Seneca discovered that sympathy was derived from bloodied skin, not the truthfulness of an exploited child (260). Bearing the scars of a human pincushion served to mask the pain of psychological and sexual abuse. As a direct result of her innocence and sensitivity, Seneca agreed to be used by Mrs. Fox as a sexual plaything for money (136). At the Convent, under Connie's spiritual direction, Seneca found comfort and security.

SENIOR PULLIAM. *See* **REVEREND SENIOR PULLIAM [PA]**

SERGEANT ROSSITER [BLV]. As one of the two black soldiers traveling from Selma to Mobile with Paul D., Sergeant Rossiter rode a "Union gunboat" to West Virginia (269).

SETHE. *See* **SUGGS, SETHE [BLV]**

SETHE'S MOTHER [BLV]. For the slaves of child-bearing age, giving birth was often foreign to mothering, and Sethe's mother was no exception. There was a lot of work in the fields, and nursing a baby took slaves away from that work, resulting in financial loss for the slaveowner. So, separated at birth, many children never knew their mothers. There is, however, a bond between mother and child stronger than the restrictions of slavery.

   It was often a custom for the slave masters to brand their slaves as they did their animals. One day, as a mother desperate to give her only daughter something/anything to reinforce kinship, she revealed the branding of a "cross" and a "circle" to young Sethe. In the excitement and innocence of a child, Sethe questioned why she could not be branded too. Sethe's mother was horrified by her child asking to experience such pain and in anger, the answer came in a slap across Sethe's face (60–61).

Nan, an older slave woman, rescued Sethe from the horror of finding her mother's body in a pile of dead slaves. In an effort to lessen the child's pain, Nan told Sethe the story of how her mother had many nameless babies whom she discarded because they were conceived in rape by white men. Nan revealed that, because her father was a black man, Sethe was the only infant her mother birthed, kept, and named. Sethe was comforted in knowing that her mother cared about her (62).

SEVEN DAYS, THE [SS]. The Seven Days was a secret society of seven black men dedicated to the purpose of avenging the racially motivated deaths of Negroes. Each member was assigned a day of the week to avenge the death of any Negro(es) killed on that day by randomly taking the life of a white person. Part of the ritual, prior to death, was to whisper in the ear of the victim, "Their day had come" (262).

The group began in 1920 as an outcry to the cruel and inhumane treatment of black soldiers returning home from military service in World War I. The horrible news of a Negro veteran being castrated and hung and another being blinded after fighting for their country created the kind of hatred that fostered retaliation (155). Milkman could only identify six of the Seven Days members riding in the car as Henry Porter, the driver with Empire State, Guitar Bains, Hospital Tommy, Railroad Tommy, and Nero Brown (211). He could not recognize the seventh man (211).

SEVEN-O [BLV]. As Six-O went to his death after a failed escape from Sweet Home, he was joyful in knowing that his pregnant girlfriend escaped with his child to be named, in succession, Seven-O (226).

SHADRACK [SU]. Shadrack was a young citizen of Medallion, Ohio, who went off to war and founded National Suicide Day upon his return. Shadrock was a classic example of how societal obligations can rob a young man of his sanity and his life. The fright and atrocities of military engagement shattered his mind to the point that he lost sight of reality (7–9).

In order to control a life of constant terror, Shadrack established the third day of January as National Suicide Day for those who pursued extinction as a solution to life's misery (14). In his lunacy, there was order as the townspeople incorporated his escapades into their daily lives.

In a panic, Sula Mae Peace entered Shadrack's lodging after the death of Chicken Little. To her surprise, she found order and serenity unlike the crazy man that led the Today Is The Day To Die parades (61). Shadrock was a very lonely man, so in the belt that Sula Peace accidently left behind in his home, he created an imaginary world. To Shadrock, the belt validated his sociability because in his mind, it was proof that he had had a guest (157). He was so enthralled with Sula's visit to his home that, for the first time since its inception, National Suicide Day almost was postponed when Sula died (158).

SHALIMAR SOLOMON [SS]. Heddy often called Solomon "Shalimar" after the town Shalimar, Virginia (321).

SHALIMAR, VIRGINIA (SS). When Milkman visited Shalimar, Virginia, he found pride in his ancestral history there. He visited Circe, the woman that delivered his father, Macon Dead II and his aunt Pilate and Susan Byrd, a cousin that knew about his ancestors. He discovered the cave and the truth about Pilate's treasured bones and the real message to her from Macon Dead I (261–63).

SHEARER, NORMA (1902–1983) [TB]. Jadine Childs had bad dreams of big fancy hats, the kind worn by actresses of another time and generation. Jadine did not care that these hats were the fashion statement of actresses like Norma Shearer, Mae West, and Jeanette MacDonald. All Jadine knew or cared about was that, as a twelve-year-old mourner at her mother's funeral, she hated the millinery she was forced to wear. The hats that haunted her in her dreams were just an outgrowth of a child's unhappiness and discomfort during a period of sadness in her life. Jadine was not interested in Norma Shearer, a silent film star of the 1930s honored with the Academy Award for Best Actress for *The Divorcee* in 1931 (44).

SHEEK, MR. *See* **MR. SHEEK [TB]**

SHEILA [JZ]. Sheila was a cousin of Malvonne Edwards. Joe Trace had an opportunity to meet Dorcas, at the home of her aunt, Alice Manfred, when he delivered an order of Cleopatra products to Sheila (68–69).

SHIRLEY [SU]. Sula and Nel shared a hearty laugh about how, in an attempt to copulate with a woman named Shirley, a man named John L. was so ignorant, he tried to enter her hip bone instead of her vagina. Sula justified Shirley's excess weight as the cause of John L.'s problem with intimacy (97).

***SI QUAERIS PENINSULAM AMOENAM CIRCUMSPICE* [SS].** As a resident of Michigan, Milkman did not realize that *"Si Quaeris Peninsulam*

Amoenam Circumspice" was the state motto and translated as, "If You Seek A Pleasant Peninsula, Look About You" (122).

SIMON CARY, REVEREND. *See* **REVEREND SIMON CARY [PA]**

SING DEAD. *See* **DEAD, SING BYRD [SS]**

SINGING BIRD. *See* **DEAD, SING BYRD [SS]**

SINGING LADY [SS]. Pilate Dead was the "singing lady" watching Robert Smith, the insurance salesman, jump from the roof of "No Mercy Hospital." In compliance with her deceased father's wishes, Pilate was always singing about the "Sugarman" (5).

SINGLETARY, DR. *See* **DR. SINGLETARY [SS]**

SIR WHITCOMB [BE]. Sir Whitcomb was the distant and eccentric relative of Elihue Michah Whitcomb (Soaphead Church) who sired racially mixed offspring (167).

SISTER MAGNA, MARY [PA]. Sister Mary Magna was a devoted nun who would not accept the plight of three children living in the street. After rescuing them, Mary Magna planned to place all three in an orphanage, but nine-year-old Connie stole her heart (223). Connie traveled with the Sisters to Oklahoma, where she began a new life under the tutelage of Sister Mary Magna.

Sister Mary Magna eventually became "Reverend Mother" and Connie became her most cherished disciple. The reverence for God was evidenced clearly in the Reverend Mother's life, as she worked to improve the living and educational conditions of the Indian girls sent to the school. When the financial struggles of maintaining a school with depleted funds and the ill health brought on by aging overwhelmed her, Mary Magna closed the establishment. Burdened with emotional and physical illness, Connie took over as the Reverend Mother's protector and caretaker (242).

SISTER MARY ELIZABETH [PA]. Living in the Convent with the other nuns, Sister Mary Elizabeth worked closely with the Indian girls. Chastising the girls when necessary, she was effective at closing the gap between adolescent distractions and Christianity. When funds began to dwindle, Sister Mary Elizabeth left to take an educational position in another town (232, 241).

SISTER ROBERTA [PA]. As one of the original Sisters of the Sacred Cross, Sister Roberta was there when the children were found in the street and when the mansion, filled with erotic fixtures, was stripped of lustful images and replaced with religious symbols. Responsible for Connie's expert culinary skills, Sister Roberta worked closely with Sister Mary Magna in administering to the Indian girls. She eventually went into a nursing home (242).

SISTER STATON (1931–   ) [PA]. Mavis Albright listened to the music of rock and rollers, one of which was Sister Staton. Born Aliyah Rabia in 1931, Dakota Staton started performing at the age of four. A wonderfully gifted jazz singer, she won the prestigious DownBeat award for a promising new singer in 1955. Staton had a unique sound and turned old favorites into fresh and exciting musical renditions (45).

SISTERS DEVOTED TO INDIAN AND COLORED PEOPLE [PA]. Order of the six nuns from the United States that Mary Magna headed after twelve years abroad (223).

SISTERS OF THE SACRED CROSS [PA]. Sister Mary Magna led the Sisters of the Sacred Cross in the dismantling of the erotic décor left behind by the Convent's former occupant (4).

SIX-FINGER-DOG-TOOTH-MERINGUE-PIE [BE]. Maureen Peal, the new girl in school, was too well dressed and a little too polished for Claudia and Frieda's taste. In mockery, the sisters belittled Maureen Peal by changing her name to "Six-Finger-Dog-Tooth-Meringue-Pie." The insulting name originated when Claudia and Frieda MacTeer discovered that their nemesis had a sixth finger and Meringue Pie was just another way to mess up Maureen Peal (63).

SIXO [BLV]. Sixo was a leader among the men of Sweet Home (22). He and Halle were the only two slaves who left Sweet Home—Halle for outside work to get the money to buy his mother's freedom and Sixo just for the pleasure of leaving at night (25). The men of Sweet Home looked up to Sixo because of his storytelling and wisdom (21). He was more knowledgeable than the other slaves because Sixo was more experienced about and knew about things they did not. The advice he gave to Sethe when Howard's thumb was out of joint saved him from being crippled (160). After Schoolteacher came, it was Sixo who told the slaves about the Underground Railroad.

Sixo was just more daring, as he snuck off into the woods late at night. He carefully planned the meeting with Patsy, the Thirty-Mile Woman, even asking permission to enter the Redmen Presence. When he arrived there, he was unable to find Patsy, so the wind was summoned for help. In order to protect her, Sixo wounded Patsy to provide an excuse for returning late (24–25). Sixo admired Halle and Sethe's family and wanted to start the same kind of family with Patsy (219).

When his plans for escape from Sweet Home were foiled, Sixo accepted death by laughing at his oppressors because Patsy had escaped, pregnant with the seed of his child and the beginning of his family (219).

SLAIN LEADERS [PA]. Gigi's grandfather in Alcorn, Mississippi, told her to come home in the wake of so many deaths: Martin Luther King Jr. (1929–1968), Robert F. Kennedy (1925–1968), Medgar Evers (1925–1963), Malcolm X (1925–1965) (65).

SMALL BOY [SS]. Small Boy was one of the men who went bobcat hunting with Luther Solomon, Calvin Breakstone, and Milkman in Shalimar, Virginia. Small Boy was good with the hounds and the shotgun. It was his expert shot that brought the bobcat down from the tree (271, 280).

SMITH, ARNETTE FLEETWOOD [PA]. Arnette Fleetwood Smith was the daughter of Mable and Arnold, sister of Jefferson, and wife of Coffee Smith (K.D.) who wanted to escape her home for a better life with the only Morgan nephew and heir. The Fleetwood home was dominated by the caring and feeding of her four nephews and nieces, leaving little attention for a teenage girl with growing pains. Arnette's relationship with K.D. was not going smoothly.

SMITH, COFFEE. *See* **K.D.** [PA]

SMITH, COFFEE. *See* **MORGAN, ZECHARIAH (I.E., BIG PAPA)** [PA]

SMITH, COFFEE, (I.E., PRIVATE SMITH) [PA]. Coffee Smith was the husband of Ruby Morgan and father of K.D. His wife was given to him as a gift by her brothers, Steward and Deacon. The union yielded one son, but shortly thereafter, Private Smith died in military service abroad. Little was known about him by his wife or the people of Ruby, Oklahoma (191).

SMITH, ROBERT [SS]. As a North Carolina Mutual Life Insurance agent, Mr. Smith was well known throughout the neighborhood, but only a few knew why he donned sky-colored wings to leap from Mercy Hospital (5–8). The families whom he visited for monthly collections opened their wallets, but not their hearts. Mr. Smith was a necessary nuisance and no more. They knew nothing of the other side of his double life, which weighed too heavily on his heart: avenging the death of black people as a member of the Seven Days (158).

SMITH, RUBY MORGAN [PA]. Ruby Morgan Smith was the younger sister of Elder, Deacon, and Steward Morgan; wife of Private Coffee Smith; and mother of Coffee "K.D." Smith. It is mentioned that the Morgan twins gave young Ruby to their military buddy, Private Smith. The Morgan twins were quite domineering, so one would think that she had little say in the matter. Her husband died in Europe, so no one really knew a lot about him except that he fathered a son (191).

When Ruby fell ill, there was a desperate attempt by her brothers to find medical help, first in Demby and then in Middleton, but neither town's hospital admitted colored people. When pressured by Ruby's relatives to do something, the hospital personnel summoned an animal doctor instead of a medical doctor. During the pleading with the hospital personnel in Middleton, Ruby Morgan Smith died (113). Shortly after Ruby's funeral and subsequent interment on Steward's ranch, the women of New Haven decided to rename the town Ruby, in her honor (17).

SMITH, TEA [PA]. Tea Smith was the twin brother of Coffee Smith (Zechariah Morgan). When his brother, the politician, fell out of favor, Tea Smith took the decline in family prestige personally. Years later, the two brothers were confronted by whites who demanded entertainment through a double dance routine. Tea responded to the gun in his face and proceeded to dance. Coffee declined, and was shot in the foot. Tea's choice of survival over suffering signaled disloyalty to his brother. As Coffee spearheaded the move to Oklahoma, he chose to exclude his brother, and the two men never spoke again (302–3).

SNOW CARNIVAL PARADE [TB]. On a business trip to Maine, Valerian Street saw a girl that looked "like candy" riding a float in a Snow Carnival parade. He was taken with her youth and beauty, and shortly thereafter she became his wife (16).

SOANE BLACKHORSE MORGAN. *See* MORGAN, SOANE BLACK-HORSE [PA]

SOAPHEAD CHURCH (I.E., ELIHUE MICAH WHITCOMB) [BE]. Soaphead Church was the grandson of a religious zealot and son of a schoolmaster known for fits of anger. Born Elihue Micah Whitcomb, Soaphead Church changed his name to escape his family. Velma, his wife for just a few months, left an imprint on his heart that could not be erased (170). Educated, yet emotionally and socially limited, Soaphead became a spiritual counselor and psychic healer to people seeking answers to life's problems. A pedophile by nature, he seized every opportunity to take advantage of little girls (166). When Pecola Breedlove came to Soaphead

Church desperately looking for blue eyes, he tricked her into poisoning his landlady's dog by promising her blue eyes (175).

SOLDIER [TB]. Soldier was an army buddy of Son (William Green) and the husband of Ellen. Soldier could not contain the joy of seeing Son after missing him for so many years. Soldier, Son, and Drake chatted for hours. When he had an opportunity to talk with Jadine Childs, Son's lady friend, Soldier revealed that they had tried to dissuade Son from marrying Cheyenne, but to no avail. As the current girlfriend and a fashion model, Jadine felt threatened when she learned that Cheyenne was not attractive but just convincingly lascivious (245–46, 254).

SOLOMON, LUTHER [SS]. Luther Solomon was one of the men in the hunting party with Milkman in Shalimar, Virginia. He was one of the skillful hunters who killed the bobcat (271).

SOLOMON, MR. *See* MR. SOLOMON [SS]

SOLOMON/SHALIMAR [SS]. Solomon/Shalimar was the husband of Ryna and father of Jake (Macon Dead I) and twenty other children; grandfather of Macon Dead II, Pilate, and great-grandfather of Macon (Milkman) Dead III. Milkman heard about Solomon or Shalimar from Susan Byrd, his maternal cousin, when he visited Shalimar, Virginia. Susan knew that Solomon/Shalimar was one of the "flying Africans" from Africa, but she was unsure of his correct name. According to the story, Milkman's grandfather had many children; one day he left his wife and family to fly back to Africa with Jake, his youngest son in tow. In flight, Solomon/Shalimar dropped Jake and in time his wife, Ryna, alone with twenty children to raise, lost her mind (322–23).

SOLOMON'S LEAP [SS]. Solomon's Leap was the ridge from which Solomon (Shalimar), the Flying African, took off to fly back to Africa (304).

SON (I.E., WILLIAM GREEN) [TB]. William "Son" Green was a stowaway on the *Seabird II*, the son of Franklin G. Green, and a lover of Jadine Childs. From a hiding place in a bedroom closet to a place setting at the dinner table, Son benefitted from Velarian Street's bizarre household on the Isle des Chevaliers. For eight years Son traveled around the world, running from the law in Eloe, Florida. He was wanted to stand trial for the murder of his wife, Cheyenne. When Jadine Childs and Margaret Street disembarked from the boat, Son left after them, but he insisted that he was not following the two women (83, 233–39).

Son had been on the lam for eight years and his physical attraction to Jadine was instant and intensive. The relationship evolved slowly with caution, but both Jadine and Son had strong unmet sexual drives. It was not smooth sailing, as he was raised with strong ethnic values, and race and culture were only secondary to Jadine's ego. Son felt that Jadine's selfishness ignored the plight of her people (145). He resented the way everyone in the Street household called Gideon "Yardman" (265). Desperately trying to bridge the cultural gap between Jadine and himself, he took Jadine to Eloe, his hometown, for a visit and risked imprisonment.

SONNY'S SHOP [SS]. The thirty-year reputation of Sonny, the former shopkeeper, was so ingrained in the minds of the community, when Macon Dead II took over the storefront as his office, he chose not to alter the sign saying "Sonny's Shop." So Sonny's Shop became Macon Dead's office (17).

SON'S NORTHERN GIRL [TB]. "Son's Northern Girl" was the name given to Jadine Childs by the neighborhood women when she visited Eloe, Florida (250).

SORBONNE [TB]. Sorbonne was the prestigious university Jadine Childs attended in Paris. She credited Valerian Street as her benefactor when she should have credited Ondine and Sydney Childs (116).

SOSA, CONSOLATA (I.E., CONNIE) [PA]. As a young street urchin, Connie was given a new lease on life by Sister Mary Magna. Connie's love and devotion for Sister Mary Magna, the nun who rescued her from a life of despair in the streets, spanned more than thirty years (224). In Mary Magna's humanity, Connie found spiritual meaning, contentment, and a God that she could trust. As the years raced by, Connie found that the most cherished gift under the Sister, who evolved in rank to Reverend Mother, was the gift of patience.

In time, religious conviction, coupled with a genuine feeling for humanity, drove Connie to be a beacon to all who entered the Convent (242, 262). As a religiously trained disciple of Mary Magna, Connie showed love to those in pain. When Mavis (38), Gigi (70), Soane (238), Seneca (129), Sweetie (129), Pallas (175), Billie Delia (152), Arnette (247), and even Menus (165, 278) came to Connie's door at the Convent, they were welcomed without questions. Connie easily recognized the distress and confusion that followed a broken spirit. She never wavered in her willingness to share her home.

Connie's thirty-year commitment to the Reverend Mother was deep, but there were moments of shame that rattled Connie's soul. The brief affair with Deacon Morgan (228–29) and the saving of young Scout Morgan's life (245) were both uncomfortable times for her. Connie's friendship with Soane Morgan, the wife of her brief lover, first began as a visit from a betrayed and desperate woman in trouble. The second time the two women met, Soane was grateful to Connie for saving her son's life. Finally, they found a common ground and bonded as sisters. In the final hours, when the Convent was under siege, Deacon's hands—hands that once caressed her body—could not deter a brother's rage that ended Connie's life (289).

SOUTH SUZANNE, MAINE [TB]. South Suzanne, Maine, was the hometown of Margaret (Margarette) Lenora Lordi, teenage wife of Valerian Street (84).

SOUTHERN SKY RAILROAD [JZ]. Joe and Violet rode north in the Negro section of the Southern Sky Railroad line (30). Later on, Joe got a job putting down track for Southern Sky (126).

SOUTHSIDE, DETROIT, MICHIGAN [SS]. Macon Dead II owned and rented out tenement houses in the Southside neighborhood of Detroit, Michigan. It was Milkman's responsibility to collect the rent in that area (15).

SPENCER, LILA [JZ]. Lila Spencer wrote one of the letters stolen by Malvonne's nephew for the money. The dollar that Miss Spencer had enclosed for an application fee to a law school was missing when Malvonne read the letter. In sympathy for Miss Spencer, Malvonne attached a note promising to send the dollar later if it really was needed (42).

SPIDER [PA]. Spider was one of the physically well-developed young men of Ruby in attendance at Arnette and K.D.'s wedding reception (157).

ST. AUGUSTINE. *See* AUGUSTINE, SAINT, BISHOP OF HIPPO [PA]

ST. CATHERINE OF SIENA. *See* SAINT CATHERINE OF SIENA [PA]

STACEY [TB]. Stacey was the daughter of Cissy and Frank and niece of Valerian Street and Margaret Lordi Street. When Stacey married, Margaret Lordi Street was furious because only their son, Michael, was invited to the wedding. Margaret felt that not being invited was an insult because Cissy and Frank did not like her (69).

STAGGERLEE [TB]. After fleeing Eloe, Florida, Son (William Green) wandered aimlessly around the world, characteristic of men like Staggerlee. According to John A. Lomax and Alan Lomax, "His folklore legend's name was Stack Lee" (Lomax and Lomax, 93). In the ballad based on the legend, Staggerlee was a black man who worked on steamers in

Memphis, Tennessee. One day, in a game of dice, Staggerlee (or Stack Lee or Stagger Lee or Stagolee) lost an expensive Stetson hat to Billy Lyons. Feeling cheated, he got a gun and returned to shoot Billy Lyons to death. The ballad has been recorded by many artists, but one of the more successful renditions was recorded in 1959 by R & B vocalist Lloyd Price. Price's version of the song became the top Rhythm and Blues Record of the Year (166).

STAMP PAID (I.E., JOSHUA) [BLV]. Stamp Paid (Joshua) was the runaway husband of Vashti. When Joshua could no longer tolerate his young master's sexually abusing Vashti, he ran away, extracting his value as a slave. Joshua became "Stamp Paid" when he certified his declaration of payment (232–33).

Thereafter, Stamp Paid devoted his life in the north to shepherding his brothers and sisters to freedom. He took great pride in his work as an underground agent helping many to cross over into freedom. He helped the three Suggs toddlers who were traveling alone to their grandmother's house on Bluestone Street in Ohio; later he helped the Suggs daughter-in-law and her newborn, who touched his heart. Stamp had devised a special signal for transporting children (90–91). He was impressed by the infant birthed in transit and wanted to celebrate Denver's survival.

Stamp Paid loved and admired Baby Suggs for her strength and considered her, "the mountain to his sky" (170–71). He pleaded with her to return to the Clearing for preaching after the death of her grandchild, but Baby Suggs refused. Stamp Paid witnessed the loss of Baby Suggs' grandchild at the hands of Sethe that fateful day, but he never fully realized the magnitude of her pain until Baby Suggs ignored his pleading to return to the Clearing to preach the "Word" (178–79).

STATE, EMPIRE [SS]. It was rumored that Empire State was the victim of "graveyard love," the kind of love that renders one insane when the passion leaves. The French wife whom Empire State brought home from the war promised to love and obey, but it proved to be a lie when Empire found another black man in his marital bed. The trauma of this hurtful discovery resulted in Empire State's loss of voice and some fraction of his mental capacity (128).

Given a menial job in the barbershop, Empire State functioned within a circle of protective friends. It is very possible that Empire State saw his membership in the Seven Days as a way to avenge his white wife's betrayal (110, 153).

STATE INDIANS [PA]. The walking man led Zechariah and the seventy-nine travelers leaving Fairly, Oklahoma, to a spot they could call home, but it was in the possession of State Indians. It took some time, but a transfer of property was worked out (98).

STAY HIGH 149. *See* GRAFFITI ARTISTS [TB]

STERL CATO. *See* CATO, STERL [PA]

STEWARD MORGAN. *See* MORGAN, STEWARD [PA]

STONE LANE [SS]. Rev. Cooper, the minister who Milkman met and looked up to in Virginia, lived in the yellow house on Stone Lane (228).

STONE, MARTHA [PA]. Martha Stone was the first wife of Harper Jury and mother of Menus. It was rumored that she had been adulterous in the marriage (197).

STOR KONIGSGAARTEN, H.M.S. [TB]. As a fugitive, Son (William Green) found work aboard the *Stor Konigsgaarten*, a ship that sailed the high seas. *Tar Baby* opens at night as he decides to jump ship and swim to shore (3–4).

STOREHOUSE, THE [BLV]. Beloved's presence in 124 was constrictive for Paul D., so he moved into the storehouse for comfort. He didn't know that Beloved would follow him out to the storehouse looking for sexual validation. Filled with shame, Paul D. had to leave 124 until Beloved was gone for good (115–16).

STOVER, LOUIS [TB]. Louis Stover was one of aliases that Son (William Green) used when he on the lame from the police in Eloe, Florida, after causing the death of his wife, Cheyenne (174).

STRANGER, THE [PA]. The Stranger was the young man who wandered through Dovey Morgan's yard one day when she was lonely and needed conversation. Dovey enjoyed talking to the Stranger and looked forward to his visits (90–93).

STREET BROTHERS CANDY COMPANY [TB]. The Street Brothers Candy Company was the business owned by the Street family. As an employer, they were civic oriented and they worked hard to maintain jobs in the community. Young Valerian Street was in line to take over management of the Street Brothers Candy Company (52).

STREET, MARGARET (MARGARETTE) LENORA LORDI [TB]. Margaret Lenora Lordi Street was the wife of Valerian Street and mother of Michael.

For Margaret Lordi, beauty was a curse that robbed her of her parents' love (57). As the only child born with beautiful red hair in the Lordi family, her parents thought they needed biological confirmation to avoid suspicious rumors among their friends. A Lordi-sponsored trip to Maine was given to the two red-headed Buffalo aunts for genetic validation of Margaret's striking hair color (56). Margaret's beauty was always a curse that served to color her life and self-perception. She was never able to develop as a person because both her parents during her adolescent years and then her husband in her married years responded to her outward features, negating her inner beauty.

Valerian Street married the Principal Beauty of Maine because he was a divorced old man who desired a trophy. After the honeymoon, Margaret's marriage to Valerian Street was froth with dominance and insults that resulted in further emotional depravation for the young woman barely out of high school (57). Marriage to a man who often called her "stupid" (66) and an "idiot" (70) caused Margaret to retreat into a world of fantasy. The emotional abuse experienced as a child by the parents whom Margaret loved and trusted caused her to seek pleasure by inflicting pain on her innocent child (208). Her forgetfulness (55), confusion (63), and dementia (53) were all part of the emotional breakdown that plagued her existence.

As a child, she was starved for parental love, and motherhood found her incapable of showing normal maternal emotions. Margaret was jealous of any of Valerian's meaningful relationships that excluded her. Sydney and Ondine Childs, his butler and housekeeper, were mocked because of their loyalty to her husband. She often referred to the couple as "Scared Kingfish" and "Beulah" (31).

Maternally depraved, Margaret knew that she was supposed to love her son, Michael, but how to love him escaped her. As an emotionally starved child who became a mother, Margaret was not equipped to give what she never had herself.

When Ondine finally revealed the truth about the abusive mother/son relationship, initially Margaret was angry, but later relief set in, and she begged Valerian to punish her (239).

STREET, MICHAEL [TB]. Michael Street was the only son of Margaret and Valerian Street. Born to a young, inexperienced mother too fragile for parenting, Michael suffered during his developmental years. He was smothered and abused by his mother and too confused to communicate his pain to his father. The questions that should have been asked by a father seeing his son hiding under a cupboard were left unattended (76–77). The strange, unexplainable behavior of the toddler was overlooked as just a maternal parenting flaw. Ondine Childs, the cook, knew, but cultural mores limited her intervention until it was too late (208–9).

As Michael grew, he took advantage of the maturity he had gained to distance himself from the parents who had distorted his childhood. He became involved in solving cultural problems as a way of life (199). An invitation for Christmas with his family at L'Arbe de la Croix in the added company of one of his favorite professors could not entice him to the Caribbean.

STREET, VALERIAN [TB]. Valerian Street's name was derived from Valerian (Publius Licinius Valerianus), the roman emperor. He was the husband of Margaret, father of Michael, and employer of Ondine and Sydney Childs. As the only male nephew, Valerian was born with an obligation to the Street Family Candy Company that he resented (50). Vowing to retire at the age of sixty-five, he fulfilled his familial obligation (53). After a failed marriage and an unpleasant divorce (51), Valerian spied the Principal Beauty of Maine on a business trip and wanted her for his prized possession (54). He did not love Margaret, because he never took the time to know her. It was her youth and attractiveness that influenced his proposal of marriage.

After marriage and the birth of their son Valerian began a campaign of undermining and belittling his young bride. When Margaret's loneliness and despair sought comfort and companionship with the servant, Ondine, Valerian interceded with negative comments (59).

Upon Valerian's retirement from the Street Brothers Candy Company, his purchase of a Caribbean home served two purposes: a retreat in which to spend his twilight years and a place to get Margaret far away from Michael (77). Valerian knew that something was wrong with his son, but he never imagined the horror of the abuse he underwent at Margaret's hands. The confusion and lack of understanding surrounding Michael's strange behavior fueled Valerian's resentment toward his wife. Valerian's inviting to dinner a stranger, found hiding in Margaret's closet (80), in addition to catering to Michael's smiling face, which came to him at night, were his ways of humiliating her (143–44). Margaret's screams at finding Son in her closet gave Valerian an opportunity to exercise his dominance over the household. As an astute man, he saw fear in the faces of Margaret, Ondine, Sydney, and Jadine when the black man was found in the closet, and he reveled in their discomfort as it showed his power as master of the house (144–45).

Learning of Margaret's abuse of his son Michael shattered Valerian's sense of dominance and dignity (207).

STUCK [JZ]. After relocating to New York City, Joe Trace found a good friend in Stuck, one of his card-playing buddies. Stuck was often in the company of Gistan, and both men were considered allies to Joe. Out of loyalty to a friend, there were times when Stuck and Gistan protected

Joe from street gossip about his wife Violet's strange behavior. Joe Trace felt close to Stuck and Gistan, but not close enough to share any of the information about his affair with a local teenager (123).

SUGAR BABE [BE]. Sugar Babe was a little girl whom Soaphead Church sexually abused. Reminiscently, through distorted reasoning, Soaphead Church tried to lessen the guilt of his perversion for sexual contact with little girls. He is comforted by the belief that, if the little girls whom he seduced with candy really were harmed in any way, they would not return to his home. Sugar Babe came into his home with Doreen, another one of his victims (181).

SUGARMAN [SS]. Sugarman was a character in a song first sung by Pilate, the "singing lady," watching Robert Smith, the insurance agent, jump to his death from "No Mercy Hospital" (9). The song was sung again by Pilate, Reba, and Hagar as Macon Dead II, the angry brother, listened outside their window (49).

SUGGS, BABY [BLV]. "Jenny Whitlow" was written on the papers, but Baby Suggs was drafted in her heart. As a slave, she knew that her husband, who called her "Baby" and who escaped with a shared promise not to look back, would never receive news of her without their married name attached (142). It was very obvious that, through the pain and suffering of slavery, family was always important to Baby Suggs. It was her son's love that set her free (141); after freedom, it was her desire for a reunion with lost children that prompted a letter-writing campaign back to the Whitlow's (143); it was a granddaughter's death and a daughter-in-law's pain that shattered her heart (150–51); and it was the spirit of kinship that inspired her to practice as an "unchurched preacher," gathering the townspeople in the Clearing for worship services (87–89). Baby Suggs wanted to share her love of freedom and family with everyone.

As caring and conscientious white people, the Garners and Bodwins were genuinely kind to Baby Suggs. However, the loss of seven children in slavery, a disabled hip, working in the fields, freedom purchased by a son's excessive hours of labor, yard invasion by a slave master, and the matricide of a grandchild were too much misery at the hands of white folks to warrant her forgiveness. Baby Suggs' last breath was taken in declaration that white people were the only source of "bad luck" in the whole wide world (104).

SUGGS, BUGLAR [BLV]. Buglar Suggs was the son of Sethe and Halle Suggs, brother of Howard, Denver, and Beloved, and grandson of Baby Suggs. Buglar, at age thirteen, left home with his brother when the confusion in their haunted home became unbearable. Long before the shattered mirror, Buglar slept holding hands with his brother (120) and shied away from his mother, whom he had seen shed the blood of his baby sister (183).

SUGGS, DENVER [BLV]. Denver Suggs was the daughter of Sethe and Halle; sister of Howard, Buglar, and Beloved; and granddaughter of Baby Suggs. Her birth and her name embodied the hope and unity of two young women of different races who shared a common force for life. Denver was named for Amy Denver, the white woman who aided her birth in the woods. Arriving at 124 Bluestone, she joined her other siblings at the home of the grandmother she never knew. Shortly thereafter, a spiritual force moved into 124, demanding recognition and dominance (78–85). As Denver grew, her world shrunk with the departure of two brothers frightened off by the ghost (3–4), a grandmother pondering colors as she prepared to die, and a town full of people who refused to socialize with the family of a woman who could take her child's life.

The enchantment of stories, told by Baby Suggs of her father's love and courage made Denver long to know him. When the spirit imagined became a human form, Denver just knew that her loneliness was over. In time, her joy turned to sadness as she witnessed the destruction and deterioration within her home. Denver had welcomed Beloved into her heart and home as a sister, but now, that same person was dominating her mother in a cruel and controlling manner. Denver braved her fears by reaching outside of 124 Bluestone Road for food and counsel. In doing so, she found acceptance and kindness from the women of the town.

SUGGS, HALLE [BLV]. Halle Suggs was the son of Baby Suggs, husband of Sethe, and father of Buglar, Howard, Denver, and Beloved. Halle was ten when his mother had the accident that shattered her hip. It was her painful gait that led to Halle's desire to buy her free (139). Mr. Garner honored his request to work Sundays outside of Sweet Home to accomplish his goal (141). Of the five Sweet Home men, Halle was the husband chosen by Sethe because of his love for his mother. Together the couple had six years and four children (25).

When Schoolteacher came to Sweet Home, the lives of the slaves drastically changed for the worst. A plan for escape was put into action. However, as Halle's wife and children escaped to freedom, his future was uncertain. Baby Suggs' stories of her son's love and devotion told to the lonely Denver empowered her when forbearance was a distant thought (208–9).

SUGGS, HOWARD [BLV]. Howard Suggs was the son of Sethe and Halle, brother of Denver and Buglar, and grandson of Baby Suggs. Long before Howard ran away with his brother to escape life in the haunted house, he had lived in fear. He was afraid because he was there in the barn when his mother took the life of his baby sister (183). When the fingerprints appeared on the cake, Howard knew that was the signal for him and his brother to leave the home (3).

SUGGS, MRS. *See* MRS. SUGGS [SU]

SUGGS, SETHE [BLV]. Sethe was the wife of Halle Suggs, mother of four children, and daughter-in-law of Baby Suggs. As a child born into slavery, Sethe had little contact with her biological mother. Forced to work in the field, Sethe's mother wanted some way to bond with her only daughter, so she took Sethe aside to reveal the scar that served as her identity. In innocence, Sethe asked for a similar marking, only to receive a slap across the face from her protective mother (61). At fifteen, Sethe replaced Baby Suggs in the Garner home (10) and received the respect of five sex-starved men. Later, she chose for a husband Halle, the man whose devotion had set his mother free (23). She gave birth to three children at Sweet Home under the watchful eye of a midwife (159), and, basically, she had the makings for a good life as an unpaid servant. That is, until Mr. Garner died and Schoolteacher arrived (36).

Life at Sweet Home was no longer sweet for the slaves, and Sethe knew that crucial decisions had to be made. It was Schoolteacher's savage treatment of the slaves that set forth plans of escape by the Sweet Home men with Sethe and her children in tow. The savage, near-death beating by Schoolteacher's nephews, forced a pregnant and valiant, but frightened, Sethe to flee Sweet Home unaware of her husband's whereabouts (16–17). She thought she was safe until, after only twenty-eight days of freedom, Schoolteacher's arrival at 124 Bluestone Road prompted her attempt to save her child's life through death (95).

Sethe could not have asked for a better mother-in-law than Baby Suggs. The three children that Sethe sent on the caravan were in her good care. When Sethe arrived bruised and beaten with a newborn baby, Baby Suggs nurtured and healed the physical and emotional wounds. However, the pain of Schoolteacher's trespassing on 124, the death of one grandchild, and Sethe's imprisonment with Denver in tow was too painful for Baby Suggs to endure (148–53). Soon after Sethe's release from jail, Baby Suggs allowed her broken heart to rest (95).

Sethe's home with Baby Suggs at 124 Bluestone was riddled with flying objects and fleeing sons (3). Paul D. lost his valiant battle with the ghost when he left Sethe's bed for the shed. At this point, role reversal became a necessary element of Beloved's vengeance as Sethe became the child to her parenting. Sethe had to be disciplined, and Beloved was a willing agent. It was Denver's love for her mother, as well as the fortitude she inherited from Baby Suggs and the father she never knew, that enabled her to leave the house in search of help. Armed with that courage and forethought, Denver was able to get the help of the town's women and restore sanity to 124 (244–45).

SUICIDE DAY. *See* NATIONAL SUICIDE DAY [SU]

SUKY [BE]. Suky was the young girl who paired with Jake, Cholly Breedlove's cousin, after Great Aunt Jimmy's funeral. The two went for walk in the woods after the rites (143–44).

SULA MAE PEACE. *See* PEACE, SULA MAE [SU]

SUNDOWN HOUSE [SU]. During her employment at the Sundown House (a whorehouse) in New Orleans, Rochelle gave birth to a daughter who was raised by her mother. Birth in an establishment that offered leased love and languished dreams was a life-long problem for Helene Sabat. She worked hard at developing a life that could contradict her birth. Under her grandmother's watchful eye, Helene became a refined lady and a conscientious mother and wife (17).

SUNNYDALE [SU]. Sula Mae Peace signed her grandmother, Eva Peace, into Sunnydale, a residential home for senior citizens and regarded as inferior by the women of Medallion (112).

SUPRA MARKET IN THE 19eme ARRONDISSE [TB]. Supra Market in the 19eme Arrondisse was the market in Paris where Jadine Childs encountered the African woman (44).

SUSAN [SS]. Grace Long enjoyed telling Milkman that Susan, a cousin of Susan Byrd, was denying her racial heritage by passing for white (290).

SUSAN BYRD. *See* BYRD, SUSAN [SS]

SUSANNAH MORGAN. *See* MORGAN, SUSANNAH [PA]

SUTTERFIELD, FLORIDA [TB]. After leaving a job playing the piano in Sutterfield, Florida, one night, Son came home to find his wife, Cheyenne, in bed with a teenager (176).

SWAMP NIGGER [TB]. In anger, Sydney Childs, butler for the Streets, called Son (William Green), a "swamp nigger" after he was found hiding in Margaret Street's closet. Sydney was angry because Valerian Street risked the safety of the people in the house by inviting the intruder to stay as a guest (159).

SWEET [SS]. Sweet was a pretty, kind, and available woman in Virginia who pampered Milkman's tired body and soul. Bathing was recreational and reciprocal. Milkman was grateful and sorry to leave (285–86).

SWEET HOME [BLV]. Sweet Home was the farm in Kentucky owned by Mr. and Mrs. Garner. It was the home of Paul A., Paul D., and Paul F. Garner; Baby and Halle Suggs; Sixo; and Sethe (10–11).

SWEET HOME MEN [BLV]. Halle, Paul A., Paul D., Paul F., and Sixo were five young slaves whom were groomed by Mr. Garner, a slave master who believed in grooming men, not boys (10–11). In fact, the Sweet Home men were so confident living as men/slaves at Sweet Home, their self-pride became an integral part of their beings. The Sweet Home men had liberties uncommon to slaves under Mr. Garner's charge: Halle was able to arrange freedom for his mother and was allowed to marry, Sixo left at night to visit his woman, and they all rode mounts of their choosing, handled firearms without supervision, and had lessons about the written word (25).

Their Negroid masculinity always was respected, never donated, controlled, or bartered for favors by Mr. Garner. Long on desire, but short on prospects, the Sweet Home men remained with the cows until the new girl (Sethe) had made her selection of a mate.

However, their right to be men was shattered when Mr. Garner died and Schoolteacher took over with bigotry and ignorance that undermined all of their progress. When Schoolteacher took charge, food rations were cut and the men resorted to stealing. All of the men were frightened and desperate, at least until Sixo told them about the Underground Railroad. In unity, the Sweet Home men planned an escape knowing that, with freedom came separation, and once across the river, they would go different ways (191).

SWEETBACKS [JZ]. Joe Trace envied the "Sweetbacks," a class of young men residing in the City who wore fancy clothes and matching ensembles. Everyone knew that the Sweetbacks were appealing to young women (132).

SWEETIE FLEETWOOD. *See* FLEETWOOD, SWEETIE [PA]

SWEETNESS (I.E., WILLIAM YOUNGER; LITTLE CAESAR) [JZ]. Malvonne Edwards affectionately called the nephew she raised "Sweetness," but his given name was William Younger, which he changed to "Little Caesar." The freedom of evening hours without supervision while his aunt worked afforded Sweetness a life of mischief. Sweetness carefully concealed his theft of the mail so that it was discovered by his aunt only upon his departure (41–42).

SYDNEY CHILDS. *See* **CHILDS, SYDNEY [TB]**

T

TAR BABY (I.E., PRETTY JOHNNIE) [SU]. A boarder in Eva Peace's home, Pretty Johnny was renamed "Tar Baby" by Eva Peace because of his fair skin. He was a quiet man who kept to himself most of the time (39–40). Even without a job, Tar Baby was resourceful at getting money for cheap wine. Even though he was talented in voice and song, his soulful melodies at Wednesday night prayer services could not alter his self-destructive nature. Church members enjoyed his voice, but never attempted to enjoin his soul (40).

TARZAN (COMIC/MOVIE CHARACTER) [TB]. Son (William Green) joked with Jadine Childs, comparing Valerian Street, the master of L'Arbe de la Croix, to Tarzan, the king of the jungle. Valerian dominated the piano that Son wanted to play, just as Tarzan dominated the greenery in the jungle; Valerian Street was "king" of L'Arbe de la Croix as Tarzan was 'king' of the jungle (156).

Tarzan, a comic book super-hero who lived in the jungle amidst animals, was introduced in 1912 by his creator Edgar Rice Burroughs (1875–1950). Inspired by the works of H.M. Stanley (1841–1904), the African explorer who wrote *In Darkest Africa*, Burroughs wrote *Tarzan of the Apes*. According to John Taliaferro, "Before Tarzan nobody understood just how big, how ubiquitous, how marketable a star could be" (Taliaferro,

5). The first film Tarzan was Elmo Lincoln in the 1918 version of *Tarzan of the Apes*.

TEA SMITH. *See* SMITH, TEA [PA]

TEAPOT [SU]. Teapot was the neglected five-year-old son of Betty, a woman called "Teapot's Mamma" by the community. Teapot's habit of begging bottles from neighbors at such a young age justified the condemnation and renaming of his mother by the community. Teapot was basically on his own, as Betty spent most of her time at the local pool hall. However, one day the threat of harm to her son at the hands of the notorious Sula Mae Peace changed all of that. Teapot's Mamma became "Mamma of Teapot," as she began to take an active interest in the well-being of her son. On the other hand, Teapot disliked the new maternal consciousness because he was no longer allowed to eat chocolate and soda for breakfast (113). However, time did not allow Teapot much comfort under his mother's care and civility as he was jolted back to reality when Sula Peace died. Teapot's Mamma returned with the inability to cope as a parent and the continuation of the physical abuse at home (153).

TEAPOT'S MAMMA (I.E., BETTY) [SU]. Mother of a five-year-old son named Teapot, Betty was her identity, but the people renamed her "Teapot's Mamma." She was perceived by the community as a trifling mother, and the community's renaming of her broadcasted those maternal deficiencies.

However, when Betty thought that the notorious Sula Peace recklessly had injured Teapot, she rose to his defense as an outraged parent. Reveling in the attention received because of the incident, Teapot's Mamma actually began to act responsibly, like a caring mother (113–14). When Sula Peace died, the charade ended, and Betty once again became Teapot's Mamma, the malcontent (153).

TEDDY BOYS [TB]. Teddy Boys were candies manufactured by the Street Brothers Candy Company that was first created for a relative and later promoted as a tribute to President Theodore Roosevelt (53).

TEEN. *See* GRAFFITI ARTISTS [TB]

TEMPLE, SHIRLEY (1928–) [BE]. It was the face of Shirley Temple, child actress, that mesmerized Pecola Breedlove from the cup of milk in the MacTeer home. For Pecola, drinking milk from that blue-and-white cup was more than thirst quenching, but soul quenching, too. Pecola wanted to trade her insecurity and sadness for Shirley Temple's joy and confidence. Frieda was less enamored, but she shared Pecola's admiration for Shirley Temple. Her sister, Claudia, was not initially impressed because in a film Shirley Temple had dared to dance with Mr. Bojangles, her idol (19).

More than two quarts of milk missing within twenty-four hours alarmed Mrs. MacTeer. She was furious about the amount of milk that had disappeared within a short period of time. As a caring mother, Mrs. MacTeer might have been more tolerant if she had known the desperation behind Pecola's thirst (23).

TEMPS (I.E., TEMPTATIONS, THE) [PA]. Mavis Albright listened to the soulful music of the "Temps" as she rode with the gas station attendant back to the Convent (45). Teenagers from Texas migrated to Detroit and merged with other teenagers there to form the Temptations. Soulful music in Detroit, Barry Gordy, and a Motown Recording contract, and the rest is history. One of their early hits "My Girl," produced by Smokey Robinson, shot to the top of the charts. The music of the Temptations is one of the key elements of American Rhythm and Blues history.

TENDERLOIN DISTRICT [JZ]. Violet Trace was not always disoriented; in an aggressive manner, she fought her way out of the "Tenderloin District" of New York. This section of the city runs from below Forty-second Street west of Broadway. The naming of Tenderloin is connected with certain civic employees being able to buy a better cut of meat by looking the other way on community crime (23).

TEX RITTER. *See* RITTER, TEX [SU]

THERESE FOUCALT. *See* FOUCALT, MARY THERESE [TB]

THERESE, THE THIEF [TB]. After being dismissed for stealing the apples, Valerian Street disparagingly called Mary Therese Foucalt, "Therese, the Thief" (201).

THIRTEENTH STREET STATION [TB]. Valerian Street complained that all the traffic to and from his house was similar to the traffic through the Thirteenth Street Station in Philadelphia, Pennsylvania. Located on Market Street between Twenty-ninth and Thirtieth Streets, this large train station houses the corporate offices of Amtrak and is the second most active railroad station in America (19).

THIRTY-MILE WOMAN [BLV]. Patsy, Sixo's young love, was called the Thirty-Mile Woman. Living at Sweet Home, Sixo made two thirty-four-mile trips on foot to convince her to meet him along the trail (24).

THOMAS BLACKHORSE. *See* BLACKHORSE, THOMAS [PA]

THOREAU, HENRY DAVID (1817–1862) [TB]. Son's lack of enthusiasm for monetary gain sparked Jadine Childs to chastise his behavior with, "Don't give me that transcendental, Thoreau crap." After calling Son "stupid," Jadine refused to elucidate on who Thoreau was or what transcendentalism was (171).

A brief explanation about how Thoreau was a world-renowned philosopher who, in 1849, wrote an essay, "Resistance to Civil Government" (later known as "On the duty of Civil Disobedience"), that encouraged the doctrine of nonviolent resistance to unfair laws which inspired great humanitarian leaders like Mahatma Gandhi and Martin Luther King Jr. would have satisfied Son's curiosity. On the other hand, transcendentalism would have taken a little more time to explain, but the theory is rooted in the works of Ralph Waldo Emerson (1803–1882) and has a moral core in that it puts the well-being of the individual man over institutional greed which returns the mind to more meaningful and fundamental thought.

THREE-SIX-NINE [JZ]. In 1919 the war was over, and Joe Trace was one of the many African Americans who felt the pride of the 369th Infantry Division marching through Harlem on February 17, for the Victory Day Parade. As the first African American combat unit to land in France, the military efforts of the 369th were honored by the decoration of the Cross of War at the end of World War I. The 369th was named the "Hell Fighters" by its German opponents (129).

THREE STOOGES [TB]. The description of Son's laughter was compared to that of someone watching the Three Stooges. Few knew there were actually four characters, however, audiences only saw exactly three at any given time (197).

This hilarious trio was first, the vaudeville act of the 1920s (Ted Healy and His Stooges), and then, later, Columbia Pictures renamed them the "Three Stooges." The zany, fun-loving comedians that brought laughter to so many were Shemp Howard, born Samuel Horwitz (1895–1955); Curly Howard, born Jerome Lester Horwitz (1903–1952); Moe Howard, born Moses Horwitz (1897–1975); and Larry Fine, born Louis Fienberg (1902–1975).

THREE YARD BOYS (3YB). *See* GRAFFITI ARTISTS [TB]

TIFFANY'S [JZ]. Felice's mother stole jewelry from Tiffany's, an upscale jewelry store in New York City (202).

TILL, EMMETT (1941–1955) [SS]. Members of the Seven Days, a secret society formed to avenge the death of Negroes discussed Emmett Till, a fourteen-year-old black boy from Chicago, Illinois, who was killed while spending the summer with family in Money, Mississippi. Freddie, the town gossip connected the death of Emmett Till to the death of a white boy in the schoolyard shortly thereafter. He intimated that Empire State committed the murder to avenge Till's death and was now being shielded from the police by Guitar Bains (111).

Race relations in the South were unusually volatile in 1955 because many white Mississippians were still very angry about the *Brown v. Board of Education* case that forced their children to attend school with blacks. When Emmett Till, playfully egged on by his friends, made a flirtatious remark to Carolyn Holloway Bryant, a white female cashier, this action led to his death on August 27, 1955. Emmett Till's badly bruised body was later pulled from the Tallahatchie River. The husband and half-brother of the offended waitress wanted revenge for the assumed insult to Carolyn. Christopher Waldrep, who wrote about racial violence and trials, reported that, "Authorities accused Roy Bryant and J.W. Milam of the crime and put the pair on trial" (Waldrep, 238). Bryant and Milam were both acquitted.

TILL, JACKSON [BLV]. Sethe Suggs remembered Jackson Till as the man who preferred to sleep under the bed, instead of in it (97).

TIME & A HALF POOL HALL [SU]. Time and a Half Pool Hall was the establishment slated for destruction in Medallion, Ohio, to replace the Bottom up in the hills (3).

TRACE, JOE (I.E., JOSEPH) [JZ]. Joe Trace was the husband of Violet and lover of Dorcas. Shunned at birth by his mother, an inhabitant of the woods, he braved maternal rejection early in life (170). The Williams family took young Joe Trace in to their home of six children where he found love and security (123). Their youngest son, Victory, became Joe's best friend.

Joe Trace and Victory Williams were inseparable. When Joe asked Mrs. Rhoda about his family, she answered, "O honey, they disappeared without a trace." Joe adopted Trace as his surname and Victory was the first to know (124). Victory was paired with Joe when the Hunters Hunter shared his knowledge of the woods (125). After Vienna was burned, Joe and Victory walked many miles to Palestine (126). Joe did not feel ashamed when he told Victory that the wild woman was his mother (178–79), and it was Victory who Joe missed the most when he needed a confidant to discuss his experiences with a girl named Dorcas (180).

Joe's marriage to Violet was strained from the beginning because the "yes" to a proposal was closely linked to the "no" he received from a mother who could not claim him as her son (181). Joe Trace was tormented by the rejection from mother, he lived with a wife who rejected reality, and he found meaning in the arms of a teenager rejected by her peers. When Dorcas chose to end the relationship, Joe was so devastated that he hunted her down. In taking her life, he also lost his own (192).

TRACE, VIOLET [JZ]. Violet Trace was one of Rose Dear's five children, granddaughter of True Belle, and wife of Joe Trace. She was the third child born to an illusive father, who gave presents instead of presence, and a mother who succumbed to the loneliness and confusion of parenting without spousal support (98).

A few years after True Belle, the grandmother whom she'd never known, arrived to help the destitute family, Violet became infatuated with the boy with hair of gold about whom True Belle told stories. Joe Trace was not Violet's first love, as Golden Gray already had stolen her heart through the stories told by her grandmother (139, 143, 208). Four years after her grandmother arrived, Rose Dear jumped into a well, to her death. Heartbroken, Violet vowed to bypass motherhood forever. However, the purchase of a doll and the desire to kidnap a neighbor's infant contradicted those feelings (102, 107, 108).

When her husband killed Dorcas Manfred, his teenage sweetheart, the mourners attending the funeral in the church witnessed Violet's attempt to mutilate the dead body. Violet, however, disassociated herself from the incident by attributing the strange behavior to "that Violet." It was "that Violet" that took a knife to the church, "that Violet" that walked the streets in a daze, and "that Violet" that people did not relate to or understand (90–93). A few days after, still distraught and confused, Violet pestered Dorcas' aunt, Alice Manfred for information about the teenager. The irony lies in the fact that the two women were initially at odds, but started to bond in sisterhood through common experiences of betrayal and deceit (83–87).

TREASON RIVER [JZ]. Whites considered Treason River to be dangerous territory because of the overgrowth of weeds and vines. It was common knowledge that crossing the Treason River was treacherous (182–83).

TRENTON, NEW JERSEY [BLV]. Paul D. was disturbed by the dead bodies en route from Mobile because the war was over and somehow the sight of death contradicted his perceptions of freedom. It was not until he arrived in Trenton, that he experienced the air of deliverance that defied bondage (269).

TRUE BELLE. *See* BELLE, TRUE [JZ]

TRUELOVE, DIVINE (I.E., DEE DEE) [PA]. Divine Dee Dee Truelove was the mother of Pallas and Jerome and ex-wife of Milton Truelove. Selfishness robbed her of credibility as a wife and mother. It is difficult to know who seduced whom, but the end result was the same (168–69): Pallas was betrayed by two people whom she loved. Carlos was Pallas' beau and, in the face of decency that should have meant off-limits to her mother. Milton called Dee Dee a "bitch mother," but disallowing biology, someone without maternal qualities is just a bitch (254).

TRUELOVE, JEROME. *See* JEROME [PA]

TRUELOVE, MILTON [PA]. Milton Truelove was the ex-husband of Dee Dee and father of Pallas and Jerome Truelove. As a successful attorney, he provided his two children with a lavish lifestyle. However, his world of working with important people kept Milton Truelove busy and away from home and family. The breakup with his wife was unpleasant, and he took every opportunity to complain about her lifestyle and lack of character (253–54).

TRUELOVE, PALLAS [PA]. Pallas Truelove was the daughter of Milton and Divine (Dee Dee) and sister of Jerome Truelove. As a sheltered young woman living a charmed life with her father, brother, and servants, Pallas was no match for Carlos. A stalled car, a thank-you gift, and a hot dog does not constitute an affair between a high school student and a good-looking custodian-type person. In a high school with many students, why was Carlos attracted to the daughter of a rich successful lawyer? Pallas was starved for attention and responded in kind to him. She never realized that weekend dates without sex and laced with conversations about marriage was a little strange (164–67). News of her mother's life in an art colony naturally piqued Carlos' interest, and, once again, the hint of adventure for a starry-eyed teenager clouded good judgment. Pallas foolishly trusted Dee Dee Truelove, the absentee mother who mailed holiday greetings from afar while dismissing the responsibilities of motherhood.

The introduction of Dee Dee to Carlos enjoined two selfish and uncaring people. Discovering their secret lovemaking, shattered Pallas' world. Fleeing the house in a state of panic behind the wheels of an automobile, she lost all sense of caution (168–69). Death was near in the wreckage and, later, in the lake, but it was not her time. A series of rescues would bring her to the Convent. The traveling Indians preceded Billie Delia with compassion for a disillusioned young woman without a voice, but only Connie's spirituality and reverence for life could ease the pain of rejection and emotional upheaval (172–73).

Pregnant and confused, Pallas tried to leave the Convent to return home, but her father's outrage toward Dee Dee and constant bantering made her life there unbearable. Emotionally, the events of her life had aged her, but legally, she was still a student and required to attend school. The corridors were filled with stares; real or imagined they were too much for Pallas to bear: Christmas in Chicago, and then a limousine ride back to the place of acceptance and tranquility. So, fate found Pallas Truelove at the Convent the morning the men came armed with guns and ignorance.

TRUMAN, HARRY S. (1884–1972) [SS]. When anyone raved about the good works for civil rights done by President Harry S. Truman, Milkman always defended FDR (Franklin Delano Roosevelt). Milkman felt that they shared a bond because of his bad foot and FDR's bout with polio. As Franklin Delano Roosevelt's successor to the presidency, Harry S. Truman, in December 1946, appointed a distinguished panel to serve as the President's Commission on Civil Rights, which issued a report in October 1947 entitled *To Secure These Rights*, recommending protection of civil rights for the people of the United States (62).

TUILERIES [SS]. Sydney Childs cautioned his niece, Jadine, about referring to L'Arbe de la Croix as the "jungle" because Valerian Street, the master of the home, called it the "Tuileries" (39). Built in the sixteenth century as a home for royalty in Paris, the Tuileries are an important part of French history.

TULSA RACE RIOTS [PA]. More than ten years after Zechariah Morgan and others traveled to look at the black towns, riots broke out in Tulsa, Oklahoma (108, 112).

In racially mixed, but segregated Tulsa an elevator, a bruised foot, and a white woman's outrage led to race riots in May 1921. Dick Rowland, the nineteen-year-old black man stumbled into Sarah Page, the white operator, as he entered the elevator. Sarah page screamed and Dick Rowland ran away. In an exhaustive study of the Tulsa riots, R. Halliburton Jr. wrote that the atmosphere in Tulsa was primed for racial problems because, "The absence of race relations was interpreted as good race relations" (Halliburton, 334).

Tulsa had a history of racial problems, but according to a well-researched book about the Tulsa riots, Tim Madigan writes, "This time, the lawlessness was blessed with the highest degree of legitimacy, vigilantism endorsed, even instigated by the *Tulsa Tribune* and its owner, the man with such a public affinity for Abraham Lincoln; Richard Lloyd Jones himself" (Madigan, 70). The outbreak of violence was over within twenty-four hours, but the damage done to the community was devastating. The violence resulted in the arrest and imprisonment of many people. The governor declared martial law, and the Oklahoma National Guards were called in to patrol the streets. There was tremendous loss in fires, hundreds of residences were completely destroyed, businesses and churches were desecrated, and there were many deaths.

TURNER, TINA. *See* **IKE & TINA GIRL [PA]**

TURTLE, EDDIE [PA]. As Seneca's romantic acquaintance of less than six months, Eddie Turtle was incarcerated for a vehicular incident involving a child. In the relationship Eddie was manipulative and condescending. Even behind bars, he ordered Seneca to do four things, one of which was to go and see his mother for the purpose of getting money to pay a lawyer (131–32).

TURTLE, MRS. *See* **MRS. TURTLE [PA]**

TUXEDO JUNCTION [JZ]. Felice, a close friend of Dorcas, had parents who worked in Tuxedo Junction. Felice lived with her grandmother, as her parents were home infrequently (198).

TWO-HEADED MAN [BLV]. The carnival crowd enjoyed watching the Two-Headed Man artfully engage himself in conversation. Seth, Denver, and Paul D. were in the crowd that watched his antics unfold (48).

237 CLIFTON PLACE [JZ]. Little did Joe Trace, the neighborhood salesman, know that an order of Cleopatra Products delivered to Sheila, one of his customers at 237 Clifton Place (the home of Alice Manfred), would lead to an introduction, a sexual interlude, and a shooting. Dorcas Manfred, Alice's young niece, opened not only the door that fateful day, but also the heart of a desperately lonely married man. A relationship born in sin and secrecy, ended in death and destruction (68).

TYLER, MISS. *See* **MISS TYLER [TB]**

TYSON'S FEED & GRAIN STORE [BE]. Young Cholly Breedlove met Blue Jack while working at Tyson's Feed and Grain Store (133).

U

UNCLE ADOLPH [TB]. When Lenora Lordi needed money to buy a fancy gown for her daughter Margaret's entrance into the beauty contest, she turned to Uncle Adolph. Mrs. Lordi went out of her way to secure funds to guarantee the showcasing of the same physical traits in her daughter that Joseph, her husband, wanted to stifle (86).

UNCLE BILLY [SS]. Uncle Billy was the great-uncle of Guitar Bains who came to assist his sister, Mrs. Baines, in the rearing of her grandchildren when their mother left. In gratitude for his relocation from Florida to help the fatherless family, Guitar placed Uncle Billy near the top of his "when-I-get-my-share-of-the-dead-man's-gold-gift-giving" list (307).

UNCLE O.V. [BE]. Uncle O.V. was Great Aunt Jimmy's brother who came to take charge when she died. If Cholly Breedlove had not left town to find his father, Uncle O.V. would have become his guardian (140).

UNCLE RICHARD. *See* RICHARD [PA]

UNIA (UNIVERSAL NEGRO IMPROVEMENT ASSOCIATION [JZ]. The uniformed UNIA men who bedecked the streets were a symbolic element of New York City's tapestry (8). Marcus Mosiah Garvey Jr. (1887–1940) founded the Universal Negro Improvement Association (UNIA) in Ja-

maica in 1914 to promote black accomplishments through cultural independence within white society. Under the doctrine of "One God! One
Aim! One Destiny!" the UNIA worked to create a separate social and
economic strata for blacks. This uniformed group of blacks was a great
source of pride, displaying colors of red, black, and green.

V

VALENTINE [SU]. Valentine was a girlfriend of Hannah Peace (56).

VALERIAN (CANDY) [TB]. As an enticement for young Valerian to join the Street Brothers Candy Company as the chief executive officer, his uncles introduced a newly developed candy in his honor. The "Valerian," a red-and-white gumdrop served to flatter its namesake, but on the market the mint and strawberry flavored treats did not sell.

The irony lies in the fact that, years later in the Caribbean, Son, a traveling fugitive remembered the Valerian candy when introduced to Valerian Street (146).

VALERIAN STREET. *See* **STREET, VALERIAN [TB]**

VALERIAN'S FATHER [TB]. A mishap with a horse-drawn milk wagon left Valerian's father bedridden until his death. Young Valerian Street found comfort for his loss in the company of the washerwoman who came on Wednesdays (140).

VASHTI [BLV]. Vashti was the wife of Joshua (Stamp Paid). As the wife of a slave, she was forced to give conjugal rights to the master's son, which was a common practice during slavery.

Distraught and demeaned, Joshua tried unsuccessfully to end this

practice by confronting the culprit's wife. At one point, Joshua wanted
to hurt Vashti for succumbing to the master's demands, but that was
pointless. Overwhelmed, Joshua was confident of two things: as a slave,
he was powerless to affect change, and, as a slave, his absence would
mean money lost. So, he took flight north to Cumberland, Ohio, where
Joshua, the slave became Stamp Paid, the free man. Cleverly embedded
in his renaming was a symbol of atonement for his loss and suffering
(232–33).

VELMA [BE]. Soaphead Church met Velma, fell in love, and married his
own "Beatrice." Shortly after the marriage, Velma felt smothered and
unhappy in the relationship and left him. She never looked back, and
Soaphead Church never recovered from his loss (169–70, 177).

VERA LOUISE GRAY. *See* **GRAY, VERA LOUISE [JZ]**

VERNELL [SS]. Vernell was the woman who was called to fix breakfast
after the hunting party returned with the slained bobcat. During the
meal, Milkman asked if anyone knew of his relatives. Vernell responded
with tales about "Old Heddy," the Indian mother who did not want her
grandmother, a black child, to play with her daughter. In spite of parental opposition, the two young girls would sneak off to play together.
Milkman learned that the Indian daughter of Old Heddy was actually
his grandmother (284).

VESPER COUNTY, VIRGINIA [JZ]. As the birthplace of Vera Louise Gray,
True Belle, and Joe Trace, Vesper County, Virginia, played a pivotal role
in the plot. Henry Les Tory/Lestory, the Hunters Hunter taught young
Joe Trace and Victory Williams the finer points of hunting in the woods
of Vesper County, and it was there too that Gray Golden found his colored father (123).

VICTORY WILLIAMS. *See* **WILLIAMS, VICTORY [JZ]**

VIENNA, VIRGINIA [JZ]. Joe Trace was born and raised by the Williams
in Vienna, Virginia (123). When the Klu Klux Klan (KKK) torched the
town, Joe and his friend Victory walked to Palestine (126).

VILLANUCCI, ROSEMARY [BE]. Introduced in the first chapter of *The Bluest Eye* as the "next door friend" of the MacTeer children, she was anything but that. Rosemary was a young white girl daughter whose father
owned a café and a car. The jealousy she evoked in Claudia and Frieda
MacTeer was of some magnitude. Once, as she was sitting in her father's
car, the girls become jealous and threatened to "beat her up, make red

marks on her white skin" (9). Always snooping around, it was Rosemary who tattled misinformation to Mrs. MacTeer, resulting in a spanking for Frieda when Pecola came into womanhood (30).

VIOLENT (TRACE) [JZ]. The neighbors renamed Violet Trace "Violent" after she tried to mutilate the corpse of Dorcas Manfred in the church at the funeral. It was not enough that her husband Joe had shot the gun that killed his teenage lover, Violet (Violent) wanted to make sure that her young rival was dead (75).

VIOLET TRACE. *See* **TRACE, VIOLET [JZ]**

W

WAGON, JANEY [BLV]. Janey Wagon was the housekeeper for brother and sister Bodwin. When Baby Suggs arrived at the Bodwin home with Mr. Garner, she was met and befriended by Janey Wagon. Though years apart in age, the two women became friends right away (143–44). Later, the memory of that friendship encouraged Denver to engage Janey's help in finding work with the Bodwins. Denver recalled the kindness of the gifts given to Baby Suggs, her grandmother, and Janey was eager to be her spokesman with the Bodwins (253–55).

WALKING MAN [PA]. The walking man was an image of a slightly built man with small feet who made a loud sound when he walked. Zechariah Morgan believed that the walking man, who carried a satchel, was guiding the seventy-nine who left Fairly, Oklahoma, to their new home. Finally, the walking man faded away and a guinea fowl was left to signal the spot of a new beginning (97–99).

WALTER [JZ]. Felice's father, Walter, worked a live-in job with her mother for the Nicholson family in Tuxedo Junction (199).

WASHERWOMAN [TB]. In the employ of the Street family, the washerwoman was an illiterate servant who may have drank too much. However, for young Valerian the washerwoman was a source of comfort and conversation when his father was bedridden with loss of mobility after a tragic accident. On Wednesdays the washerwoman would come to do the laundry and she always inquired about the well-being of Valerian's father. Valerian would fantasize and give good news of his father's condition. Unable to grasp the seriousness of his father's medical state, Valerian needed a diversion and the washerwoman provided it.

The washerwoman recognized the pain of the little boy when his father passed away, and she promptly busied Valerian with laundry scrubbing to divert the anguish. The appearance of Valerian's knuckles aroused suspicions about the washerwoman's motives and soon she was let go. Years later, during the holidays at L'Arbe de la Croix, his retirement home in the Caribbean, Valerian remembered the washerwoman with comforting kindness (141, 187).

WASHINGTON, BOOKER T. (1856–1915) [JZ]. Joe Trace was inspired to move to New York City with his wife after he heard the news that Booker T. Washington, a Negro ambassador, educator, and statesman dined with a white president in the White House (127). Theodore Roosevelt was the president of the United States who broadened racial boundaries in dining etiquette. His presidency began on September 14, 1901, but he had been acquainted with Booker T. Washington's work since 1898, and both men were in Elmira, New York, with Frederick Douglas in 1899. The two men were friends because—several months before moving into the White House on March 21, 1901—Roosevelt wrote a short note from Oyster Bay commenting on how he and Mrs. Roosevelt enjoyed Washington's book, *Up From Slavery*. It seems that Washington had sent Roosevelt a copy of the book, as the letter ended, "With hearty regards and many thanks. Very sincerely yours" (Washington, 251).

Roosevelt respected Washington and knew early in his presidency that help was needed in the area of racial matters, so on October 16, 1901, a little over a month after taking office, President Theodore Roosevelt invited Booker T. Washington to the White House for dinner. Louis R. Harlan, who studied the life of Booker T. Washington wrote, "Roosevelt's choice of Washington as an adviser was partly intuitional, for the black man was the kind he could 'cotton to' " (Harlan, 306). Seth M. Scheiner also wrote that, "The Booker T. Washington dinner was the first incident that involved President Roosevelt in the question of Negro rights" (Scheiner, 171). The white press reacted negatively and quickly to formal socializing between a white president and a Negro. The two men remained friends, but they never publicly shared a meal together again.

WASHINGTON, HENRY (I.E., MR. HENRY) [BE]. Henry Washington was the roomer in the MacTeer's home who disarmed Claudia and Frieda

MacTeer with flattery at their first meeting. When he wanted the sisters to leave him alone in the house, he charmed them with candy money.

Mr. Washington was an opportunist who took liberties when the family was out of the house. He would invite women into the home for entertainment. Mr. Henry knew that Mrs. MacTeer would be horrified at his having loose women in her home, so he did it behind her back. He really overstepped his boundaries when he made sexual advances toward Frieda, the landlady's daughter. The MacTeers were furious, and Mr. MacTeer threatened to kill him if he ever returned to their home again (12, 98).

WATERGATE LAWYERS [PA]. In conversation, Mrs. Turtle related "slick lawyers" to the "Watergate lawyers." She refused to give Seneca money to hire a lawyer to defend the reckless behavior of her son, Eddie (134).

Watergate is actually a hotel complex in Washington, D.C. But the term has become synonymous with political scandal, abuse of power, tax fraud, crime in politics, and other issues of legal misconduct in American history from 1972 to 1974, during the presidential administration of Richard M. Nixon. The scandal began with the burglarizing of the Democratic National Committee office within the Watergate complex on June 17, 1972. The court hearings that followed were televised. On August 8, 1974, President Richard M. Nixon resigned from his presidency as a result of the Watergate scandal.

WATTS FAMILY [TB]. The Fisher family was one of the families that left Isle des Chevaliers (39).

WEAVER WOMAN [BLV]. Paul D. hid for three years with the "weaver woman" in Wilmington, Delaware (268).

W.E.B. DUBOIS. *See* **DR. ALBERT SCHWEITZER [SS]; DUBOIS/ WASHINGTON DEBATE [PA]**

WEIMARANERS [SS]. Weimaraners were the large dogs of a breed originating in Weimar, Germany, that belonged to the Butler family. Known as the "Weimar Pointer" in the early days of the breed, the Weimaraner was developed by the noblemen of the Court of Weimar to hunt large game. There were strict rules governing who could own and breed the canines. When the Butler family died off, Circa, the maid, allowed the dogs to roam free within the home (240).

WEST, MAE (1893–1980) [TB]. Jadine Childs had nightmares about the kind of large, glamourous hats often worn by Mae West, a vaudeville star of the silent screen. Known for a racy style of comedy, Mae West once was arrested for authoring a play called *Sex* (44).

WHITCOMB, ELIHUE MICAH (I.E., SOAPHEAD CHURCH) [BE]. "Elihue Micah Whitcomb" was the given name of Soaphead Church before he adopted a new one.

WHITCOMB, SIR. *See* SIR WHITCOMB [BE]

WHITLOW, JENNY [BLV]. Baby Suggs asked Mr. Garner who Jenny was. It was then that she found out that "Jenny" was the name on her bill of sale received from Mr. Whitlow. This was news to Baby Suggs; she had never known any name but "Baby Suggs" (142).

WHITLOW, MR. *See* MR. WHITLOW [BLV]

WILD [JZ]. Wild was the mother of Joe Trace. Uncivilized but resourceful, she lived untamed in the woods amongst the animals. Biting Henry Les Tory/Lestory as he tried to comfort her during childbirth earned her the "Wild" name (166). With sincerity of heart, yet, without verbal verification, the Hunters Hunter let young Joe Trace know that Wild was his mother. Primitive in nature and mental capacity, Wild was never able to acknowledge Joe Trace as her son (167, 175–79).

WILD AFRICAN SAVAGE [BLV]. Paul D. enjoyed responding in good humor when the Wild African Savage made noises to the crowd at the carnival he, Sethe, and Denver visited (48).

WILEY WRIGHT. *See* WRIGHT WILEY [SU]

WILKENS, MRS. *See* MRS. WILKENS [SU]

WILLIAM GREEN (I.E., SON). *See* SON [TB]

WILLIAM YOUNGER. *See* SWEETNESS (I.E., LITTLE CAESAR) [JZ]

WILLIAMS, ADA & FOWLER [BE]. Ada and Fowler Williams were the parents of Pauline, the wife of Cholly Breedlove (112).

WILLIAMS, CHICKEN [BE]. As the twin brother of Pie, Chicken Williams was under the care of his big sister Pauline when no one was at home (112).

WILLIAMS, FRANK. *See* MR. FRANK; WILLIAMS, RHODA & FRANK [JZ]

WILLIAMS, LUCILLE M. [BLV]. When Lucille M. Williams, one of the women from town, heard of the problems in the home of Sethe Suggs, she started leaving the family bags of food by the tree stump at the edge of the yard (149).

WILLIAMS, PAULINE [BE]. Pauline "Williams" was the maiden name of Pauline Breedlove (112).

WILLIAMS, PIE [BE]. Pie, the twin brother of Chicken, was under the watchful eye of his sister, Pauline, when their parents were not at home (112).

WILLIAMS, RHODA (MRS. RHODA) & FRANK [JZ]. Even though the Williamses already had a large family with six children, there was room for one more. Young Joe Trace was birthed by a wild woman that lived in the woods who never acknowledged him as her son. Adopted by the Williams family, Joe Trace was nurtured by Mrs. Rhoda, but he never forgot that he was taken in and not birthed into the family. The Williamses gave young Joe love, shelter, and a place amongst the six children, one of whom was Victory Williams who became his confidante and his best friend.

Curious, one day Joe asked Mrs. Rhoda about the whereabouts of his family. In her very candid response about them leaving without a trace, Joe assumed that the "trace" they left without was the "Trace" he longed for in a surname (123–24).

WILLIAMS, VICTORY [JZ]. Son of Rhoda and Frank Williams and the best friend of Joe Trace, Victory was the youngest of the Williams' six children and closest in age to Joe Trace. The two became best friends and shared many adventures. Victory was selected with Joe to experience the knowledge of hunting by the Hunters Hunter (125). The two friends walked to Palestine after Vienna burned to the ground (126). Joe missed Victory when he wanted someone with whom to share his first encounter with Dorcas (123).

WILLIE PIKE. *See* PIKE, WILLIE [BLV]

WILLY FIELDS. *See* FIELDS, WILLY [SU]

WILMINGTON, DELAWARE [BLV]. Paul D. walked from Georgia to Wilmington, Delaware, where he found the weaver woman. After sleeping in and around whatever nature provided, he was overjoyed to sleep with a mattress beneath him and a cloth cover on top of him (115).

WILSON, BUDDY [BE]. One of the four boys that taunt Pecola chanting "Black e mo. Black e mo. Yadaddsleeps nekked" (87).

WINDEMERE [JZ]. Joe Trace waited tables at Windemere (122).

WINNIE BOON. *See* BOON, WINNIE [TB]

WINSOME CLARK. *See* CLARK, WINSOME [JZ]

WISDOM POOLE. *See* POOLE, WISDOM [PA]

WISH, ARIZONA [PA]. Mikey Rood told his girlfriend, Gigi, that the statue of two lovers was in Wish, Arizona (63).

WITHERS, JANE (1926–) [BE]. When Frieda MacTeer and Pecola Breedlove swooned over Shirley Temple, the child movie star, Claudia MacTeer told the two starstruck admirers that she preferred Jane Withers, who played the role of Joy Smythe in the 1934 Shirley Temple movie, *Bright Eyes*. The irony lies in the fact that, in that film, Jane Wither's character was a nasty little rich girl who attempted to run over poor little Shirley Blake, Shirley Temple's character, with a tricycle and the baby buggy. Jane Withers was so convincing as a brat, she upstaged Shirley Temple, the star (19).

WONDER WOMAN (COMIC BOOK CHARACTER) [TB]. Valerian Street sarcastically called his wife, Margaret, "Wonder Woman" (22). Associating Margaret with the heroine Wonder Woman was probably one of the few compliments (though sarcastic) Valerian ever paid her. Under the pseudonym of Dr. Charles Moulton, Dr. William Moulton Marston (1893–1947), a Harvard psychology graduate, created the cartoon character of Wonder Woman and had Harry G. Peters illustrate it in 1941. As a Harvard-educated psychologist, author of *Emotions of Normal People* (1928), and the inventor of the polygraph lie detector, Marston felt that "Comics speak without qualm or sophistication, to the innermost ears of the wishful self" (Marston, 36).

After many years of studying human behavior at Harvard, Marston strongly believed that women had tremendous power and compassion; in contrast, the male comic hero Superman had power and strength, but could not show love or compassion for fear of being considered weak. Marston created a "superwoman" who had compassion as well as nerves of steel. Marston wrote that he wanted a heroine with "the strength of a Superman and all of the allure of a good and beautiful woman" (Marston, 43). As an icon for women everywhere, Wonder Woman graced the inaugural cover of *Ms. Magazine* under the direction of feminist Gloria Steinen in July 1972.

WOODROW CAIN. *See* **CAIN, WOODROW [BE]**

WOODRUFF, ABLE [BLV]. The brother of Scripture Woodruff, Able Woodruff was a laborer who worked for the Bodwins. Brother and sister Bodwin were the friends of Mr. Garner who gave Baby Suggs a home. Able Woodruff was kind enough to give Baby Suggs a ride to her new home at 124 Bluestone (146).

WOODRUFF, SCRIPTURE [BLV]. Stamp Paid recognized Scripture Woodruff, the sister of Able Woodruff, in a conversation with Paul D. as an example of the good people in town who would be willing to take him in for lodging (232).

WORDSWORTH, VIRGINIA [JZ]. Wordsworth, Virginia was the county seat of Vesper County. True Belle left Wordsworth, Virginia, in bondage, but she returned years later as a free woman (138).

WRIGHT, HELENE SABAT [SU]. Helene Sabat Wright was the wife of Wiley Wright, daughter of Rochelle, granddaughter of Cecile Sabat, and mother of Nel. As a young girl, Helene was raised by her religious grandmother who was given a second chance at parenting. She worked hard to eliminate the stigma of her granddaughter's birth to a Creole whore. Helene responded well to her grandmother's nurturing by becoming the kind of parent who enjoyed uplifting the quality of her family. Marriage to Wiley Wright took the couple to Medallion, where Helene was considered a well-respected wife and mother. Helene saw the birth of her daughter as an opportunity to practice her grandmother's strict parenting techniques that had benefitted her (17–18).

With the illness and the ultimate death of her grandmother, Helene, with Nel in tow, traveled down South to New Orleans. As a protective parent, Helene was careful to monitor the threat of any negative influence upon her daughter when introducing her to Rochelle. Rochelle was aloof and self-centered, and the conversation between the mother, daughter, and granddaughter reflected coldness and disinterest (25–27).

WRIGHT, WILEY [SU]. Wiley Wright was the great-nephew of Cecile Sabat, husband of Helene, and father of Nel. Wiley took Helene to Medallion, Ohio. As a good provider, he had to work a job that kept him away from home for weeks at a time (17).

Y

YACABOWSKI, MR. *See* MR. YACABOWSKI [BE]

YARDMAN. *See* GIDEON [TB]

YOUNGER, WILLIAM. *See* SWEETNESS (I.E., LITTLE CAESAR) [JZ]

Z

ZANESVILLE [PA]. Mavis Albright left New Jersey and headed west. She picked up the first female hitchhiker, Dusty, who wore dog tags and ate Mallomar cookies, outside of Zanesville, Ohio. Mavis dropped Dusty off in Columbus, Ohio (33).

ZECHARIAH MORGAN. *See* **MORGAN, ZECHARIAH (I.E., BIG PAPA; COFFEE SMITH) [PA]**

APPENDIX: ALPHABETICAL LISTING OF ENTRIES BY BOOK

BELOVED (1987)

The setting for this historical novel is Cincinnati, Ohio, during the 1800s, centered primarily at the house at 124 Bluestone Road. Sethe Suggs escapes Sweet Home in Kentucky along the Ohio River to rejoin her children already in the safe care of Baby Suggs. Free from chains in Alfred, Georgia, and with Sethe Suggs as a magnet, Paul D. travels to Alfred, Georgia; Wilmington, Delaware; Northpoint and Mobile, Alabama; West Virginia, and Trenton, New Jersey; until he reaches 124 Bluestone Road near Cincinnati, Ohio.

Abu Snake Charmer

Alfred, Georgia

Angel Man

Arabian Nights Dancer

Aunt Phyllis

Beaver River

Beloved

Bishop Allen

Bleached Nigger

Bodwin, Brother & Sister

Boston, Massachusetts

Brandywine

Brother (Tree)

Buffalo Men

Carnival Acts

Cherokee Indians

Children of Baby Suggs

Chipper & Sampson (Dogs)

Chokecherry Tree

Cincinnati, Ohio

Clearing, The

Denver, Amy

Devil's Confusion

DeVore Street

Ella & John

Garner, Lillian

Garner, Paul A.

Garner, Paul D.

Garner, Paul F.

Giant

Grandma Baby

Hazelnut Man

Headless Bride

Here Boy (Dog)

Hi Man

Iron-Eyed Woman

Jesus

John Shillito's

Joshua (i.e., Stamp Paid)

Judy

Keeping Room

Lady Button Eyes

Lady Jones

Licking River

Lot's Wife

Lu

Ma'am

Midget

Mister (Chicken)

Mr. Buddy

Mr. Garner

Mr. Sawyer

Mr. Whitlow

Mrs. Buddy

Nan

Nanadine

Nathan, Joe

Nelson, Lord

Nephews, The

Northpoint Bank & Railroad Company

Oglethorpe, James Edward

Ohio River

One-Ton Lady

124 Bluestone Road

Onka

Patsy (i.e., Thirty Mile Woman)

Pike

Pike, Willie

Princess (Horse)

Private Keane

Pulaski County, Kentucky

Red Cora

Redmen Presence

Reverend Pike

Rochester

Saturday Girl

Schoolteacher

Sergeant Rossiter

Sethe's Mother

Seven-O

Sixo

Stamp Paid (i.e., Joshua

Storehouse, The

Suggs, Baby

Suggs, Buglar

Suggs, Denver

Suggs, Halle

Suggs, Howard

Suggs, Sethe

Sweet Home

Sweet Home Men

Thirty-Mile Woman

Till, Jackson

Trenton, New Jersey

Two-Headed Man

Vashti

Wagon, Janey	Williams, Lucille M.
Weaver Woman	Wilmington, Delaware
Whitlow, Jenny	Woodruff, Able
Wild African Savage	Woodruff, Scripture

THE BLUEST EYE (1970)

Narrated in the voice of young Claudia MacTeer, this story is set in Lorain, Ohio, during the 1940s. A little girl's search for meaning evolves around traditional and nontraditional family settings. The migration of characters from all points are artfully interwoven into the plot: Soaphead Church from Chicago, Geraldine and family from the South, and the Breedloves from Kentucky, all headed for Lorain, Ohio.

Alighieri, Dante	Doreen
Angelino, Luke	Dostoevsky, Fyodor M.
Appolonaire, Marie	Dreamland Theatre
Audrey	Emancipation Proclamation
Aunti Julia	Fisher Family
Bay Boy	Fisher Girl
Beatrice	Ford, Henry
Big Mama	Foster, Essie
Big Papa	Fuller, Samson (i.e., Fuller Foolish)
Bob (Dog)	Gable, Clark
Breedlove, Charles	Garbo, Greta
Breedlove, Cholly	Geraldine
Breedlove, Pauline Williams	Gibbon, Edward
Breedlove, Pecola	Gobineau, Joseph Arthur, Comte de
Breedlove, Sammy	Grable, Betty
Brown Girls, The	Great Aunt Jimmy
Bullet Head	Grinning Hattie
Cain, Woodrow	Hamlet
Candy Dance	Harlow, Jean
CCC (Civilian Conservation Corps)	Iago
Colbert, Claudette	Isaley's
Darlene	Ivy
Desdemona	Jack, Blue
Dick & Jane Series	Jake
Dillinger, John Herbert	Johnny
Dog Breedlove	Junior (i.e., Louis Jr.)

Junie Bug

Lady in Red

Lake Shore Park

Lamarr, Hedy

Li'l June

Lorain, Ohio

Louis

Macon, Georgia

MacTeer, Claudia

MacTeer, Frieda

Magdalene, Mary

Mary Jane (Candy)

M'Dear

Melba's Boy

Michelena

Mildred

Miss Alice

Miss China

Miss Della Jones

Miss Dunion

Miss Erkmeister

Miss Forrester

Miss Marie (Maginot Line)

Miss Poland

Mr. Bojangles (i.e., Bill Robinson)

Mr. Buford

Mr. MacTeer

Mr. Yacabowski

Mrs. Cain

Mrs. Gaines

Mrs. Johnson

Mrs. MacTeer

Nisensky, Ralph

Old Honey (Dog)

Old Slack Bessie

Ophelia

Othello

Peal, Maureen

Peola

Peggy

P.L.

Polly

Precious Jewel

Prince, Dewey

Reese, Bertha

Rogers, Ginger

Sage, Anna

Sir Whitcomb

Six-Finger-Dog-Tooth-Meringue-Pie

Soaphead Church (i.e., Elihue Micah
    Whitcomb)

Sugar Babe

Suky

Temple, Shirley

Tyson's Feed Grain Store

Uncle O.V.

Velma

Villanucci, Rosemary

Washington, Henry (i.e., Mr. Henry)

Whitcomb, Elihue Micah (i.e., Soap-
    head Church)

Williams, Ada & Fowler

Williams, Chicken

Williams, Pauline

Williams, Pie

Wilson, Buddy

Withers, Jane

JAZZ (1992)

Set in Harlem, New York, this novel takes place during the 1920s. Characters who migrate from Vesper County, Virginia, or Baltimore,

Maryland, adopt the city life with ease. Vesper County, Virginia, serves as a backdrop for pertinent history in the lives of some of the fictional characters. Joe and Violet Trace meet and marry in Virginia. With visions of a better life in Baltimore, Maryland, the attractions of New York City alter their path, so the "City" became their home.

Acton

Alice Manfred's Brother-in-law

Alice Manfred's Sister

Armistice Day

Bede, Clayton

Belle, True

Birds of Violet Trace

Blind Twins

Brothers, The

Bubba (Pig)

Bud

Catholic Foundling Home

Clark, Winsome

Cleopatra Products

Cottown, Tennessee

C.P.T.

C.T.

Daddy Sage

Dear, Rose

Dolls (i.e., Rochelle, Bernadine, & Faye)

Duggie's

Dumfrey Women

East St. Louis Riots

Edison Street

Edwards, Malvonne

Felice

Felice's Grandmother

Felice's Parents

Galveston Longshormen's Strike of 1920

Gistan

Goshen, Virginia

Grandfathers, The

Gray, Colonel Wordsworth

Gray, Golden

Gray, Vera Louise

Honor

Hot Steam

Hunters Hunter, The

Hunting Party in Shalimar, Virginia

Indigo, The

King (Cat)

Les Tory/Lestory, Henry

Manfred, Alice

Manfred, Dorcas

Manfred, Louis

Martin

May

Mexico

Miller, Frances

Miller, Neola

Miller Sisters

Minnie

Moore, Helen

Mr. Frank

Mrs. Rhoda

My Parrot (Bird)

Opportunity: A Journal of Negro Life

Palestine, Virginia

Patty

Philly

Readjuster Party

Rochelle

Rome, Virginia

Ricks, Harlon

Roosevelt, Theodore

Sheila

Southern Sky Railroad

Spencer, Lila

Stuck

Sweetbacks

Sweetness (i.e., William Younger; Little Caesar)

Tenderloin District

Three-Six-Nine

Tiffany's

Trace, Joe (i.e., Joseph)

Trace, Violet

Treason River

Tuxedo Junction

237 Clifton Place

UNIA (Universal Negro Improvement Association)

Vesper County, Virginia

Vienna, Virginia

Violent (Trace)

Walter

Washington, Booker T.

Wild

Williams, Rhoda & Frank

Williams, Victory

Windemere

Wordsworth, Virginia

PARADISE (1998)

As an epic, this historical novel is mainly set in an all-black fictional town of Ruby, Oklahoma, during the 1970s. The struggle of ancestors in past generations plays a key role in the survival and structure of the town. Flashbacks to the past provide the reader with pertinent historical and social facts. The events in the 1800s in Haven (Oklahoma Territory) and the move from Haven to Ruby (Oklahoma State) in the 1900s are significant to the story line. Military service is used to identify historical time frames within the text. A father fights in World War II (1942) and loses sons in the Vietnam War (1954–1975). The deaths of political leaders serve as benchmarks to chart national civil rights issues. Traditionally, generations live according to the customs of each particular time period, but that is not the case in this novel. The New Fathers make decisions based solely on the memories and actions of Old Fathers.

Abyssinian Baptist Church

Albright, Frank

Albright, Mavis

Albright, Merle & Pearl

Albright, Sally, Frankie, & Billy James

Alcorn, Mississippi

Arapaho Girls

Atenas

Augustine, Saint, Bishop of Hippo

Aunt Alice

Beauchamp, Luther

Beauchamp, Ossie

Beauchamp, Ren

Beauchamp, Royal & Destry

Ben (Dog)

Bennie

Best, Delia

Best, Faustine

Best, Fulton & Olive

Best, Patricia

Best, Roger

Big Daddy (i.e., Rector Morgan)

Blackhorse, Celeste

Blackhorse, Drum

Blackhorse, Ethan

Blackhorse, Peter

Blackhorse, Thomas

Brother Otis

Carlos

Cato, August

Cato, Billie Delia

Cato, Billy

Cato, Bitty Friendship

Cato, Fawn Blackhorse

Cato, Jupe

Cato, Sterl

Cato, William

Charmaine

Che

Children in Christmas Play

Children of Zechariah & Mindy Flood
    Morgan

Christ the King School for Native
    Girls

Churches in Ruby, Oklahoma

Clarissa & Penney

Compton, Praise

Convent, The

Creek Nation

Daddy Man

David

Dice

Dinah Baby

Dr. Martin Luther King Jr.

DuBois/Washington Debate

Dunbar, Paul Lawrence

DuPres, Fairy

DuPres, Family

DuPres, Juvenal

DuPres, Linda

DuPres, Lone

DuPres, Mirth Morgan

DuPres, Moss

DuPres, Nathan

DuPres, Pious

Dusty (i.e., Sandra)

Eight-Rock Families

Embezzler, The

Embezzler's Folly

Fairly, Oklahoma

Fleetwood, Arnold (i.e., Fleet)

Fleetwood, Esther

Fleetwood, Jefferson

Fleetwood, Mable

Fleetwood, Ming

Fleetwood, Noah

Fleetwood, Save-Marie

Fleetwood, Sweetie

Flood, Able

Flood, Ace

Flood, Anna

Flood, Charity

Fox, Leon

Fox, Norma Keene

Gibson, Manley

Golightly, Kate Harper

Good (Dog)

Goodroe, Birdie

Grace, (i.e., Gigi)

Hard Goods (Horse)

Harry

Haven, Oklahoma

Sister Mary Elizabeth

Sister Roberta

Sister Staton

Sisters Devoted to Indian & Colored
    People

Sisters of the Sacred Cross

Slain Leaders

Smith, Arnette Fleetwood

Smith, Coffee (i.e., Private Smith)

Smith, Ruby Morgan

Smith, Tea

Sosa, Consolata (i.e., Connie)

Spider

State Indians

Stone, Martha

Stranger, The

Temps (i.e., Temptations The)

Truelove, Divine (i.e., Dee Dee)

Truelove, Milton

Truelove, Pallas

Tulsa Race Riots

Turtle, Eddie

Walking Man

Watergate Lawyers

Wish, Arizona

Zanesville

SONG OF SOLOMON
(1977)

The main setting for this novel is the Southside of Detroit, Michigan, during the 1930s. There is a sojourn to search for family ties from the Susquehanna to Danville, Pennsylvania, to Shalimar, Virginia, where African folklore reigns with flying ancestors and children with song.

Amanuensis

Aunt Florence

Aunt Jemima Act

Bains, Guitar

Beavers, Louise

Becky (Dog)

Black Jake

Blood Bank District

Breakstone, Calvin

Brown, Nero

Butler Family

Byrd, Crowell (Crow)

Byrd, Heddy

Byrd, Susan

Cency Bains

Circa

Corrie

Daudet, Alfonse

Daudet Contes de (Stories of Daudet)

Dead, First Corinthians

Dead, Macon I (i.e., Old Jake)

Dead, Macon II

Dead, Macon III (i.e., Milkman)

Dead, Magdalene called Lena

Dead, Pilate

Dead, Ruth Foster

Dead, Sing Byrd (i.e., Singing Bird)

Djvorak, Anna

Djvorak, Ricky

Dr. Albert Schweitzer

Dr. Foster

Dr. Singletary

Dunfrie

Edward, King

Erie Lackawanna

Fairfield Cemetery

Father Padrew
Faubus, Orval
Feather
Flying African
Four Little Girls
Freddie
Freedmen's Bureau
Garnett, Fred
Gerhardt's Department Store
Graham, Michael-Mary
Grant, Ulysses S.
Hagar
Hansel & Gretel
Helmut (Dog)
Honore Island
Horst (Dog)
Hospital Tommy
Hunters Cave
Hunting Party in Shalimar, Virginia
John
Judd, Winnie Ruth
Kennedy, Robert
King Edward
King Edward's Gas Station
King of the Mountain
Lee, Robert E.
Lilah
Lily
Lincoln, Abraham
Lincoln, Mary Todd
Lincoln's Heaven
Linden Chapel Funeral Home
Long, Grace
Macon Dead's Hearse
Marcelline
Mary
McQueen, Butterfly
Mercy Hospital

Miss Mary
Montour County
Moon
Mr. Bradee
Mr. Solomon
Mrs. Bains
Mrs. Butler
Mrs. Esther Cooper
Nephew
92nd Infantry Division
No Mercy Hospital
Nommo
O'Hara, Scarlett
Omar
Porter, Henry
Railroad Tommy
Reba (i.e., Rebecca)
Red-Headed Negro Named X (i.e., Malcolm X; Little Malcolm)
Reverend Coles
Reverend Cooper (i.e., Coop)
Roosevelt, Anna Eleanor
Roosevelt, Franklin Delano (i.e., FDR)
Ryna
Ryna's Gulch
Saul
Seven Days, The
Shalimar, Virginia
Si Quaeris Peninsulam Amoenam Circumspice
Singing Lady
Small Boy
Smith, Robert
Solomon, Luther
Solomon/Shalimar
Solomon's Leap
Sonny's Shop
Southside, Detroit, Michigan
State, Empire

Stone Lane	Truman, Harry S.
Sugarman	Tuileries
Susan	Uncle Billy
Sweet	Vernell
Till, Emmett	Weimaraners (Dog)

SULA (1973)

This novel is set in the Midwest, in the Bottom section of Medallion, Ohio, during the late nineteenth and early twentieth centuries. As the story opens, a planned golf course turns the Bottom, once the home of blacks, into a suburban neighborhood. This novel is rich in community and social mores. The reader experiences the problems facing the people living in the Bottom through a series of events outlined in the story. The central characters are the Peaces, a family of free-spirited women whose moral and social mores are juxtaposed against community values. All of the fictional characters are emotionally tied to the community; some connected by choice and others by consequence. There are those who travel outside of Medallion, Ohio, only to return with more of an emotional attachment to the lives within.

Ajax	High John the Conqueror
Bargeman, The	Hodges Funeral Home
Beechnut	Irene's Palace of Cosmetology
Beechnut Cemetery	Ivy
Bottom, The	John L.
Boyboy	Kentucky Wonders
Chicken Little	King, Dewey
China	Laura
Cora	Martin, Henri
Dessie	Medallion City Golf Course
Deweys, The	Medallion, Ohio
Dick's	Mickey
Edna Finch's Mellow House	Mr. Finley
Fields, Willy	Mr. Hodges
Garland Primary	Mrs. Jackson
Greater Saint Matthew	Mrs. Rayford
Greene, Jude	Mrs. Reed
Greene, Nel Wright	Mrs. Suggs
Ham's Son	Mrs. Wilkens
Heatter, Gabriel	National Suicide Day

New River Road

Number 7 Carpenter's Road

Patsy

Peace, Eva

Peace, Eva (Called Pearl)

Peace, Hannah

Peace, Ralph (i.e., Plum)

Peace, Sula Mae

Porter's Landing

Reba's Grill

Reed, Buckland

Rekus

Reverend Deal

Ritter, Tex

Rochelle

Sabat, Cecile

Shadrack

Shirley

Sundown House

Sunnydale

Tar Baby (i.e., Pretty Johnnie)

Teapot

Teapot's Mama

Time & a Half Pool Hall

Valentine

Wright, Helene Sabat

Wright, Wiley

TAR BABY (1981)

This contemporary novel takes the reader from a luxurious retirement home in the Caribbean, and via memories to Philadelphia, Baltimore, and Maine, while the glamor of the fashion world of Europe and New York City is contrasted against the small-town atmosphere of Eloe, Florida.

African Woman

Aisha

Algeria

Alice Tully Hall

A.M.E. & Good Shepherd Baptist
   Churches

Anarchic(s)

Andrew

Aunt Rosa

Bach, Johann Sebastian

Beatrice

Betty

Beulah

Blind Race

Boon, Winnie

Bow-tie

Brandts, The

Bride of Polar Bear

Bridges, B.J.

Brown, Sally

Caliban

Candy King

Carl

Catherine the Great

Celestina & Alicia

Cestaire, Aime

Childs, Jadine (i.e., Jade)

Childs, Ondine (i.e., Nanadine)

Childs, Sydney

Chocolate eater

Cissy & Frank

Copper Venus

CUNY
Dawn
Dorcus
Dowing, May
Dr. Robert Michelin
Drake
Ellen
Eloe, Florida
Estee, Alma
Fast Ass
Finn, Huck
First Wife of Valerian Street
Fong, Nina
Fontaine, Joan
Foucalt, Mary Therese
Frisco (i.e., San Francisco)
George
Gideon (i.e., Yardman)
Gideon, The Get Away Man
Graffiti Artists
Grandmother Stadt
Green, Francine
Green, Frank G.
Green, Franklin G. (i.e., Old Man)
Green, Horace
Green, Porky
Gregory, Dick
Hatchers, The
Haydn, Franz Josef
Helmut (Dog)
Henry, John
Isle des Chevaliers
Itumba Mask
Jigs (Jigaboos)
Kingfish
("Scared Kingfish")
L'Arbe de la Croix
Leonard

Listz, Franz
Little Prince
Lordi Extended Family
Lordi, Lenora & Joseph
MacDonald, Jeannette
Machete-Head
Marshall Plan
Marys
Mikell's
Miss Tyler
Mount Kilimanjaro
Mr. Broughton
Mr. Sealskin
Mr. Sheek
Nanadine
Nigger Jim
Night Moves Café
Night Women
Nommo
Old Queen Hotel
Paul, Ernie
Philadelphia, Pennsylvania
Picasso, Pablo
Pie Ladies
Principal Beauty of Maine
Queen of France
Rampal's Rondo in D
River Rat
Ryk
Seabird II
Sein de Vielles
Shearer, Norma
Snow Carnival Parade
Soldier
Son (i.e., William Green)
Son's Northern Lady
Sorbonne

South Suzanne, Maine

Stacey

Staggerlee

Stor Konigsgaarten

Stover, Louis

Street Brothers Candy Company

Street, Margaret (Margarette) Lenora Lordi

Street, Michael

Street, Valerian

Supra Market in the 19eme Arrondisse

Sutterfield, Florida

Swamp Nigger

Tarzan (Comic/Movie Character)

Teddy Boys

Therese, The Thief

Thirteenth Street Station

Thoreau, Henry David

Three Stooges

Uncle Adolph

Valerian (Candy)

Valerian (Name Origin)

Valerian's Father

Washerwomen

Watts Family

West, Mae

Wonder Woman (Comic Book Character)

BIBLIOGRAPHY

BOOKS AND ARTICLES

Ansorge, Rick. "African-American Traditional Remedies Have a Rich History." *Florida Times–Union* (Jacksonville, FL), 30 March 1999, C1.

Atwood, Rufus B. "The Origin and Development of the Negro Public College, with Especial Reference to the Land Grant College." *Journal of Negro Education* 31.3 (summer, 1962): 240–50.

Augustine, Saint, Bishop of Hippo. *Tractates on the Gospel of John*. Trans. by John M. Retti (*Joannis Evangelium Tractatus*) Washington, DC: Catholic University of America Press, 1988–1995.

Biddiss, Michael Denis. *Father of Racist Ideology: The Social and Political Thought of Count Gobineau*. New York: Weybright and Talley, 1970.

Boyce, Charles. *Shakespeare A to Z*. New York: Facts on File, 1990.

Campbell, James, "Obituary: David Baldwin: Brotherly Back Up." *The Guardian* (London), 12 July 1997, p. 19.

Clarke, John Henrik. *Malcolm X: The Man and His Times*. Trenton, NJ: Africa World Press, 1990.

Clement, Rufus E. "Problems of Demobilization and Rehabilitation of the Negro Soldier After World Wars I and II." *Journal of Negro Education* 12.3 (summer 1943): 533–42.

Deen, Edith. *All of the Women of the Bible*. San Francisco: Harper, 1955.

Demaris, Ovid. *The Dillinger Story: The Dramatic Story of John Dillinger—Gangster, Bank Robber, Killer and Public Enemy*. Derby, CT: Monarch Books, 1961.

De Saint-Exupery, Antoine. *The Little Prince*. Trans. and ed. by Katherine Woods. New York: Harcourt-Brace, 1971.

DuBois, W.E.B. "The Black Man and Albert Schweitzer." *The Albert Schweitzer Jubilee Book*. Ed. by A.A. Roback. Westport, CT: Greenwood Press, 1970.

DuBois, W.E.B. "The Freedmen Bureau." *Atlantic Monthly* 87 (1901): 354–65.

duCille, Ann. "The Shirley Temple of My Familiar." *Transition* 73 (1997): 10–32.

Dunning, John. *On the Air: The Encyclopedia of Old-Time Radio*. New York: Oxford University Press, 1998.

Edmunds, R. David. *World Book*, v. 17. S.v. "Sauk Indians."

Fisher, Ada Lois Sipuel and Danney Goble. *A Matter of Black and White: The Autobiography of Ada Lois Sipuel Fisher*. Oklahoma: University of Oklahoma Press, 1996.

Frazier, Edward Franklin. *The Negro Family in the United States*. Chicago: University of Chicago Press, 1939.

Fultz, Michael. " 'The Morning Cometh' ": African-American Periodicals, Education, and the Black Middle Class, 1900–1930." *Journal of Negro History* 80.3 (1995): 97–112.

Grimm, Jacob. *Grimm's Fairy Tales: Stories and Tales of Elves, Goblins, and Fairies*. New York: Harper & Brothers, 1917.

Halliburton, R., Jr. "Tulsa Race War of 1921." *Journal of Black Studies* 2.3 (1972): 333–57.

Harlan, Louis R. *Booker T. Washington: The Making of a Black Leader (1856–1901)*. New York: Oxford University Press, 1972.

Haskins, James and N.R. Mitgang. *Mr. Bojangles: The Biography of Bill Robinson*. New York: William Morrow, 1988.

Hill, Mozell C. "The All-Negro Communities of Oklahoma: The Natural History of a Social Movement: Pt. 1." *Journal of Negro History* 31.3 (1946): 254–68.

Hine, Darlene Clark. *Black Women in America: An Historical Encyclopedia*. New York: Carlson Publishing, 1993.

Jordan, David P. *Gibbon and His Roman Empire*. Urbana: University of Illinois Press, 1971.

Kesting, Robert W. "Conspiracy to Discredit the Black Buffaloes: The 92nd Infantry in World War II." *Journal of Negro History* 72½ (1987): 1–19.

Leckie, William H. *The Buffalo Soldiers: A Narrative of the Negro Calvary in the West*. Norman: University of Oklahoma Press, 1966.

Lewis, David Levering, ed. "On Being Ashamed of Oneself: An Essay on Race Pride." In *W.E.B. DuBois A Reader*. New York: Henry Holt & Co., 1995.

Lomax, John A. and Alan Lomax. *American Ballads and Folk Songs*. New York: Macmillan Company, 1965.

Madigan, Tim. *The Burning: Massacre, Destruction and the Tulsa Race Riot of 1921*. New York: St. Martin's Press, 2001.

Malcolm X. *The Autobiography of Malcolm X*. With the assistance of Alex Haley. New York: Grove Press, 1965.

Marston, William Moulton. "Why 100,000,000,000 Americans Read Comics." *The American Scholar* 13 (1943–44): 35–42.

Moore, James T. "Black Militancy in Readjuster Virginia (1879–1883)." *Journal of Southern History* 41.2 (1975): 167–86.

New York Times (Late Editorial). "Belated Justice in Birmingham." 23 May 2002, A30.1.

New York Times. "Fifth Avenue Cheers Negro Veterans." 18 February 1919, 1.2.

New York Times. "Gabriel Heatter, Radio Newsman, Dies." 31 March 1972, 32:1.

Phillips, Susan A. *The Dictionary of Art*. Ed. by Jane Turner. New York: Grove, 1996. S.v. "Graffitti."

Randel, Don Michael, ed. *New Harvard Dictionary of Music*. 2nd ed. Cambridge, MA: Belknap Press, 1986.

Roosevelt, Eleanor. "Race, Politics and Prejudice." *New Republic*, 11 May 1942, pp. 135–36.

Scheiner, Seth M. "President Theodore Roosevelt and the Negro (1901–1908)." *Journal of Negro History* 47.2 (1962): 169–82.

Schweitzer, Albert. "Letter to W.E.B. DuBois, 5 December 1945." In *The Correspondence of W.E.B. DuBois*, ed. by Herbert Aptheker. Amherst: University of Massachusetts Press, 1978.

Siroto, Leon. "A Mask Style from the French Congo." *Man* 54 (Royal Anthropological Institute) (October 1954): 149–50.

Spaulding, Phinizy. *Oglethorpe in America*. Chicago: University of Chicago Press, 1977.

Taliferro, John. *Tarzan Forever: The Life of Edgar Rice Burroughs*. New York: Scribner, 1999.

Trace, Arther S. *Reading Without Dick and Jane*. Chicago: Regnery, 1965.

Walcott, William H., Sr. "Twenty Years at Tuskegee." *The Brown American* 37 (1939).

Waldrep, Christopher. *Racial Violence on Trial: A Handbook with Cases, Laws, and Documents*. Santa Barbara, CA: ABC-CLIO, 2001.

Washington, Booker T. *The Booker T. Washington Papers*. Ed. by Louis R. Harlan. Urbana: University of Illinois Press, 1972.

Washington, Booker T. *Up From Slavery*. New York: Dover Publications, 1995.

Wickett, Murray R. *Contested Territory: Whites, Native Americans, and African Americans in Oklahoma 1865–1907*. Baton Rouge: Louisiana State University Press, 2000.

Williams, Carla. "Reading Deeper: The Legacy of Dick and Jane in the Work of Clarissa Sligh." *Image* 38 (fall/winter 1995): 2–15.

Williams, Charles. *The Figure of Beatrice: A Study in Dante*. London: Farber and Farber, Ltd., 1943.

COURT CASES

Separate but Equal Doctrine (Supreme Court)

Plessy v. Ferguson, 163 U.S. 16 S.Ct. 1138 (1896). The language of "to provide equal, but separate" facilities for Negroes appeared first in the *Plessy v. Ferguson* case of 1896. The Homer Adolph Plessy (plaintiff) case applied to discrimination on the railroad and trains, but the language and intent of the "separate but equal" doctrine was expanded to include schools and all public accommodations.

Fifty-eight years later, in *Brown v. Board of Education* et al. (347 US 483, 74 S.Ct. 686 [1954]), Chief Justice Earl Warren wrote in the Court's unanimous decision, which ruled for the plaintiffs, struck down the "separate but equal" doctrine, and mandated desegregation of schools throughout the United States. "We conclude that in the field of public education, the 'separate but equal' doctrine has no place. Separate educational facilities are inherently unequal. . . ."

Case History of Thurgood Marshall's Integration Attempts of the Law School of University of Oklahoma

Sipuel v. Board of Regents of U. of Oklahoma, et al. (199 Okla 36, 190 P2d 135 (1947). After defeat, Marshall petitioned the Supreme Court in *Sipuel v. Board of Regents of U. of Oklahoma et al.* (332 US 631, 68 S.Ct. 299 (1948).

INDEX

About the Author

GLORIA GRANT ROBERSON is Associate Professor and Reference Librarian at Adelphi University and was the bibliographer for the *Toni Morrison Society Newsletter*.

Roberson, Gloria G.

The world of Toni
Morrison.

8/03

$49.95

DATE			